MW00630374

The Clayton Tribune
1902

Compiled by Dawn Watson

BONE DIGGERS PRESS
WWW.BONEDIGGERSPRESS.COM

ALSO AVAILABLE:

Rabun County, Georgia, Newspapers, 1894 – 1899

Rabun County, Georgia, Writs, 1836 – 1859

Slave Importation Affidavit Registers for Nine Georgia Counties, 1818 - 1847

PUBLISHED BY BONE DIGGERS PRESS, CLAYTON, GA

ISBN 978-1-943465-72-9

Preface

The Clayton Tribune was first published in 1898, one of many newspapers published and distributed within Rabun County, Georgia, from 1894 into the 1920s. It later became the county's legal organ, making it a useful resource for supplementing official legal records.

The first extant issue of The Clayton Tribune is from 1899; all known extant issues for that year were abstracted and compiled into the volume Rabun County, Georgia, Newspapers, 1894 – 1899, along with other extant Rabun County newspapers from that era.

Many issues of The Clayton Tribune are missing until around 1930. Through 1905, no issues are known to be extant for the years 1898, 1900, 1901, and 1904.

This volume covers only the year 1902. Several issues for this year are missing, but many remain. Extant issues for 1902 include: January 2, January 9, February 13, February 20, February 27, March 13, April 3, April 10, April 17, May 1, May 8, May 15, June 12, June 19, July 10, July 24, July 31, August 14, August 28, September 4, September 11, September 18, September 25, October 2, October 16, October 30, November 13, November 20, November 27, December 4, and December 11.

Items contained in this volume were abstracted from digitized microfilm created and maintained by the University of Georgia's Georgia Newspaper Project. UGA's main library in Athens contains one of the largest collections of Georgia newspapers on microfilm. Digitized versions of many microfilmed newspapers, including The Clayton Tribune, are located online at dig.usg.edu.

Several issues were encountered during the abstraction process, including pages that were too dark to read or that were cut off. See notes within the compilation for more information.

METHODOLOGY

The contents of this volume are arranged chronologically by the extant issue, earliest to latest, from the first page to the last as they were published.

Local items were included in their entirety whenever possible, if brief, and with pertinent details if not, where "local" is defined as anything directly affecting or pertaining to residents of Rabun and surrounding counties in Georgia, North Carolina, and South Carolina. Nearly all local items were extracted in their entirety.

For advertisements, the name and nature (if not obvious from the name) of the business, its location, and the names of the proprietors or managers were retained, at the least. Advertisements and legal notices were included only once, generally for the first issue in which they appeared. This includes notices for the payment of debts, and notices intended to warn trespassers.

Mentions of non-local items were usually excluded as these are believed to have been published in and/or covered adequately by other newspapers from the same era.

Local community columns were treated as one item.

Most of the local community columns were submitted by correspondents via letters to the editor. These correspondents often used nicknames or pseudonyms that make it virtually impossible for modern-day readers to ascertain the identity of the writer. Unless the correspondent's full name was given in the original, his or her name was omitted entirely here.

Words were transcribed as given within the original, especially proper names. Spelling was incredibly fluid at that time. Many instances of apparent typographical errors represent the actual appearance of the word in the original record. This includes instances where words and letters were inadvertently omitted, reversed, or otherwise mislaid by the typesetter.

Some punctuation was added to improve clarity, uniformity, or readability, especially within lists. The formatting of items as they appeared in the original issues was generally not retained due to space considerations.

While every effort was made to accurately transcribe or abstract items from these newspapers, it is always advisable to refer back to the originals.

[THIS PAGE LEFT INTENTIONALLY BLANK.]

January 2, 1902
Volume 4, Number 50

§   Germany

Mr. Luke Fowler and wife, who have made their home at Toccoa, Ga., are spending a few days with Mr. and Mrs. James Colenback.

Mr. Ed Almon and family spent Xmas day with Mrs. Crawford, on Scott's Creek.

Mr. James Colenback carried a load of rye to Clayton Friday.

Mr. I. M. Justus visited his grandparent Mr. J. M. York on Persimmon Thursday.

Mr. Bill Norton and son Ed passed through Germany Friday.

Mr. D. L. Dodgins, from Westminster, is spending a few weeks with friends in Germany.

Mr. Anderson Coffee is very feeble at this writing.

Mr. Isaac Ramey and family are spending a few weeks with Mr. John Holcomb.

Walter Rembert is spending a few days with Mr. John Hollifield.

Mr. Bill Wellborne is building him a new residence on Timpson Creek.

Mr. Marvin Powell spent Xmas on Wolf Creek.

Mr. Ambros Louin passed up through Germany Friday.

Georgia Justus spent Christmas hunting rabbits.

Mr. John and Virgil Keener visited C. F. York and family Friday.

Mr. A. E. Dickerson has purchased some feed from John Justus.

Mrs. Marion Justus spent Friday night with Miss Lizzie Dillingham.

Mr. Jeffie Holcomb is peddling some this week.

§   Mortgage Foreclosure. Taylor & Sweet vs. Lizzie M. Robson. Foreclosure of mortgage in Rabun Superior Court, February adjourned term 1901. It being represented to the court by the petition of Taylor and Sweet, a partnership, the individual members of which are J. R. Taylor and W. R. Sweet that on the 3rd day of July, 1900, Lizzie H. Robinson executed and delivered to said Taylor and Sweet a mortgage on certain real estate lying in said county described as follows to-wit: All that tract of land known as the Robinson Hotel Place in the town of Tallulah Falls, being parts of original land lots Nos. 175 and 184 in the 13th district of Rabun county Georgia, commencing at the corner of Spring and River streets and running east 175 feet along said River street, thence south 75 feet, thence west 41 feet, thence south 75 feet to a alley, thence slightly south west 150 feet along said alley to Spring street, thence slightly west of north 280 feet along Spring street, to the beginning corner together with all and singular the rights, members and appertinances thereto belonging or in any wise appertaining for the purpose of securing the payment of a certain mortgage note for one hundred and fifty dollars principal executed and delivered by said Lizzie H. Robinson to said Taylor and Sweet on the 3rd day of July 1900, due October 1st 1900, and stipulating for interest from maturity at the rate of eight per cent per annum and ten percent attorney fees in case of suit. It is ordered that the defendant said Lizzie H. Robinson do pay into this court by the first day of the next term the principal, interest, attorney's fees and costs due on said note or show cause why she should not pay the same or on[?] default thereof the aforesaid mortgage be foreclosed and the equity of redemption of the said Lizzie H. Robinson therein be forever barred and that service of this rule be perfected on said Lizzie H. Robinson according to law. This May 11th 1901[[?]. J. R. Estes, J. S. C. ... Rabun Superior Court, August Term, 1901. It appearing to the Court that the defendant in the above stated case has not been served with the petition and rule ni si in the above stated case as required by the former order of this court. It is therefore ordered that this case stand continued and that said defendant Lizzie H. Robinson be served with said rule ni si as required by law before the next term of this Court... August 3th 1901. John S. Candler, J. S. C.; W. S. Paris, Plaintiff's Att'ys... I, J. S. Ramey, Clerk of the Superior court of Rabun County Ga. do hereby certify that the foregoing orders are two copies of the records on minutes Superior Court of Rabun County Ga. Witness my hand and seal, This Oct. 25, 1901. J. S. Ramey, Clerk.

§   The Tallulah Falls Railroad Company. Time Table No. 21. In effect Sunday, Sept. 22, 8 a. m. 1901., Eastern Time. Stations... Tallulahe Falls... Tallulah Lodge... Turnerville... Hollywood... Anandale... Hills[?]... Clarksville... Demorest... Cornelia... No. Twelve will run to Tallulah Falls regardless of No. Eleven. All southbound trains have right of tract over trains of class moving in opposite directions. W. S. Erwin, G. P. A., S. C. Dunlap, Gen. Manager.

§   Mortgage Foreclosure. W. S. Whitmire vs. J. L. Hamby. Foreclosure of mortgage in Rabun Superior Court, August Term, 1901. It being represented to the court by the petition of W. S. Whitmire that on the 20th day of September 1897, J. L. Hamby executed and delivered to the said [petitioner] a mortgage on certain real estate lying in said count and described as follows to-wit: The lot on which the W. S. Whitmire store house now stands and described as follows: Commencing at a point three feet north of the north west corner of the front piazza to the said store house, thence east and parallell with the east end or wall of said store house sixty eight feet, thence west parallell with the south wall of said store house sixty five feet, thence north sixty eight feet to the beginning corner, containing one ninth of an acre more or less, for the purpose of securing the payment of a certain promissory note for $200 executed and delivered by the said J. L. Hamby to said W. S. Whitmire on the 20th day of September 1897. Done on the 1st day of January, 1900 after date, and stipulating for interest from maturity a the rate of eight per cent, per annum... This 25th day of August, 1901. Jas. R. Grant, Petitioner's Att'y... John S. Candler, Judge Superior Court Stone Mountain Circuit, Presiding. Georgia—Rabun County. I, J. S. Ramey, Clerk of the Superior court in and for said county of Rabun do hereby certify that the foregoing rule [ni] si is a true copy from the minutes of Rabun Superior Court... Sept. 30th, 1901. J. S. Ramey, Clerk.

§ Sheriff's Sales. Georgia—Rabun County. Will be sold, on the first Tuesday in February next, at the public outcry at the court house in Clayton, said county, within the legal hours of sale, to the highest bidder for cash, certain property of which the following is full and complete description: A one fourth undivided interest in lot of land 83 in the 13th land [district] of originally Habersham, now Rabun County. Levied on as the property of defendant W. S. Baker to satisfy two executions issued from the Justice's Court of the 1275th Dist. G. M., of said county, one in favor of C. T. Wilbanks, the other in favor of V. C. Taylor and preceeding for the benefit of C. T. Wilbanks transferee. Both against said W. S. Baker. Levy made and returned to me by Loma Gipson, L. C. This the 20th day of December 1901. J. R. Ritchie, Sheriff.

Also part of lot [No.] 13 in the third land District of Rabun county containing 17 acres more or less bounded as follows [beginning] at a stake in the state line between Georgia and North Carolina at the north west corner of Eva Watkins land 1500[?] feet from the north west corener of said lot, thence south 1230 feet, thence north 84 degrees west 850 feet to a white oak, thence north 6 degrees west 400 feet to a chestnut, thence north 2 degrees east 815 feet to the state line, thence west along the state to the [beginning] corener. Levied on as the property of George Jacobs by [virtue] of an execution issued by Joseph L. Dickerson Tax Collector of said county to satisfy his state and county Tax for the year for 1901.

Written notes given defendant in terms of the law. This Dec. 23, 1901. J. R. Ritchie, [Sheriff].

§   Administrator's Sale. Georgia, Rabun County. By virtue of an order of the court of Ordinary, will be sold, on the first Tuesday in Jan., 1902... Part of lots of land Nos. 52 and 53 in the 4th land district of said county, and described as follows: Beginning on the west original line at a conditional corner, and running east a conditional line to an apple tree in the gap of the ridge, thence east to a poplar tree, thence east to a black gum, thence east to the original line, thence north to the original line to the original corner, thence west a conditional line to the top of Joe[?] mountain, thence down the dividing ridge to J. F. Godfrey's draw bars, thence south-east along the road to the public road, thence south west the conditional line to the original line, thence south the original line to the beginning corner, containing 150 acres more or less. Terms of sale one half cash and balance o nsix months time with notes and approved security. This 3rd day of Dec., 1901[?]. J. F. Godfrey, administrator of the estate of Ansel Godfrey, deceased.

§   Libel for Divorce. Wm. G. Taylor vs. Palestine Taylor.... To Palestine Taylor: You are hereby notified to be and appear either personally or by attorney at the next Superior court of Rabun county, to be held on the fourth Monday in February 1902 next, to answer the complaint of W. G. Taylor in an action for total divorce. In [illegible] thereof the court will proceed as to justice shall appertain. Witness the honorable J. B. Estes, Judge of said court, this October the 1st 1901. J. S. Ramey, C. S. C.   Jas R. Grant, Libelants Attorney.

§   Ordinary's Citations. Georgia—Rabun County. M. L. and H. M. Hopper, administrators upon the estate of Henry Hopper, late of said county, deceased, having filed their petition for discharge, this is to cite all persons concerned to show cause against the granting of [illegible] at the regular term of the court of Ordinary for said county to be held on the first Monday in January, 1902. This Sept. 3d, 1901. W. S. Long, Ordinary.

§   Georgia—Rabun County. M. L. Dickerson, administrator upon the estate of W. T. Dickerson, late of said county, deceased, having filed his petition for discharge this is to cite all persons concerned to show cause against the granting of this discharge at the regular term of the court of Ordinary for said county to be held on the first Monday in February, 1902. This Oct. 29, 1901. W. S. Long, Ordinary.

§   Georgia—Rabun County. Emma R. Crawford, having made application for a 12 months' support out of the estate of James J.

Crawford, and appraisers duly appointed to set apart the same having filed their return all persons concerned are hereby required to show cause before the court of Ordinary of said county on the first Monday in February, 1902. This 1st day of January, 1902. W. S. Long, Ordinary.

§ Georgia—Rabun County. John B. Dockins, administrator upon the estate of Benjiman Dockins, late of said county, deceased, having filed his petition for discharge, this is to cite all persons concerned to show cause against the granting of this discharge, at the regular term of the court of Ordinary for said county to be held on the first Monday in April 1902. This 2nd day of January, 1902. W. S. Long, Ordinary.

§ County Directory. Judge Superior Court, John B. Estes. Solicitor General, W. A. Charters. Senator 40th Senatorial District, J. Miles Berrong. Member of Legislature, R. E. A. Hamby. Ordinary, W. S. Long. Sheriff, J. R. Ritchie. Clerk Superior Court, J. S. Ramey. [Tax?] Receiver, J. M. Marsongale. Tax Collector, Joseph L. Dicerson. County Treasurer, John W. Green. County Surveyor, J. A. Reynolds. Coroner, T. N. McConnell. County School Commissioner, A. A. O'Kelley.

§ Masonic [Directory]. John W. Green, W. M.; J. C. Dover, S. W.; W. S. Long, J. W.; R. E. A. Hamby, Sec.; W. J. Green, Treas.; A. A. O'Kelley, S. D.; J. A. Reynolds, J. D.; W. E. V. Cathey, Tyler.; R. L. Whitmire, Chap.; W. T. York & D. J. Duncan, Stewarts.

§ Church Directory. Westley Chapel first and second Sundays at 11 a. m., Saturday before the first at 11 a. m. Blue Ridge first Sunday at 3 p. m. Wolffork, third Sunday at 3 p. m. Clayton second Sunday at 11 a. m. New Hope second Sunday at 3 p. m. Pine Mountain fourth Sunday at 3 p. m. L. L. Landrum, P.

§ Mrs. Jesse McCurry is quite feeble.

§ Uncle Jeff Duncan is not feeling well.

§ Vig Arrendale went down to Cornelia yesterday on business.

§ Robt. Singleton will represent the Tribune on Chechero.

§ Dr. W. J. Green and Col. R. E. [missing] Hamby are in Atlanta.

§ Geo. W. Lovell, of Clarkesville, Ga., was in town Friday.

§ Rep. Howell C. Blalock, of Burton, was in town yesterday.

§ Mrs. J. I. Langston is clerking the absence of her husband.

§ J. Marcus Bleckley will represent the Tribune on Moccasin.

§ Misses Ema and Bulah Dover were shopping in town to-day.

§ Next Tuesday is the regular meeting of the Board of Education.

§ Ordinary Long is very busy attending to the applicants for pensions.

§ Miss Fannie Donaldson, of the Valley, is visiting Mrs. W. C. Donaldson.

§ Prof. A. A. O'Kelley has been spending the week with relatives at Harmony Grove.

§ J. M. Arrendale was here Tuesday arranging for board for his daughter, Miss Eliza.

§ A. J. Grist, of the Tennessee Valley, was the first to appear on our new list of subscribers.

§ Frank Singleton is home from his school, on Flat Creek and will enter school next week.

§ The County Union Meeting was a failure on account of the inclemency of the weather.

§ James Green, of the Tribune force is canvassing the county in the interest of the Tribune.

§ D. M. Green and daughter Miss Beulah were in town to-day. Miss Beulah speaks of attending school here.

§ One of our citizens who is connected with the revenue department received a severe shock a few days ago.

§ The Masonic Hall will be lighted and heated in a few days. The craft will be comfortable Saturday the 11th when they meet for instruction.

§ Marriage license was granted yesterday to a Mr. Morton and Miss Ella Goble and the last seen of them they were going in the direction of the home of Esquire Pickett.

§   Judge J. B. Estes has issued a restraining order against Judge W. S. Long and Jesse McCurry, road overseer, from removing gates on the Chechero road through the farm of Mrs. E. A. Bell. All other gates on this road were removed yesterday.

§   J. I. Langston was appointed superintendent of public roads yesterday by Ordinary W. S. Long at a salary of $300 per year and bond fixed at two thousand dollars and Jas. R. Grant is preparing the bond of Mr. Langston.

§   Samuel Speed, the young man whom we reported in our last issue as being the victim of a very serious accident, is said to be little improved, except he is not suffering the intense pain that he did for the first few days. It will be remembered that Mr. Speed was shoemaking and was in the act of kneeling to the floor to cut some leather, his knife was on the floor, with blade half open with point sticking up, when he came down on it, entering the blade between the bones of the knee point. A surgical operation has been done but the piece of blade was not removed since it was ascertained that the point would have to be considerably mutilated to accomplish the object at the time. His surgical attendants report that within a short time they hope to dislodge and remove the offending substance. Mr. Speed was brought to Town Tuesday p. m. and will remain indefinitely. We regret the accident very much and extend our sincere sympathies. Mr. Speed is a highly respected man in the community[.] He is best known in, and leads a life, we are informed, exemplary in every way.

§   There will be a call meeting of Rabun Gap Lodge No. 265 F. & A. M. on the evening of Jan. the 11th, 1902, at 8 o'clock sharp, for the puprose of instruction. A full attendance is earnestly requested. John W. Green, W. M. R. E. A. Hamby, Sec'y.

§   Teachers Take Notice. In order to receive your pay for this year's teaching, you must make your reports and have them filed in my office by Monday, Jan. 6th, 1902. Teachers, in every instance, sign and return the receipts that accompany your checks. This Dec. 26th, 1901. A. A. O'Kelley, C. S. Com.

§   Grove
Christmas passed off quietly.
The people have gone to work again.
John V. Arrendale is at home again from the North Georgia Agricultural College. He is taking Christmas.
John Arrendale and John McClain, of Burton, were at Grove Monday.

Lenard Lovell, of Toccoa, was visiting relatives in the community Tuesday.

Lester Arrendale was the champion hunter in this community Xmas as he killed the most game.

Loma Gipson, of Stonepile, was in the community Thursday.

The people of Grove regret the announcement of Hon. R. E. A. Hamby's not being a candidate for re-election for representative as he has been so faithful to the people for the past six years.

Wm. Ritchie caught the largest owl Wednesday night on record as it measured four feet and ten inches from tip to tip of its wings. M. L. Arrehdale [*sic*] has it caged now.

§   Upper Chechero

Christmas is over and we are all feeling good.

Miss Georgia Woodall leaves here for Pelzer, S. C., where she is expected to become the bride of Mr. Beard.

Ask a certain young man who attended the Xmas tree at Tiger if he thinks peas are cheap.

Mr. Dover's school at Ivy Hill closes Dec. 31st.

§   Blalock

Ask Mr. J. C. Howard who visited Mr. Andy Justus Christmas day.

Ask Mr. Lester Nichols who lost one of his shoes coming home from G. H. Thomson's.

Ask Rosa Thompson and Harley and Milas, who shed their toe nails just after Xmas.

Mr. Tom Coleman has returned from jail. He says he is as fat as ever and to go over to Towns Co. if you want bear meat.

Ask J. D. York who is going to the west before long.

We suppose that Mr. J. M. Bleckley is going to teach school at Boiling Spring for the next two months so I must close.

§   Burton

It is just rain and mud these days.

The river and creeks are on a rise to-day.

We had a Christmas tree at Burton. Everything passed off nicely. We think everyone was remembered that was present. Some of the girls got some nice dolls from the Christmas tree and were well pleased with them. Mr. David Parker was presented with a pair of little pants, the cutest we have ever seen. We had some nice music by Messrs. Tom and Jim King.

Mr. E. O. Marsingale is visiting friends at Burton.

Misses Dora and Della King, May Justus and Sallie Parker, of Persimmon, spent Christmas at Burton.

§   Tiger

Christmas is on in Old Tiger and the boys are trying to get their share.

Four boys went out with four guns, started four rabbits, made four shots and killed nothing.

At the adjourned conference last week Tiger church unanimously elected Bro. D. D. Taylor as pastor for the next year.

Prof. H. C. McCrackin is home from Atlanta, where he has been attending the medical college.

A candy pulling at Mr. Gambols Christmas night.

Two of Mr. F. A. Taylor's boys went out one day and killed 15 squirells [*sic*].

Mr. H. C. Ramey and Isaac Worley went hog hunting and killed five squirrels.

A lawsuit at Tiger last Friday between Mr. W. E. Jones and Mr. Albert Williams. The result was Mr. Williams was bound over to court.

There was a Christmas party at Mr. John Jenkin's Tuesday night.

We are informed that some one who has learned the combination got into Mr. E. W. Shirley's place of business Christmas eve night and helped themselves to some wine.

§   Dillard

Miss May Donaldson and Mr. Charlie Grist went to Clayton Sunday.

Mr. Oscar Powell is up from Atlanta with home folk this week.

Will Dillard was all smiles Sunday, especially when he saw his best girl coming from Clayton.

Mr. Frank Scruggs, who has been at Demorest, going to school, is at home for a few days.

A sociable was enjoyed at Mr. Ira Holden's Tuesday night.

Mr. James Hopper has returned from Oklahoma where he has been visiting relatives.

John Godfrey is off to Blairsville this week.

A nice dinner was enjoyed at W. C. Scrugg's Saturday.

Mr. Hiram Dillard went to Clayton Sunday.

A singing was enjoyed at Mr. John Howard's Friday night.

Miss Beulah and Sallie Grist visited Miss Lula Howard Saturday night.

§   Flat Creek

Snow and rain is the order of the day.

Ask Mr. Charley Benfield where he got his pet o'possum that he is carrying persimmons for. He says that he has not got enough o'possums to feed his persimmons to and is trying to feed them to the girls.

We think someone had a corn shelling the other night as they had the Christmas tree decorated with cob pipes. We think women have gone to smoking as they received the pipes.

Miss Rebecca and Gussie Lovell are up from Toccoa visiting relatives.

Ask Mr. W. J. Shed and Will Arrendale who got a hard fall Christmas eve but not seriously hurt.

Christmas is on...a boom.

§ Quartz

Xmas is over and everybody is thinking of the new year next.

Old Santa Clause made hearts [full] of joy. Some of them hung up their stockings around the fireside at night, and next morning they were up bright and early, some saying law! law!, and some would say God bless "old Santa Clause", I do love him. If we all could live as happy as the children are on [Xmas], it would be almost heaven here on earth.

Rev. Brooksher, with one of his cousins, is on Persimmon. Ha, ha! Texie York is all smiles.

M. B. York has returned to his school.

Prof. Howard is at home for a few days.

G. F. York has Erysipelas in one of his legs. We hope he will soon recover.

The little daughter of E. B. Philyaw is sick at this writing.

We wonder if Prof. Bleckley has forgotten the way back to Persimmon. We were looking for him Xmas.

Mr. M. V. York and wife were glad to get their Xmas gifts Mineola, Tex., sent them by Dessie and Montine York. They wish to thank them through the Tribune for their presents.

The girl that they call Belle has had toothache and sty for Xmas.

§ Trespass Notice. The public are hereby warned not to trespass by hunting, fishing or entruding upon in any way land lot No. 62 in the 4th land district of Rabun County. This Dec. 3rd 1901. M. W. Swafford, E. D. Swafford.

January 9, 1902
Volume 4, Number 51

§ Col. Estill Endorsed by Home People. The Retail Merchants Association, comprising practically all of the merchants of Savannah, has indorsed Col. J. B. Estell for Governor...

§ Mud Creek

Messrs. Ed Page and Jim Dodgins visited Mr. and Mrs. Geo. Martin Sunday.

Mrs. Julia Grist is very sick at this writing. We hope she will soon recover.

Mrs. Laura Grist, of the Flats, visited her father Mr. W. A. Martin a few days last week.

Miss Addie Fuller was all smiles Sunday.

Mr. and Mrs. John Godfrey visited Mr. and Mrs. Reed Dillard Sunday.

Mr. Ben Long has moved to Mud Creek.

Mr. Bud Martin and family visited Mr. George Grist Friday.

Mr. Bob Long, of the Flats, was in the Valley one day last week.

§ Grove

Weather fine.

Mr. S. M. Arrendale and Eddy Marsingale passed through Grove Monday.

Mr. J. M. Arrendale and a crowd of young people attended the entertainment at Tiger Tuesday.

Mr. Andy Davidson, one of Towns County's best citizens was [in] Grove Wednesday.

Josey Meece was at Grove Thursday.

Cicero FinCannon died at his home Wednesday night. His wife woke up during the night and discovered that he was dead.

John V. Arrendale returned to Dahlonegah to school, after taking a stay of a week with home folks.

Monroe Kragg, of Stonepile, was at Grove Friday.

§ Dillard

Fine weather for the past few days.

Mr. W. H. Greenwood, after spending the holidays with his family here, has returned to his work.

Mr. and Mrs. Allen Turpen are at Turnerville on a visit.

Mr. Ed Holden is at Demorest going to school.

Mr. John Holden went to Hiawassee last week.

Mr. James Green is in this community this week, collecting for the Tribune.

Mr. Logan Turpen is making new improvements to his father's house.

Mr. Oscar Powell has returned to Atlanta after spending the holidays with home folks.

Mr. Bob Dillard's child, which has been sick, is improving.

New year is here and I wonder how many citizens of the county are taking the Tribune, which should be the most interesting paper the people of Rabun county could take.

Mr. Zack Dillard went to Tallulah Falls Monday.

Mr. Wade Hamlin and Miss Fannie Scruggs went to ride Sunday evening.

Mr. and Mrs. B. R. Dillard visited Mr. and Mrs. A. J. Grist Saturday night.

Several of the people here are making preparations for entering school at Clayton.

§ Change of Business Firm. Notice is hereby given that the firm of Ritchie and Keener has been dissolved and that H. A. Keener has purchased my interest and will collect and pay all debts incurred by the firm. All persons indebted to me either by account or note will settle with H. A. Keener until the 20th inst., after then with "him who is mightier than I." Your Respectfully, R. L. Ritchie.

§ For Representative. At the solicitation of friends from all parts of the county, I hereby announce my candidacy for representative, subject to the action of the democratic party. I promise you, fellow-citizens, if honored to this high office to serve you faithfully and to the best of my ability. Yours to serve, James E. Bleckley.

§ After due consideration and consultation with friends, I hereby announce myself candidate for representative, subject to the democratic primary, promising if elected to serve you honestly and faithfully. This Jan. 3, 1902. Yours & etc., J. H. Derrick.

§ W. D. Manley vs. E. M. Manley. Libel for Divorce. You are hereby notified to be and appear either personally or by attorney at the next Superior Court of Rabun county to be held on the fourth Monday in February 1902 next, to answer the complaint of W. D. Manley in an action for total divorce. In default thereof the court will proceed as to justice shall appertain. Herein fail not. Witness the Hon. J. B. Estes, Judge of said court. This 19th day of December 1901. J. S. Ramey, C. S. C. Jas. R. Grant, Libelant's Attorney.

§ J. R. Grant went down to Clarksville Saturday.

§ Heman Earl is at home from Atlanta for a few days.

§ W. C. Scruggs was meeting friends here Saturday.

§ Thanks to Clemy Rogers for a load of wood on subscription.

§ H. A. Keener, of Rabun Gap, was here on business Saturday.

§ Miss Liza and Mary Arrendale came in Monday to attend school.

§ Miss May Ramey was the guest of her brother J. S. Ramey Monday.

§ L. C. Hollifield is at his Timpson farm most of his time of late days.

§ M. L. Arrendale was here Monday and gave us two paid up ads. Thanks.

§ F. A. Taylor was in town Monday. He will hustle for the Tribune in Stonepile.

§ The hour of the Masonic meeting Saturday has been changed from 8 to 6 o'clock.

§ Henry Long of S. C. was here Saturday arranging for his children to attend school.

§ Mr. J. Z. Ford of the Valley was in town Monday arranging for two of his children to enter school.

§ F. A. Taylor rent the Simmons house Monday, and his children will occupy it and attend school.

§   B. E. Ellerd of Flat Creek was here Monday. He will start for a town in the west in a few days with a view of locating there.

§   A yoke of oxen for sale on time till fall with note and security. Apply to H. K. Cannon, Clayton, Ga.

§   We call attention to the announcement of John H. Derrick, Jr., of Burton for representative. Mr. Derrick is a young man, a hustler and a good citizen.

§   Lost—A fingered pair of home knit gloves. The finder will be rewarded by bringing them to my office. W. S. Paris.

§   Miss Fannie Scruggs and Miss Beulah Green, of the Valley, gave our office a call Saturday. We think they called to see the traveling representative of The Tribune.

§   We call attention to the announcement of James E. Bleckley as a candidate for representative. "Jim" is a good man and has many friends who will be gratified to hear of his candidacy.

§   Dr. C. L. Marlatt, of the United States Department of Agriculture, has announced that the 17 year locusts will be with us here in North Georgia the coming summer. So we may expect the monotonous P-h-a-r-o-h.

§   A restraining order is presented to Judge Estes prohibiting the ordinary from proceeding with the alternative road law. The people will anxiously await the result. Col. Jas. R. Grant represents the petitioners.

§   Jerry Burton of Burton, probably the oldest man in the county, died at his home this morning. He was about 90 years old and a highly respected citizen. As time rolls by the old landmarks go out.

§   School opened here Monday with bright prospect of building up a standing high school at Clayton. Prof. O'Kelley [followed] by Prof. M. B. York made a nice opening address to the school and everything started off warm and lively. We predict a good and lively school this term.

§   For rent—Forty acres of good bottom land on the O'Callagan farm, two and a half miles from Clarksville, Ga. Good pasture on premises. Address, Mrs. E. A. Cartell, Clarksville, Ga.

§   We are again obligated to James L. York for a load of good hickory wood on subscription.

§   V. A. Green leaves to-morrow for Wrightsville, Johnson Co., Ga., to accept a position as teacher. The best wishes of his many friends here go with him to his new field of labor. The Tribune commends him to the good people of Johnson Co.

§   We hear encouraging news about the railroad. We are reliably informed that bills of lumber have been put in the hands of saw millers to build the trestle in Tallulah Falls, and contracts are being offered. There is a rumor that a few miles have been let. So it appears that the building has begun and we will now have a railroad.

§   Capt. S. S. Hall, an experienced miner who is in possession of the Barclay gold mines continues to bring to town exceedingly fine specimens of gold ore. This mine has been lying [dormant] for 50 years for lack of enterprise and capital.

§   Friend Rol Cannon of the Falls spent Wednesday night at the Blue Ridge hotel.

§   Wanted. Reliable man for Manager of a Branch Office we wish to open in this vicinity. A good opening for the right man. Kindly give good references when writing. The A. T. Morris Wholesale House. Cincinnati, Ohio. Illustrated catalogue 4 cts stamps.

§   Pine Mountain

We have plenty of cold weather now. Old Boreas seem to be whispering a tempest in the trees on the hill tops and in the vales.

Mr. Americus Ramey's children have scarlet fever at this writing.

Profs. J. M. Bleckley and G. N. Bynum have gone to Persimmon. Perhaps J. M. can help G. N. get "Justus".

Mr. W. F. Holden has returned from the Gate City, and reports a lively time.

Miss Ella Goble and Mr. Morten were happily married last Thursday Mr. Crain officiating. We wish them a long and happy life.

Miss Dovie Carver, formerly of this county, died at her sister's at Westminister, S. C., last week.

Mr. Jesse Hamby is in Colorado again.

It is reported that Mr. Hughes "cut up Xmas, and carried off the 'devil's' dinner pot."

§   Burton

School begins here next Monday.

A pound supper was enjoyed at Mr. V. T. Stonecypher's New Years night. A large crowd attended.

Mr. Cicero Fincannon of Habersham, formerly of Rabun, died at his home Thursday morning. He was a kind and affection [*sic*] husband and father. He will be missed in his community. We extend our heartfelt sympathy to the bereaved family.

Mr. Lyon and wife of Texas are visiting relatives here.

Miss [illegible] and Coloma Wood spent new years night with Mr. and Mrs. J. F[?]. Arrendale.

Miss Sallie Smith and Messers Willie Stonecypher and James Smith attended Prof. Dover's entertainment at Ivy Hill.

Miss Texie Wood and Miss Rosa Wilson spent New Years night with Miss Lula Arrendale.

Messrs. Graver Daniels and Connie Barron of Habersham attended singing here Sunday evening.

Mr. Lum FinCannon of Newman, Ga., is with home folks this week. He came to attend his brother's funeral.

Mr. Alfred and Tom Cook of Indian Territory is visiting friends and relatives here.

Mr. James FinCannon who has had Typhoid fever is improving.

§   Glassy

Cold weather.

Hog killing is the order of the day.

The People of this section had the pleasure of going to a nice entertainment at Ivy Hill Dec. 31st. We saw three last days in one: last day of school, last day of month, and last day of year.

The boys had the fun of putting up footlogs after to high waters.

Guess what young man fell in the creek last Sunday night as he was on his way home and the foot logs were washed away.

Ask what young man missed his dinner at the house raising the other day.

We are sorry to say that V. G. Dixon's child is very ill.

Jerry Vickers and Horace McCurry was in this section after a load of fodder the other day.

§   Stonepile

Weather very cold.

There was a big day at Stonepile Saturday. Col. Owens, of Toccoa, was attending court there in the interest of G. H. Lovell.

Mr. C. H. Benfield says he did not mean those persimmons as a gift, only to make the girls grown tail. Some of them stopped growing too soon or were pulled and dried up.

The girls of Flat Creek think the young men ought to furnish something nicer on a Christmas tree than cob pipes.

The people are going to soon have a new church house at Flat Creek which will add to the improvement of the community.

Mr. W. S. Ellard and wife are out from the west visiting their connection, M. B. Ellard and others. He will leave in a few days. He seems to have made money since gone. We wish him a prosperous life as he was the baby of one of our best friends.

Wild turkeys are scratching in the fence corners.

Rev. R. L. Whitmire will preach at Eden church the third Saturday and Sunday.

§   Chechero

Mr. George Dickson is visiting on Chechero.

Miss Dovie Williams had a candy drawing not long ago.

The son of Mr. W. J. McCrackin is very sick at this writing.

School has begun at Chechero again.

Mr. James Alison Jones moved from Chechero to Wolf Creek to his old home.

§   Blalock

Fine weather.

The roads are in bad fix.

Mr. Bud Elliot has moved two miles the other side of Hiawassee.

Ask Horley Thompson who saw the finest time when he was moving the other day.

Miss Texie and Belle York have gone to Cornelia to go to school.

I suppose Miss May Justus was all smiles Christmas day.

Thos. E. King has commenced keeping store again.

§   Quartz

The deaths that occured last night is astonishing to you.

The New Year has begun with a beautiful and brilliant day. We trust that the glory of God might be realized through the sunshine even to the extent that it will cause new resolutions to be formed and carried out by his people to his...glory.

J. F. York is off to Cornelia to carry the children down to enter school Those that went were Richard, Henry, Belle and Helena York.

Texie York has gone to her school at Blue Ridge.

Washington Coleman has returned from market. He was gone twenty one days.

There was another sea of water on Persimmon the 29th inst.

Prof. Howard left for his school last week where he will stay until it closes. He informs me that he has a school on Wolf Fork for this year.

A. A. Darnell is at work on a chimney for I. P. Coleman.

No sickness at this writing as far as we know. H. A. Parker has been very bad off but is better.

§   Germany

Mr. J. A. Alman and wife visited John Justus Friday.

Mr. D. L. Justus is recovering a granery this week.

John Colenback had a corn-shucking Thursday.

Mr. Emory Hollifield was among friends here Sunday.

Miss Della Moore from Wolf Fork was the guest of her sister, Laura Justus this week.

Mr. Netherland Bynum and J. M. Bleckley spent Sunday night with C. F. York and family.

Mr. M. B. York passed through this community Sunday.

Mr. M. L. Keener and wife, of Tennesee Valley, visited James Powell Sunday.

Mr. J. N. Justus gave the young folks a nice singing Sunday night.

Mr. C. F. York and J. W. Alman started on a market trip Monday.

§   Tiger

Did we tell you that Mr. Thomas Dotson traded his big mule for oxen? Well he did.

Mr. Frank Shirley has moved to Vandiver.

It is reported that Rena Hunter will moved to Vandiver.

It is reported that Mary Worley's husband has come back. (Mr. Bill Potts.)

Mr. Willie Sutton Ellard, a young friend and neighbor who has been in the west for several years, is visiting his brother Mr. M. B. Ellard of Stonepile District.

Mr. H. J. Taylor is moving back from Habersham County to settle again on their old home in old Rabun.

Mr. F. A. Taylor has succeeded in getting a settlement of the differences in account with Mrs. Roena Hunter.

Miss Susie Taylor and brother attended the school entertainment and Christmas tree at Ivy Hill.

Miss Ada Green was at Tiger preaching Sunday. She is always a welcome visited.

February 13, 1902
Volume 5, Number 4

§ Big Blaze in Elberton. Plucky Georgia Town Suffers Loss of Over $100,000 by Fire. Fire broke out in the heart of the business section of Elberton, Ga., at an early hour Sunday morning, and before the flames were checked over $100,000 had gone up in smoke. Two of the main business blocks of the city are in ruins and the loss is estimated at $194,500. Of this less than half was covered by insurance, the total amount of insurance on the burned buildings and stocks amounting to only $41,750. The fire is by all odds the most disastrous in the history of the Granite City. The buildings burned were on McIntosh street, the principal business street of Elberton.

§ As I have never entered a political campaign before it is necessary for me to make a few remarks in regard to my political principals. Mr. Ritchie said in our contest that I was deprived of the office of C. S. Comm'r on account of my being a republican. I made no reply to this because I did not believe any member of the Board knew anything about my political standing. I have never voted a full democratic or republican ticket as I remember of. I would have voted a republican ticket for president if I had gone to the last presidential election. I have often said that we, the people of north Georgia, had more money and could get better prices for our stock under a republican administration. As to the principals of the two parties, I don't yet thoroughly understand them, therefore am unable to make a permanent decision, but am making this race subject to the action of the democratic party and will appreciate all the help I can get, let it be democratic or republican. Yours truly, C. J. Crunkleton.

§   Wolffork

Mrs. E. A. Moore is very sick at this writing.

Uncle Jeff Hopper, of N. C., was up visiting friends here the other day.

The infant child of Sheriff Ritchie was buried here Friday.

Rev. Barret preached a very interesting Sermon Sunday.

Mr. Isaac Justus visited his best girl Sunday.

Mr. Jesse Justus, Georgia and Marvin Powel were on Wolffork Sunday.

Ask Miss Ella and Della Moore if they got disappointed Saturday night.

Little Bryant Dickerson visited Mr. J. B. Moore Saturday night.

Mr. John Keener was absent Sunday and some of the girls were very uneasy about him.

Mr. Luther Dickerson is building him a new residence.

Some of the boys visited Mr. D. G. Dover's log rolling Saturday.

I will agree with the Pine Mountain dots about popping [sic] the question. I think there would be fewer and better weddings if the girls would propose.

§   Warwoman

Mr. A. L. Beck returned to his home in N. C. Saturday.

Mr. Will Holden, of Pine Mountain, passed through here on his way to Clayton last week.

Mrs. S. M. Beck is real sick at this writing.

Mary Beck and Josie Swofford spent a few days on Checheroe last week.

Mrs. Mart Beck spent Saturday night with parents, Mr. and Mrs. Powers.

§   Georgia—Rabun County. To all whom it may concern: J. S. Ramey has in due [form] applied to the undersigned for permanant letters of administration on the estate of T. J. Coffee, late of said county, deceased and I will pass upon said application the first Monday in March, 1902. Given under my hand and official Signature. This 6th day of February, 1902. W. S. Long, Ordinary, Rabun Co.

§   V. T. Stonecypher, Administrator of the estate of Wm. Stonecypher, deceased, vs. A. W. Irvine, trustee. Foreclosure of mortgage in Rabun Superior court, Feb'y adjourned term 1901. It being represented in the court by the petition of V. T. Stonecypher, administrator of the estate of William Stonecypher, deceased, that on the 28th day of December, 1898, A. W. Irvine, as trustee for Frederick W. Vest, Ella E. Irvine and Jennie C. Taylor, of the county of Hall, executed and delivered to the deceased intestate, William Stonecypher, a mortgage on certain real estate lying in said county and described as follows, to-wit: All the mineral on, under or in the following described lands: Beginning at a point marked with a stone monument to the conditional line between the Smith and Stonecypher property, thence running a course west of north and following the line of an old field in the rear of Stonecypher's house past a red oak tree marked on nits upper side with a letter "M" in a straight line to the intersection with main road to Hightower Pass, thence northeasterly along said road to its intersection with upper line of Stonecyphers property, thence southeasterly to its intersection with the conditional line between Smith and Stonecypher, thence with said Smith and Stonecypher conditional line to the place of beginning, with all rights, members and appurtenances to the said property in anywise appertaining and belonging, for the purpose of securing the payment of 8 certain promissory notes for the sum of one hundred and twenty-five dollars each besides interest and attorney fees, executed and delivered by said A. W. Irvine, trustee as afore said, to said William Stonecypher on the 28th day of December, 1898, due "one each three months thereafter until all are paid" and stipulating for interest after maturity at the rate of seven per cent per annum and ten per cent attorney fees. It is ordered that the defendant A. W. Irvine, trustee as aforesaid, do pay into this court by the first day of next term the principal, interest, attorney fees and costs due on said notes or show cause why he should not pay the same... This May 11th 1901. J. B. Estes, J. S. C.

§   Rabun Superior Court, August Term, 1901. It appearing to this court that [the] defendant A. W. Irvine trustee has not been served with the petition and rule in the within stated case as required by the former order of this court. It is therefore ordered that this case stand continued and that said defendant A. W. Irvine trustee be served with said rule as required by law before the next term of this court... August 30, 1901. John S. Candler, J. S. C.   H. H. Dean and W. S. Paris, Plaintiff's Attorneys.

Georgia—Rabun County. I, J. S. Ramey, Clerk of the Superior Court of Rabun County, Ga., do hereby certify that the foregoing orders are true copies from the minutes of the Superior Court of Rabun County. Witness my hand and official signature, this Sept. 3rd, 1901. J. S. Ramey, Clerk.

§   Dillard
Dock Parker is off to the Falls this week.
Frank Godfrey is not very well at this writing.
There occured something very funny in the Valley Sunday. Mr. John Parker hauled wood [illegible] day and did not know it was Sunday until noon. He was making all[?] preparations of keeping Monday the Sabbath. John is a hustler.

The roads are getting very bad. Mr. Leo Lyle had a horse to [illegible] down in the public road near Mr. Ira Holden's Sunday that weighed over twelve hundred pounds. It took eighteen men to pull the horse out and they said if two of the party had not had a little "mountain dew" it would not have been such an easy task.

On last [illegible] Mrs. John Lamb[?] died[?]. She was takened suddenly ill the night before her death. Also on the previous evening on going to milk Mrs. R[?]. Lamb dropped dead as she was [illegible] the fence.

Mr. M. L. Scruggs takened[?] dinner with J. W. Godfrey and son Frank Sunday. Ask M. L. who did the cooking.

Mrs. Laura Dockins came near being burned to death on last Thursday morning by her clothing catching on fire.

Mrs. Lizzie Howard is very sick at this writing.

Mrs. Sallie Powell spent Saturday and Sunday in Clayton.

Rev. Brown, of Gainesville, preached at the Baptist Church Sunday.

Zoie Godfrey is mad at this writing.

Ed McConnell was in this section Saturday night.

§   Attention Young Men. The state, recognizing the necessity of your obtaining an education, has established at Dahlonega, a college where you can have the advantage of a $40,000.00 equipment and a faculty, each man a specialist in his department. Tuition is free and board is only $8.00 a month in dormitory. It is your college, built for you, supported by you, and stands ready to help you. It is not a town school but a real college, being one of the five male colleges of the state. It costs no more to go to a real college than to one only in name. Don't cheat yourself by going to a school without library or scientific labatories. Write for catalogue to J. S. Stewart, President, Dahlonega, Ga.

§   Notice is hereby given to all creditors of the estate of Ancil Godfrey, late of said county, deceased, to render in an account of their demands to me within the time prescribed by law, properly made out. And all persons indebted to said deceased are hereby requested to make immediate payment to the undersigned. This 3rd day of Feb. 1902. J. F. Godfrey, Administrator of Ancil Godfrey.

§   Having been advised by many of my friends to make the race for clerk superior court I hereby announce myself a candidate for clerk subject to the action of the democratic party. If elected will serve you to the best of my ability. Yours truly, C. J. Crunkleton.

§   To the voters of Rabun county. I hereby announce myself a candidate for re-election to the office of clerk of the superior court, subject to the actions[?] of the democratic party and thank my friends in advance for their patronage and grateful[?] to them for past favors. J. S. Ramey.

§   At the solicitation of friends from every district in the county: I hereby announce my candidacy for the office for Sheriff. If a primary election ordered by the democratic party of Rabun county my candidacy is subject to the result of such primary. Thanking the people for the hearty and enthusiastic support formerly given me, and promsing if again elected not to betray the trust so generously reposed. I am respectfuly, John B. Dockins.

§   After due consideration and consultations of friends I hereby announce myself a candidate for representative, subject to a democratic primary, promising, if elected, to serve you honestly and faithfully. E. H. Baker.

§   To the voters of Rabun county: I hereby announce myself a candidate for re-election to the office of Tax Receiver, subject to the action of the demorcratic party. I thank the people for their support in the past and will be thankfull for any support in the future. John M. Marsingale.

§   Oweing[?] to our crowded column last week Mr. C. J. Crunkleton's explanation did not appear in our last issue, we print same in this issue.

§   The school continues to increase.

§   Dan Dover reports that his family are all sick.

§   Miss Stella Langston will keep boarders court week.

§   Col. Paris visited Gainesville and Atlanta the past week.

§   Miss Amanda Earl has returned home from Otto, N. C.

§   Dr. Green is improving his acre property near the Baptist church.

§   Thanks to L. N. Robins for a subscription to his boys Bert and Jesse in the far west.

§   Our good friend Lafayette Wall was in town to-day. He never forgets the Tribune.

§   Nelson Tilley will pay county [illegible] in the absence of John W. Green[?], Treasurer.

§ Robt. Crisp, of Walhalla, S. C., is the guest of children, Mr. and Mrs. L. N. Robins.

§ The post office cancellations here have increased considerably since school began.

§ Beulah Dixon, col., died of Typhoid fever Sunday and was buried at the Gipson cemetery in Tennessee Valley Tuesday.

§ Lamb-Corn. Marriage licence was issued yesterday for the marriage of Samuel Corn and Mary Lamb.

§ Joseph W. Derrick, a brother to our townsman J. E. Derrick and a native of this county, died at his home at Elem Springs, Arkansas Feb'y first 1902.

§ Miss Glenn Adams, of Thomaston, Ga., will teach music here for the next four months. She is an accomplished young lady, with rare musical talent, having graduated at Brenau Female College, Gainesville, Ga.

§ See the announcement of John Marsingale for tax receiver. Mr. Marsingale was complimented by the Comptroller General last year for his efficiency. He ever has [illegible] words for all and is a kind and genial fellow and has many friends.

§ We have 30,000 lbs of acid and guano for sale either here or at Tallulah Falls. Will take corn, cash, produce or sell on time with note and approved security. Call on or address Cannon and Thompson, Tiger, Ga.

§ We call your attention ty the announcement of E. H. Baker for representative. Mr. Baker is well known over the county and would make an able and honorable representive.

§ J. M. and C. W. McConnell represent Treeville Nursery Co., of Winstead, Tenn. This nursery is one of the finest in the south and by seeing them you can save money. The McConnell Bros. will be here court week. They are gentlemanly boys. Call and see them.

§ Marriage is an honorable institution—instituted by God himself. Our law is [illegible] makes people marry. This kind we are not [illegible]. To avoid legal complications Emory Dickson was married to Miss Paloma Gables[?] Tuesday night, J. C. Pickett officiating.

§ J. C. Richards, representing the [illegible] Bros. Nursery and Orchard [illegible] of 77 years' standing. Mr. Richards wishes us to state he will be here during court week and will be pleased to meet old friends of the nursery.

§ Between three and four hundred people met at the court house Monday for the purpose of discussing merits and [illegible] of the alternative road law. The fight will be vigorous in the courts. If nothing more becomes of it, in the event the opposition wins, the old system will be better enforced.

§ [Illegible] you will find the announcement of John B. Dockins for sheriff. Mr. Dockins was sheriff when we made our first advent in the county and his name sounds familiar to us in connection with the word. He made a good officer and no better recommendation can be given him than his past record.

§ A young man in Atlanta, after corresponding four years with one of the Robin's girls, wrote he would be delighted to have a lock of her hair. She at once proceeded to take a wisp from the fine haired shepherd dog, bound it with a blue ribbon and forwarded it to him. The young man acknowledged the receipt saying the hair was beautiful and that he had kissed it a thousand times.

§ Mrs. J. B. Dockins, while attending her little sick daughter, Irene, was seriously burned last Thursday. The child was lying before the fire and Mrs. Dockins was kneeling to attend the child with her back to the fire, when her dress caught on fire, and before Mr. Dockins could extinguish the flames, she was badly burned. Mr. Dockins' hands were also badly burned in subduing the flames. Mrs. Dockins, though narrowly[?] escaped death, was resting at last accounts.

§ The students contemplating attending school are out here by a goodly number yet. We will tell our readers, and especially those who may want to attend school, who are here and where they stay and how. The cost is small and nearly every student has left comfortable homes and in a point of comfort are making sacrifices. They are "chucked" in little [illegible] open huts, wading through mud and losing slippers, all the time seemingly happy, and in the future you will hear from these self sacrificers. Young man, make up your mind to no longer grope in darkness but come to school here and be enlightened. The students are scattered all over the town, as follows: Frank and Jesse Singleton are boarding with Esquire Pickett, Miss Deskie[?] Justus is with Mrs. L. C. Hollifield, Sanford and Virgil Taylor and ---------- Dockin are cabined in[?] the Simmons cottage; Thos. Singleton, Major York, Marvin

Powel[?], John Franklin[?] Jones, Misses Sallie[?] Parker and Ada Justus are roomed in the W. B. Duncan cottage; Miss Dovie Williams is in the FinCannon house; Misses Ethel Powell and Beulah Green are cabined in the Howell[?] house; Miss Carrie Grist is with Mrs. J. R. Grant[?]; Miss Ella[?] Ramey, Misses Mary and Eliza Arrendale and Misses Zelma and Mattie Price are with Mrs. Coffee; Miss Mary and Belle[?] Scruggs, Wallace Scruggs, Miss Lizzie and Frank Dillard and Turner[?] and Luther[?] Swofford are in Miss[?] Wall's house on Warwoman street; James[?] Guy and Misses Mary and Ada Green are rooming in the Whitmire block.

§   Germany

Rev. Ford will preach at Mountain Grove on the first Saturday and Sunday in every month.

We are having a nice Sunday School here. It has been going on for nearly two years and is still going on.

Mrs. Moore spent this week with her daughter Laura Justus.

Aunt[?] Nancy York is on the sick list this week.

Clerk J. S. Ramey and Jess Smith were among friends here Friday

J. N. Justus has been splitting rails and fencing some for pasture.

Mrs. Lizzie Arrendale spent Sunday with Dock Justus. Come again Lizzie.

Mr. Jeffie Holcomb says if he had a dollar and a half he would carry it to the [illegible]. Hurray for Jeffie!

Little Roy York spent Friday with Mr. and Mrs. James Colenback.

Mr. John Holcomb, who moved on the Tom Coffee land about two months ago, has moved back to his old place. John is a hustler.

Mr. Isaac Justus spent Sunday with his girl.

Mr. John Carnes is the boss singer on Germany.

Little Carrie York is sick at this writing.

John Justus is still in a painful condition caused by a cut on the hand.

Mr. John Keener, of Wolffork, spent Sunday night with C. F. York and family.

Little Dewey Justus has been sick for the past week.

§   Upper Chechero

Mr. Jesse Green is in this section.

Mr. Thomas Burrel has moved to Anderson S. C.

Mr. Dud Dockins went to Clayton last week.

Mr. Andrew Ramey's children are sick at this writing.

A crowd from here visited friends in the Valley last week.

Mr. V. C. Taylor is very busy [illegible] his land.

Aunt Polly Ramey is improving.

Ask Miss Zelma and Mattie Price if they found anybody they liked any better than themselves at Clayton.

Miss Lottie Swofford is improving at this writing.

Miss Mary Beck and Josia Swofford, of Warwoman, was on Chechero last Sunday.

Mrs. Mary Swofford is sick at this writing.

Miss Lucy Duncan attended preaching at Chechero Sunday.

Miss Lillie Ramey is visiting her sister Miss Mary Swofford.

Mr. Adolphus Ramey says he met some cold weather between home and Clayton.

§   Blalock

[Illegible] on Pop Corn the other day.

Look at the [illegible] weddings on Plum[?] Orchard[?].

Mr. Albert Henderson and brother visited G. H. Thompson Saturday night and Sunday.

Ask Luther Thompson who killed a bear with M. C. Warlee's gun.

Robert[?] Lunsford is very sick at this writing.

Miss Plena[?] Thompson visited her father Monday night.

You may ask little Maggie Garlet what she found in her bucket one morning.

Ask Lizzie Thompson who is her sweetheart is. She says he is a fine fellow.

§   Quartz

If it continues fair a few days longer the garden work will be going on. Then the farmers will jump on the briars and sprouts, fixing for making corn.

Thomas Nichols planked up his mill so it can be locked. He says somebody help themselves to his meal and take the sack with them.

We have some boys that like to shoot a pistol so good that they shoot[?] the school house door. We hope the Grand Jury will find them out and the judge will shoot them into the chaingang.

Well, we have not seen any candidates yet, but expecting. We would like to know whether the candidates for representative want to go to the legislature to do something for the people, or for the name of going or for that four dollars per day. If they want to do something for us we would like to know what it is so we could help them predict what would be best for us. One thing I know and that is, not so much legislation unless it was more to the people's interest.

We need a law to prohibit any one from selling or buying and relling[?] corn or provision on time for more than the market price with the lawful interest, as poor, laboring men have and[?] to pay 50 or 75 per cent above the rise in price for bread just because the seller knew he had to have it.

There is another thing comes to my mind and that is whether or not the man who lends his money at over 8 per cent could be counted as a law-abiding man or not. If he is, the law surely don't mean what it says, for it only gives 7 unless by specified contract and then only eight. Now what about that other two cents you want unlawfully? Is it right? If it not right to let us have the law changed or abide by the law one of the two. There is a certain lot of people that will come right up to the grand jury and stand up to make people abide by the law and at the same time they are imposing an unlawful per cent on their fellow-man, which is contrary to the law of justice.

§ Burton

There was a large crowd out at Sunday School and preaching Sunday evening. Prof. Burrell delivered an interesting sermon to an attentive audience.

Mr. Nelson Tilley was among friends at Burton Sunday.

Mr. Lester and Connie Barron were at preaching Sunday evening.

Mr. Jimmy King and Mr. Henry English, of Persimmon, were at Sunday School Sunday evening. Ask them if they got disappointed when they went up on the creek.

Mr. Connie Barron was with his best girl Sunday.

Mr. Willis Jones and wife visited their parents Saturday night.

Col. Wimpey attended our Sunday. He says he will give us a lectur[?] next Sunday.

Mr. John Moore and wife visited Mr. John Philyaw and family last Sunday.

§ Pine Mountain

Dr. Bell, of Walhalla, S. C., was called professionally to the bedside of J. M. Bleckley, Sr., last Friday.

Mr. Mel Houston, of this place, and Miss Belle Ballew, of Macon Co., N. C., were happily married at the bride's home last week.

Miss Mary and G. N. Bynum have gone to Clayton to enter school.

Miss Ella Hamby and her cousin Tom were the guests of J. M. Bleckley, Jr., last Tuesday night. Tom is expecting to return to Colorado soon. He is one of Rabun's brightest young men.

We wonder if the candidate of the 1275th district is going to kiss both the old and young.

Mr. Fred Bowers was with his best girl Sunday. We think he means business.

Mr. Talley is not improving any.

Mr. W. F. Holden went to Clayton Saturday on business but we don't know what kind.

February 20, 1902
Volume 5, Number 5

§   We have never "drummed" very much for the Tribune, but look out for us court week.

§   No one has announced for tax collector yet. Come on gentlemen with the announcement.

§   We are buying new type this week and ask all who are due for advertising or otherwise to aid us.

§   The Clayton Tribune and the Clarkesville Advertiser do [*illegible*] to be popular with home merchants. We ask Charlie and Miss Mattie for an explanation. We trade with our home merchants altogether. Other papers are full of ads from their home merchants.

§   Next week is court week. We wait in fond anticipation. It is then we meet the judge and the lawyers, Col. Swain, the clever court stenographer, and many who do not live in the county who are our patrons. We meet many prominent ment of our county, all of whom we are glad to see. We feel the Tribune has many friends. It has been going to many homes over four years now and to those who have unceasingly stood by us we feel truly grateful. We are glad we can truthfully say that we do not entertain any ill will toward any one, dead or living, but we just can't help having a special kind feeling for those who heartily favor us. We have asked the people for no more except to take their county apper since we have been in the county. We hold the county surveyor's office, but did not seek it and offered to announce free of charge, in our paper, any one who would serve in this capacity. We do ask and plead to the good citizens of Rabun county to take their home paper, and we are going to meet the people during court and talk the Tribune [*illegible*] we never have before and you may prepare to meet us. We are going to act as our own agent and give the people agent's commission for each subscribers. We dare say, and we say it, the people of Rabun have more ready cash according to population than any county in northeast Georgia, and we purpose to persuade you who are not already taking our paper to subscribe. We need your support and must have it and you need the paper.

§　How infinitely nicer it is to see you people striving for an education than it is to see them going into debauchery and dissipation. Here we see faces all beaming with smiles and happy. Faces are indices to the hearts. All great people are educated...

§　Important Notice. The last day of Hall Superior Court a case of small pox broke out in the jury and almost all the people were exposed to it including the Judge and the lawyers. Six cases have developed from that juror in the last three days. Owing to this threatened scourge—especially in this awful weather—it is deemed dangerous to hold Rabun Court next week. It is therefore ordered that Rabun Superior Court be, and is, adjourned, from the fourth Monday in February instant, to the first Monday in May, 1902. All parties, witnesses, jurors and officers interested in said Court, will take due notice thereof and govern themselves accordingly. The Clerk and Sheriff are directed to give publicity to this notice as far as possible, and give it notice also in the Clayton Tribune. The Clerk will enter the above on the minutes of the Court. This February 20th, 1902. J. B. Estes, J. S. C.

§　No court till May. Court is postponed. See the reason why elsewhere.

§　Col. Paris has purchased a horse.

§　There are four prisoners in Jail.

§　Marion Long has fire proof oil.

§　The court house has been neatly carpeted.

§　Mrs. J. S. Ramey is not in her usual health.

§　Grover and Miss Mary Bynum are in school.

§　Drew Wall of Scaly N. C. has entered school.

§ Col. W. S. Paris spent the first of the week in Atlanta.

§ Mrs. John H. Donaldson has been quite sick for a week.

§ Mrs. Emily Wall attended the funeral of her brother, Mr. J. M. Bleckley Sr. Wednesday.

§ Our Warwoman letter this week should be an example for some of our correspondents to go by.

§ Nelson Tilley drove to Cornelia from here and returned the same day, last Thursday, a distance of 75 miles at least.

§ It began snowing here last Friday about 10 a. m. and never ceased till about midnight when the ground was covered about 14 inches.

§ J. A. Mahaffey, who has been confined in jail here since last September court charged with perjury in the case of Chub Wall, has been quite sick.

§ Any person tresspassing on the following lands will be prosecuted to the full extent of the law: Lots of land 19, 20, 22 and 6 in the 5th land district and lot 6 and a part of 5 in the fourth land district. Miles Phillips.

§ J. M. Thos, and Miss Lena Bleckley intered [*sic*] school here this week.

§ J. M. Bleckley, Sr., aged 73, died at his home Monday morning. Mr. Bleckley had been feeling badly about a month. The direct cause of his death is thought to be heart failure. No one was present in his room at the time of his death. He passed away while lying before the fire. He has a large circle of relatives to mourn his loss.

§ Notice. All persons who have bonded lands to W. M. Turpen and D. W. McDade must bring all deeds and titles to the undersigned at once to be passed upon. If you will bring your deeds of records and those not to record to our attorney Jas. R. Grant, we will assure you of the money for every acre that you can show good title for. The reason you have not received payment for your lands long before this is because we are unable to get clear abstracts of your lands. We have been at work on these lands since Nov. 1st 1901, and fail to find them of record. Others desiring to sell their lands will present same to Mr. Grant at once for approval. W. M. Turpen, D. W. McDade.

§   Grand Jurors. Jeff D. Beck, James B. Hicks, John H. Dotson, Russell E. Cannon, Elijah B. Philyaw, Cicero C. York, Lafayette Dixon, Isaac P. Coleman, John W. Green, Thos. E. King, Wm. B. Watts, Peter E. Thompson, Pat Coleman, Andrew M. Holden, Henry N. Burrell, A. J. Kell, F. G. Holden, Bailess Nicholson, Chas. J. Crunkleton, John Howard, J. M. Arrendale, E. D. Swofford, Isaac N. Lovell, James M. Bell, Wm. H. York, Marion Jones, Virgil Stonecypher, Eli H. Baker, James F. Smith, James B. Powell.

§   Traverse Jurors. Sam J. Page, Wyly Pitts, Julius F. York, Jesse F. Philyaw, Americus A. Billingsley, Wm. A. Martin, Jas. W. Smith, Jas. E. Rickman, Allen Turpen, James L[?]. FinCannon, John R. Carver, Henry M. Pitts, Jas. H. Dillard, Abraham Jones, Columbus C. Ledford, Leander T. Teens, Wm. M. Parker, Rufus J. Parker, John P. Billingsley, Tillman M. Ramey, Geo. N. Garland, Elias N. Holden, Wm. J. Watts, Pulaski H. Garland, Samuel Hamby, Alfred E. Dickson, Andrew J. Grist. R. D. Speed, Wm. Bradley, Julius P. Dotson, James E. Callenback, James Bell, John Martin, Henry K. Cannon, John H. Hooper, John W. Alman, Levi N. Robins.

§   Upper Chechero
The deepest snow that has been in many a year came last Friday night. Some were glad and some were sorry to see it. Some of the boys went rabbit hunting but did not see any sign of rabbits. They said they looked in every hole on the side of the road and they could not see one bit of a sign.
    The health of this community is very good.
    Miss Lottie Swofford is improving.
    Ask Mary Cox which she likes best, white or black hats.
    Mr. Davis, of Anderson, S. C., is visiting relatives in this community.
    Mr. Charlie, Bron and Miss Maud Coffee and Ella Ramey visited relatives and friends in the Valley Sunday.
    Dol Ramey went to Clayton Friday.
    Miss Zelma Price visited home folks last Saturday and Sunday. Ask her if she got much cold Saturday evening.

§   Blalock
Spring is almost here.
    The Tate city mines will start up the 10th of next month.
    Rev. Warlick wishes to thank the people of Upper Tiger and Spring Hill for their kindness.
    G. N. Bynum will teach school at Cross Roads this year.

§ Dillard

News scarce this week.

Guss Hensely[?] is off to Towns County after [*illegible*].

Logan Turpen[?] [*illegible*] Turnerville last week.

Little Effie Turpen[?] [*illegible*] spending the week with [*illegible*] Godfrey.

Willie Franks is in the Valley this week.

Mr. Hiram Dillard and family have moved to Gainesvill [*sic*] where they expect to work in the cotton mills.

There fell a snow last Friday measuring from fifteen to eighteen.

Frank Wall of Warwoman was in the Valley Sunday.

§ Quartz

A big, deep snow, between 12 and 14 inches deep, the largest one in many years.

To-day would have been garden work done with many farmers but Mr. White says "wait until I get away."

T. M. Justus and wife went to the R. R. Wednesday.

A. M. and J. F. Keener have returned from market.

H. W. Barclay still carries the mail from Quartz to John M. York's.

It is said that Rev. Warleck is going to move to Burton. We hope it will be a good change for him but would be glad to have him stay with us.

There was one of the grand jurors said if you wanted to know what kind of grand jurors were in the box to ask one they call T. J. N., who says they are the biggest set of fools he ever saw—not one of them has sense enough to bead a sheep. He wants to know if they would be any the wiser if he were included with them.

Quite a crowd attended the road meeting at Clayton last Monday. It seems as if they will have a lot of money to spend anyway, and it seems like we had as well pay a road tax as to employ a man and give him a right to still employ others for it is the money they are after and they will have it if you give them a chance.

We see the [*illegible*] full, but I guess the editor would make more room unless he is partial.

§ Wolf Fork

News is scarce.

There is nothing but snow snow.

Mrs. E. A. Moore is still on the sick list.

Mrs. Hindy Dickerson and Mrs. R. L. Keener are sick at this writing.

Mr. T. F. Page and son Charlie returned home from market last week.

Rev. Landrum will preach here next Sunday.

The Revenues visited here Friday and cut up two stills.

Mr. James Pendergrass and Virgil Keener are gone to Toccoa.

§ Old Tiger

The train failed to make its run to the Falls last Saturday on account of the snow. Chance Vickors made his run alright and on average time.

Mr. J. H. Dotson is the spirit of fun among the lumber hands.

It is reported that one of the Stonepile boys built him a "turkey pen" without any cover in the woods to catch "wild turkeys"[.] Some of the other boys caught the fowl first[.] Mr. Tom Roberts laid claim to it and had the successful trappers served with a warrant.

The case is pending for Stonepile court for the justice to decide whose turkey the wild unmarked hog is.

Some of the boys went out in the snow and caught thirteen rabbits.

§ Burton.

Snow.

We are about snowed in.

Mr. John Burton and wife, of Fair Mount[?], Ga., are visiting relatives here this week.

Dr. Dover made a professional call here last week.

Col. Wimpsey and H. C. Blalock have been on the sick list for a few days.

Miles C. Canup is off below selling mules.

Mr. and Mrs. Tom Wood are visiting Mr. Frank Wood and wife.

Mr. Rufus Arrendale, of Towns Co., is visiting friends and relatives.

§ Dr. J. W. Quillian[?], D. D., will preach at Wesley Chapel church in Tennessee Valley on the first and second days of March at 11[?] a. m. Quarterly conference at some church on March first. Dr. Quillian will preach at methodist church at Clayton on first Sun. [night] in March. L. L. Landrum, P. C.

§ Warwoman.

Didn't it snow Friday?

The boys are having a fine time hunting rabbits.

Mrs. A. M. Holden spent several days with relatives at Cullasajah, N. C., last week.

Mr. Lafayette Wall is up from Atlanta.

Mr. Ed McConnell captured Besry[?] Beck here Friday.

Misses Ara and Carry Ramey were on Warwoman last week.

Miss Mary Beck was the guest of Miss Martha Wall Wednesday.

Mr. Arthur Beck left here last week for Utah.

Mr. and Mrs. J. I. Langston passed through here on their way to Walhalla last week.

Mr. Turner Page, of Wolffork, was on the Creek the other day.

E. D. Swofford made a business trip to Habersham last week.

§ Grove

Prospects for farming dull.

Quite a number of the boys went to Clayton Monday in answer to a call for a mass meeting in regard to the alternative road system.

Tom Gable says he and the correspondent at Dillard will have their photographs taken together and put on exhibition at the Tallulah Falls fair next fall, provided the Dillard correspondent will pay all expense and see who will get the prize and if the correspondent don't pay all expenses he has no more to say, but still has twenty five cents to pay for Bill Arp's photo.

Mr. M. L. Arrendale is down the country trading on mules and produce.

Mr. C. E. Cannon, of Tiger, was in this community Wednesday.

Kinney Kragg is off with a load of produce.

§ We make a specialty of second hand and new clothing. Just received a large lot from New York. New suits for only $8.00. Good coats for 1.50 and over coats for two dollars. These goods are all wool. Pants 50 cents and up, shoes 85 cents and up. Our motto is quick sales and small profits. Highest prices for produce. Come and see our stock and go away satisfied. H. A. Keener & sons, Rabun Gap, Ga.

February 27, 1902
Volume 5, Number 6

§   If the alternative road law were an issue in the election for representative, we would like to be the candidate of the opposition. We would sure take a seat in the capitol this fall.

§   The Blairsville Herald says all the good newspapers are supporting Col. Estill for Governor. This is the first complement we have received from Bro. Haralson and may be the only one deserving.

§   Elsewhere you will see the announcement of John W. Green for re-election to the office of Treasurer. For two years Mr. Green has given entire satisfaction to the administration of the affairs of the office and we unhesitatingly say that there is no better man in the county nor in Georgia. And we heartily commend him to the suffrage of the county.

§   Clayton, Ga., Feb. 24th, 1902. Mr. Editor:--I see your correspondent from Quartz attacks me in an article published in your issue of the 20th. In reply to same will say that the gentleman has not paid one cent into my fees that I know of, and if he has I will take pleasure in refunding to him his little mite. I employed associate counsel. The mass meeting of citizens ratified my acts and I am informed your correspondent was present, and if he wanted to make a kicking machine out of himself then was the time to do it, and not hold his peace until he gets home and then get under a non [sic] de plume to make of himself a kicking machine against the wishes of the majority of the people of Rabun county. Very Respectfully, Jas. R. Grant, Attorney at Law.

§   Germany

Farmers are making preparations for crops.

Miss Retha York and Pearl Almon attended preaching at Union Hill Sunday.

Mr. E. A. Dickerson returned from a market trip last week.

Mr. and Mrs. Burrell was the guest of James Almon Saturday night.

Miss Laura and Lula Justus spent Sunday with Mr. J. N. Justus.

Mr. James Collenback went to Clayton Friday.

Charley Page passed through this community Saturday.

Mr. Anderson Coffee is very feeble at this writing.

Mr. John Carns is the best hair clipper of Germany.

Mr. John Justus is improving some at this writing.

J. C. Justus spent Sunday with friends and relatives on Wolffork.

Miss Carrie and Julia Holcomb spent Saturday night with Mr. John Hollifield and family.

Little Mollie, Fannie and Carrie York spent Sunday with Miss Essie Almon.

Erastus Harvey passed through this community Sunday enroute to Wolffork.

Mr. J. C. Justus has been repairing his residence.

Mr. James Almon went to Persimmon Sunday.

§   Grove

Snow was sixteen inches deep in Grove.

Mr. J. M. Burton and wife, of Gordon county, are visiting relatives in this community.

Mrs. A. J. Meece's health is very bad at this writing.

Miss Fannie Watts[?] of[?] Stonepile is visiting relatives on Bridge Creek.

Mr. R. N. Dover went to Clayton Wednesday.

Mail Carrier Gables said while he was working for Uncle Sam a woman friend wanted to accompany him and of course he had to refuse as he did not carry anything but the mail.

Detective John Marcus was at Grove Thursday looking up business.

§   Dillard

Ed Holden is up from Demorest.

Mr. W. H. Greenwood is at home for a few days.

Several of our people are down with measles.

Thanks to Mr. Gable for working my example.

D. D. Turpen is up from Turnerville.

Mr. Lee McConnell passed through this section Saturday selling apple trees.

Mr. R. E. L. Dillard was in this section Sunday.

Mr. H. R. Penland is off to Franklin this week.

Mrs. Little Thomas, of N. C., is with her mother, Mrs. Scroggs, this week.

Mr. and Mrs. G. W. Darnell are all smiles—it's a girl.

Mr. John Liner passed through here enroute to Clayton Sunday.

§ Come and pay me the interest you are due me or I will see about getting the principal. J. A. Almon.

§ Stonepile

Mrs. Fanny Watts came home Wednesday from a visit on Bridge Creek.

Mr. Sug Ramey made a trip up the river buying cattle.

Mrs. Lily Ellard has about recovered from her illness.

James Dockins and Virgil Taylor have spent a few days at home during the snow and report a fine school and good neighbors in Clayton. We want to tender our thanks to those good people for their kindness to those boys while up there.

§ Chattooga

(The following letter should have been published two weeks ago but has been crowded out, and as we are requested to print it any how we do so.)

Miss Mary Bynum is visiting relatives on Warwoman creek.

Mr. Monroe[?] Hopper, who lives in N. C., got his barn burnt up last Saturday.

Mr. Alf[?] Whitmire killed a hog last week that weighed over four hundred pounds.

The Russell bridge across Chattooga river is reported to be dangerous.

Pine Mountain is on a boom.

Mrs. Elias Holden is ill at this writing.

Jack Holden is very bad smitten on a girl who attends school at Clayton from the Valley.

It is reported that Hattie Ivester is to get married to a young man in Walhalla, S. C. Lookout Mr. J [*illegible*]den, it is too late to do good.

Ask Genelia Bynum who visited her Sunday.

The people have organized a Sunday School at Mount Pleasant church.

Miss Martha Wall spent last Sunday night with Mrs. Martha Bynum.

§ Ordinary Long requests us to say that he has received the money to pay indigent widows and soldiers and will do so at once.

§ There will be a called convocation of Tallulah Chapter No. 68 R. A. M. in the hall on Saturday March 8th at 9 a. m. for the purpose of confering all the degrees on several candidates. All qualified companions are urgently requested to be present. By order of R. E. A. Hamby, H[?]. P., W. S. Long, Sect'y. Feb'y 27 1902.

§ There will be a called communication of Rabun Gap Lodge No. 265 F. and A. M. on Saturday March 8th at 2 p. m. for the purpose of instruction, a full attendance is desired. By order of John W. Green, W. M., R. E. A. Hamby, Sec'y. Feb'y 27 1902.

§ Letters of Dismission. Georgia—Rabun County. A. J. Grist, administrator upon the estate of W. J. Grist, deceased, having filed his petition for discharge, this is to cite all persons concerned to show cause against the granting of this discharge at the regular term of the Ordinary for said county to be held on the first Monday in June[?], 1902. [Illegible] W. S. Long, Ordinary.

§ Railroad. Do you think it will come?

§ J. A. Alman was in town yesterday.

§ Thanks to Alvin Moore for favors.

§ We want a good correspondent at Pin[?] Mt[?].

§ Miss Elsie Ramey came up to-day to enter school.

§ D. M. Smith, of Tallulah Falls, was here Monday.

§ Thanks to G. W. Thompson of Spruce for favors.

§ A. J. Kell was among our pleasant visitors Monday.

§ Nelson Tilley made a hurried trip to Burton Saturday.

§ Thanks to Mr. and Mrs. H. K. Cannon for kindness shown us.

§ Court failing to convene makes the editor's pocket book lonely.

§ Mr. T. M. Justus, of Persimmon, was with us Monday. Thanks to you.

§ Miss Lucy Duncan, of Chechero, attended Sunday School here Sunday.

§   Lee King, popular knight of the grip, is registered at the Blue Ridge hotel.

§   Miss Carrie Grist spent Saturday and Sunday with home folk in Tennessee Valley.

§   Mr. H. R. Cannon, the popular merchant of Tallulah Falls, was here Sunday.

§   We are obliged to D. M. Green for his 5th year's subscription to The Tribune.

§   The Y. M. C. A. met Sunday and had the pleasure of admitting several new members.

§   Miss Ida Ford and little brother, of Scaly, N. C., have moved to town and entered school.

§   About eight have spoken to us concerning the race for Sheriff.

§   Come on gentlemen. All good fellows, any of whom will make a good Sheriff.

§   See the announcement of J. C. York for Tax Receiver. No better man than J. C., he is popular and has served the people satisfactory in this county before.

§   J. H. Coffee has recently sold two wagon loads of fine green apples and has another load for sale now. Mr. Coffee is getting fancy price for his fruit. Again we say, set apple trees to growing.

§   We are the proudest men surely in Rabun over the news of the extention of the Tallulah Falls Ry.

§   We have never had confidence in Mr. Prentiss' assertions, notwithstanding a few glooms. Now that carloads of dynamite and powder and other things in proporion[?] are in, we are just elated. All praise to every one connected in the enterprize from the president down to the humblest laborer.

§   Work will begin on the railroad Monday.

§   There are some unsavory litigations developed and brewing, if more tongues were bridled and about nine tenths would go to work there would be better times and few violations of the law.

§   Mr. Wagoner has the contract for 6 miles of the Tallulah Falls R'y extention and will begin at once. Mr. Wagoner is at Tallulah Falls where he is waiting his paraphernalia to begin work. This is news glorious to our people.

§   William Ritchie, who is about thirty years old and born and principally reared in the county, was at Clayton Friday last for the first time. He has never taken an oath, never had a law suit and is an intelligent man.

§   Cols. McDade and Turpen have been very busy since May of 1901 in securing timber lands in this section. They have secured about 40000 acres of land. We are personally acquainted with these gentlemen and have found them to be [straight] forward and conscientious business men. It seems that these gentlemen have been slow in disposing of these lands to our people Most of us are to [sic] impatient.

Their Att'y explains this satisfactorily to the public, he has been abstracting these lands, and the only dificulty [sic] he finds is that not more than fifty per cent of the deeds of the Rabun lands are of record and since this work has been in progress their Att'y has placed 75 per cent of the deeds to the lands bonded to men McDade and Turpen on record, so soon as parties will put their titles on[?] record we predict these gentleman [sic] will place something like $1000,000 dollars in circulation in this county.

§   Germany
Intended for last week.
Isaac Justus, Damascus Allman and Miss Dora Pitts went to Mr. Dan Dover's working. They report the nicest dinner on record.
I. M. Justus and Marvin Powell visited J. B. Moore's Sunday. Guess what girl Marvin saw.
D. B. Alman has a breech loading shot gun to sell or swap for a Winchester shot gun.
Mr. Hillyer Taylor and Charley Page were among friends here Saturday. Come again.
Ask A. E. Dickesson who visited him Sunday. I guess it was a young man who came to see Letha don't you?
Mr. Isaac Justus has his mind turned toward Black Rock. Look out, Isaac is coming. He is all o. k. I wonder if I could borrow Mr. Dover's gun?
C. F. York visited J. W. Alman Sunday.
Mr. J. N. Justus went to see Mr. Almon but he was gone. Ask him

where he went.

Rev. Albridge will preach at Union Hill the fourth Sunday in April. All are respectfully invited to attend.

§   Old Chechero

Intended for last week.

Rev. J. S. Dickson delivered an interesting sermon Sunday.

Miss Sarah and Dovie Lee spent Saturday night with James York.

Grandma Ramey is still very ill.

We were glad to have Mr. Jess and Frank Singleton with us Sunday.

Mrs. Leander Ramey is sick at this writing.

W. A. Dickson is having a fine bill of lumber cut and is going to have a fine house soon. Lookout girls.

§   The Snow. It is snow, snow, the beautiful snow, that comes so noiselessly and makes such a show... Still I don't—well I don't know, if we would or would'nt [sic] have snow. Just occasionally for just a change, but the Clayton boys—just keep out of their range... And so these lines, if you want to make songs, the snow-ball gang were out at John Long's...

§   Warwoman

Mr. Ed McConnell was on Warwoman Monday.

Jeff Swofford is off to Walhalla this week.

Mr. Will McWhorter and Berry Ramey, of Chechero, spent Thursday with E. D. Swofford and family.

Mrs. S. M. Beck is real sick at this writing.

Mr. and Mrs. Jack Duncan, of S. C., were on Warwoman last week.

Mr. J. D. Beck went to S. C. Friday.

Ask Savala Bowers where he stayed the other night and whose dog broke the dish.

§   Blalock

Very deep snow—14 inches.

Mr. H. R. Lunsford is better at this writing.

Ask Henry Blalock who is going to learn how to make picture frames.

Mr. I. P. Coleman has returned from market.

Tom Coleman says no one can beat him riding. He has a fine gray to ride.

You may ask M. N. York and S. E. Thompson what they had in their hands as they passed up the other day.

§   Pine Mountain

Intended for last week.

Mr. Editor, the snow is to [sic] deep to hunt rabbits or news either.

The deepest snow that has fallen for years fell here last Friday and Friday night.

The last we heard of Jack Holden he was at Pine Mountain crying for candy.

Mr. W. C. Speed bought a hog from J. S. Bleckley that weighed 214 pounds. W. C. says he has no other money but gold to pay for pork this year.

Most all the young people have left this place and gone to Clayton to enter school. We are proud to know the young people are fitting themselves for the great work so much needed... Then what is to hinder us from uniting in a social band and roll the wheel of prosperity.

§   Stonepile

Written for last week.

There is not much news or passing in the last week.

There has been a little law and the biggest snow since the woods were burnt. It was twelve inches deep on a work bench and it seems to get away very slow.

Someone wanted to know if our correspondent was going to kiss both old and young. The promise is to all and if elected it will just be the prettiest ones. That is the way politics runs.

The Quartz correspondent beat me. We asked the Baptist Banner printer at Cummings, Ga., some years ago how it was that our laws would allow men to sell corn at [*illegible*] ½ and 8 per cent interest when it would bring only 75 cents, also charge 10 and 12 ½ per cent interest when the law only allows eight when uncertain. I asked some one to explain the difference in that and other things but got no answer but The Tribune has published his.

We would be glad if some one would make a square cut and not round up the corners and smooth up the lower planes and jump the high ones.

We are going to ask the candidates for representative to speak in our district and give their platform. Then we will find out if they are running for the money, honor or the good they can do. We expect a lively time.

March 13, 1902
Volume 5, Number 8

§ Methodists to Meet. Workers' Conference Assembles in Chattanooga on March 11. The Workers Conference of the Methodist Episcopal church [illegible] will meet in Chattanooga March 11, 12 and 13. All officers of Sunday schools and Epworth league boards, mission boards, officers of same and annual conference Epworth leagues and central missionary committies [*sic*] east of the Mississippi river are members of the conference.

§ The People's Choice, For Ratification of the Democratic Party. For Govenor [*sic*], Jno. H. Estill.

§ Estill. We have been strongly inclined to Mr. Estill from the time he first announced his candidacy for Governor... –Wrightsville Headlight

§ Col. J. H. Estill, candidate for Governor of Georgia, says that he has no platform, and does not think he will promulgate one. He says that the constitution and the laws are the platform on which the chief executive stands...

§ Warwoman
Mrs. M. V. Beck made a flying trip to Walhalla last week.
Mr. Gus Wall is off to market this week.
Miss Mary Beck spent Friday night with Josie Swofford.
Miss Della Long and her brother Charley, of S. C., passed up the road[?] the other day on their way to Clayton.
Mrs[?]. Lula Wall, who has been spending several days with relatives at Clayton, returned home Saturday.
Mr. M. V. Beck happened to a very bad accident the other day. While

crossing the river his mule fell down and came very near breaking his leg.

Mrs. Bowers spent several days with her daughter, Mrs. Jeff Swofford last week.

§   Burton

Mr. John M. Marsingale, with Mr. Stone, a drummer from Virginia, passed through this community last week.

Mr. J. E. Bleckley was among friends here Saturday and Sunday.

Miss Lola Stonecypher returned home Friday from visiting her brother at Suwannee, Ga.

Mr. L. M. Chastain has gone to Toccoa with a load of meal.

Mr. and Mrs. J. I. FinCannon went to Demorest last week.

Mr. David Parker and family are going to move to Clayton next week.

Mr. J. H. Derrick went to the Valley last week.

Mr. and Mrs. Virgil Philyaw spent Saturday with the latter's sister.

Mr. James Smith and Marion Wood went to Providence Sunday.

Mr. J. R. Stonecypher and Byrant Hill went to Clarkesville last week.

§   A Proclamation. Georgia: By A. D. Candler, Governor of said State. Whereas, Official information has been received at this Department that on the 13th day of December, 1901, in the County of Rabun, one Horace Bradshaw shot and killed James W. Thompson, and made his escape, I have thought proper, therefore, to issue this my Proclamation, hereby offering a reward of two hundred dollars for the apprehension and delivery of said Horace Bradshaw, with evidence sufficient to convict, to the Sheriff of Rabun County, Georgia. And I do moreover charge and require all Officers in this State, Civil and Military, to be vigilant in endeavoring to apprehend the said Horace Bradshaw, in order that he may be brought to trial for the offense with which he stands charged. Given under my hand and Seal of the State, this the 3rd day of March, 1902. A. D. Candler, Governor. By the Governor, Philip Cook, Secretary of State. Description. Sandy hair, beard red, reserved in conversation, and speaks low, stands erect, red complected, looks off in conversation.

§   Sheriff's Sales.

Georgia—Rabun County. Will be sold, on the first Tuesday in April next, at public outcry at the court house in Clayton, said county, within the legal hours of sale, to the highest bidder for cash, certain property of which the following is a full and complete description: Parts of lots of improved land Nos. 162, 163, 174 and 175 [lying] and being in the second land district in Rabun county, containing 100 acres more or less, and more fully described in a deed from Z. B. Dillard and Sarah C. Powell to James H. Dillard, dated January the 29th 1881, recorded in book G, record of deeds of Rabun county Ga. pages 542 and 543. Levied on as the property of James H. Dillard to satisfy two fifas issued from the justice's court of the 556th district G. M. Rabun county in favor of J. M. Rice against James H. Dillard. Levy made and returned to me Feb'y the 24th 1902 by J. [illegible] McCurry L. C. written notice given tenant in possession as the law directs. This Feb'y 28th 1902. J. R. Ritchie, Sheriff.

Also at the same time and place lot of land No. 8 in the first land district of Rabun county, Ga., said property levied on to satisfy a tax fifa issued against said lot of land by Joseph L. Dickerson T. C. said county, for taxes due the State and county for the year 1901. This March 4th 1902.

Also at the same time and place part of lot of land No. 168[?] in the second land district of Rabun county, containing 62 ½ acres, more or less, and more fully described in a deed from E. W. Thomas to Ella Wall, dated January 23, 1891 and recorded in record of deeds book M, page 376. Levied on as the property of Ella Wall to satisfy a fifa issued from the justice's court of the 556th district G. M. of Rabun county in favor of H. V. [illegible]atland, against L. M. Wall and Ella Wall, defendants in this Levy made and returned to me by J. A. McCurry L. C. written notice given tenant possession. This March 3rd 1902 J. R. Ritchie, Sheriff.

Also at the same time and place part of lot of land No. 8 in the 5th land district of Rabun county Ga. containing one hundred acres more or less and bounded as follows: On the East by lands of F. A. Bleckley, on the North by lands of John McCrackin[,] on the south by lands of A. J. Williams and on west by land of Adaline Knowell. Levied on as the property of W. E. Stancill to satisfy a fifa issued from the justice's court of the 597th district G. M. of said county in favor of Taylor and Sweet against the said W. E. Stancill. Property pointed out by Plaintiff in fifa. Levy made and returned to me by E. M. Manly L. C. This March 4th 1902. J. R. Ritchie, Sheriff.

§   Upper Chechero
Mrs. Lucy Chappell died last Saturday night.
Miss Dovie Williams visited home folk last Tuesday.
Mr. Will and John Carver went to market last week.
Miss Geneva Price went to Clayton Friday.
Mr. Marlor Swofford went to Chechero Sunday.
Miss Mary Beck was on Chechero Sunday.
Misses May and Carrie Denney visited Misses Geneva and Zelma Price Sunday.
Mr. Ben Swofford and wife took dinner at Mr. John Denney's Sunday.
Mrs. Mary Cox was all smiles Sunday.
Mr. Smithie Johnson and wife visited Mr. Sylvester Ramey Sunday.
Little Lex Ramey visited Eddie Price Sunday.
Miss Lucretia Carver has returned home from Atlanta.

§ To the voters of Rabun county: at the solicitation of friends from all parts of the county, I have decided[?] to become a candidate for Tax Receiver. As is known by all, I have served the people in this county[?] for terms[?] and my qualifications[?] are therefore known. I make this announcement subject to the democratic primary or any other action of the democratic party. If elected I promise to serve you to the best of my skill and ability, always looking[?] with an eye single, to the very best interest of our county. Thanking you, and each of you, for your kindness in the past and cordially seeking your continued support in the future. I am, as always, Your friend J. C. York.

§ For Treasurer. To the voters[?] of Rabun county: being solicited by a number of friends to offer myself for re-election to the office of county Treasurer I hereby announce my candidacy subject to the action of the democratic party. Thanking one and all for past support and courtesies and soliciting your future indulgence: I am very truly, John W. Green.

§ To the voters of Rabun county: I hereby announce myself a candidate for Tax Collector subject to the action of the democratic party. If elected will serve you to the best of my ability. I am respectfully, Will F. Holden.

§ For Solictor [*sic*] General. I respectfully announce myself a candidate for re-election for Solictor [*sic*] General of the North Eastern Circuit—subject to the Democratic primary. W. A. Charters.

§ Capt. Beck was in town yesterday.

§ Candidate James E. Bleckley was in the city Wednesday.

§ Rev. L. L. Landrum preached an interesting sermon Sunday at the Methodist Church.

§ The latest students in school are Jable[?] Cannon of Tiger and Miss Mary Neville of Rabun Gap.

§ The home of Mr. and Mrs. Thos. Mitchel was brighened [*sic*] by the arrival of a daughter on the 8th inst.

§ John M. Marsingale and John Burton are still at Tallulah Falls awaiting the arrival of Nelson Tilley's goods.

§ The Tribune extends sympathy to John Howard and family of Rabun Gap, in the death of wife and mother. Mrs. Howard was one of the best women in the county.

§ Mrs. M. B. Ellard and family, daughter of Mr. and Mrs. H. K. Cannon, will leave for Taylor, Arkansas, on March 15th. Mrs. Ellard Joins her husband, who left for the west three months ago.

§ J. A. McHaffey who has been confined in Jail for about a year is one of the most agreeable prisoners that has ever come under the charge of our Sheriff. His deportment has been such as to excite sympathy for him, not only the Sheriff but by all who know him.

§ Mrs. J. R. Ritchie received a letter last night from Sabo, Texas, containing the sad news of the death of her brother, R. L. Carter. Mr. Carter has been in ill health for some time and left Rabun only a few weeks ago. Our sympathy goes out to Mrs. Ritchie and other relatives of the deceased.

§ The Tallulah Falls R. R. extension is in a flattering condition. Hands are busily engaged cleaning off the right-of-way. Men are also [getting] out cross-ties.

§ At Tallulah Falls, the dirt road is being changed - beginning at the iron bridge and intersecting the old road near the Robinson bar. This is done by order of Mayor Cannon and the R. R. we understand is assisting. The object of the change is to make way for the R. R. since it crosses old road near the top of the Hill. We are told sub-contractor Hampton is moving on his section.

§ Gentleman and fellow citizen, in our humble judgement [*sic*] our R. R. is a certainly [*sic*].

§ J. C. York—more familiarly known as "Cal" York, was arrested last Saturday upon a warrant charging him with murdering Charlie Ramey, an aged man living about one and a half miles west of Clayton. Mr. Ramey lived on the land of Mr. York and Friday they had some difference about the possession of the land the present year. Cal York and Mrs. York went to the house for the purpose of planting a garden and Ramey became enraged with passion and hit York on the head with a rock, inflicting a wound. The evidence showed that this was resented in a gentle way by Mr. York, except the wife of the deceased, and she was not present at the time of the difficulty, but swore that Ramey said York killed him. To satisfy the minds of the Coroner's duty an autopsy was held and Dr. W. J. Green and Dr. J. C. Lloyd testified that there was no evidence of violence. The jury returned a verdict substantially that the cause of his death was unknown. J. R. Grant represented the defendant. Coroner T. N. McConnell summoned the following jury of investigation:

J. A. Reynolds, J. A. Alman, John Hollifield, J. I. Langston, L. M. Robins, Jack Wilborne.

§ Notice. A regular communication of Rabun Gap Lodge Fo. 165 F. A. M. will be held in the hall on March 21st beginning at 10[?] o'clock a. m. sharp. All qualified brethen [*sic*] are urgently requested to meet with us. By order of John W. Green, W. M. R. E. A. Hamby Sect'y. This March 12 1902.

§ Notice. A regular convocation of Tallulah Chapter No. 68 R. A. M. will be held at the hall in Clayton on March 21 at 2 o'clock p. m. Companions will please meet us promply [*sic*] as there will be work in all the degrees. By order of R. E. A. Hamby, H. P.   W. S. Long Sect'y. This March 12, 1902.

§ The People in Town. We have often thought of going around town, And picking up the citizens and writing them down. So for the place we choose to start, We've no better one than to begin with Spart. And across we go to see Judge Long, And never for the first to him wrong[,] And now we come to Jesse Dover[,] The one that woos him will be in the clover. And up the street to Nelson Tilley, If you think he a fool you're awful silly, And back to Langston's, we mean J. I., But he's up at the ridge trying to raise rye. And back we go in Duncan Dave, And for the postage there is a continual crave. Up to the Wall house to see Miss Blanch, She is riding the cycles, attending the ranch. Over the way to Marsingale's, Among the farmers he rakes with the whales. Then away over to the Greens, Many of the people from death he serenes[?]. Then around to Robin's we also go, We think all he thinks of is the plow and the hoe. Why, la me!, we've missed Jim Grant, In some of his cases he gets on a rant. And still there is Col. Rob Hamby, Well to friends he comes in very handy. Well, well, well, we forgot Mr. Earl, Whenever you see him you see him in a whirl. Why there is Mr. Picket, he's the squire, He makes the lawless feel mighty queer. And there's McCurry I mean W. J. He don't know he'll move he don't know he'll stay. But I do know there is uncle Jeff, Lived 55 all to himself. Back to Mr. Norton his[?] name is W. c. We heard him say haw but never say "G". Uncle Henry Winters everybody knows, Then there's his wife who washes our clothes. Why, I declare I just happened to think, over the road lives old uncle Pink. And closer by us still lives uncle Hamp, Black as a crow but not any scamp. And often we go over to John Longs, They pick the [illegible] songs. We come back to Sheriff Ritchie, If you don't mind he will surely get ye. At Mrs. Coffee's you may see, The girls of cabin number three. Do not get mad and don't you fume, We just want something for The "Tribune."

§   Quartz

The revenues have been on the creek, but we don't know what they done. It is reported they got one still and went to another place and found none there.

The wedding bells rang Friday about three o'clock p. m. Mr. I. P. Coleman was married at the home of the bride, Miss Justus, daughter of T. M. Justus. There were several present. E. B. Philyaw officiating. They took supper at the home of Mr. Coleman, where the table was filled full and running over with the best that could be prepared. We wish the happy couple a long and prosperous life, and may all life's troubles be turned to sunshine.

Mr. Marvin Powell and Miss Ada Justus were over from Clayton taking in the wedding.

Miss Matilda Coleman is among relatives and friends on a visit. She came over from Towns County Thursday.

Well, we are going to work our roads pretty soon. The commissioners met and appointed overseers and divided up the hands. So we will try the old system again in working the roads.

No farming scarcely done yet, but we hope the weather will soon give us a chance now as the time is here that work should and must be done.

There is a girl we call Rosy says she will make a picture frame for Pine Mountain, if she had the picture, as she is in the business.

J. M. Chastain traded his steers to Thomas Coleman for a mule, by paying some boot[?].

L. T. Teems made a trip to Highlands the other day. We don't know his success.

What do you think about a man who will buy his own glass windows? We know of one that is said to have done so.

Emory Dillingham was seen going up the road the other day en route to Washington[?]. If he keeps going, we wish him a safe journey.

Marsh Moore is cutting beard. Lookout girls, he will be smiling.

§   Mud Creek

Mr. Frank Bleckley, of Scaly, N. C., was in this community last Saturday.

Miss Mary Drymon, of Scaly, N. C., who has been visiting friends and relatives here has returned to her home.

Mr. Tom Grist spent last Monday night with Mr. G. W. Grist and family.

Mrs. Sarah Dillingham and her daughter Mary are spending a few days with her sons in Anderson, S. C.

Mr. Boraguard Carter spent last Wednesday night with Mr. G. W. Grist.

Mr. George Dillard has got his saw mill at work again.

Mr. G. R. Martin has returned from market.

Mr. Napoleon Reed spent last Monday night with Mr. W. A. Martin and family.

Miss ley [*sic*] Martin spent last Sunday with May Grist.

Mr. George Burrell, of Pine Mt. was in the Valley last Monday.

§   Stonepile

There was quite a crowd at the sale yesterday through it was very rainey [*sic*]. Everything brought a nice price. Mr. H. K. Cannon and wife attended the sale and bade off some things. We were forced to go with our head drooped to think of giving up one of the best families but we hope some good ones will fill the place.

Mr. James Dockins came home on a visit from [school] last Saturday.

Mrs. Gus Gard is up from Demorest to stay a week or two with her father F. A. Taylor.

Mrs. M. B. Ellard will leave next Saturday for Arkansas.

Uncle Bill Smith has moved to Clarkesville on ex-Ordinary Hill's land. He moved to Grannie's Camp, and one of his daughters married, then he moved up on the creek, and another married and away he went and we suppose if another marries he will move again.

There has been more moving in this section in the last year than in five years before. Next Tuesday will be the 30th year since we were married and there is only one family living where they did then. Most all the old ones have died out and young ones moved in.

§   Dillard

Garden planting is the order of the day.

Mr. D. M. Green was at Clayton Friday.

Dr. Green and Judge Long were in this section Friday. Dr. purchased a horse while here.

Judge Long reports that they are most ready to go to work on the railroad.

John Harkins is off to Franklin this week after a load of flour for Z. B. Dillard.

Mrs. Clarey Hogshed went to Clayton Thursday on business.

Mr. Ben Thomas, of N. C., passed through here enroute to Tallulah Falls Thursday.

George Dorsey is off to Gainesville.

M. L. Scruggs has gone to baching. Look out girls.

J. C. Turpen, of Warwoman, is in this community.

We notice through the Tribune that some think girls ought to pop the question. We will agree with the correspondent from Pine Mountain if the girls don't pop the there [*sic*] will be no more weddings.

Mrs. Lizzie Howard, wife of John Howard, died the 9th and was buried the 10th at the M. E. Cemetery.

Beans are so scarce in N. C. that Mr. Ben Thomas says that you can buy a two cent postage stamp for two beans.

Ask John Godfrey if he ever gets in a hurry when he goes anywhere.

Guess what boy tore his pants Sunday.

Mr. Clayton Phillips and wife, of Long Creek, S. C., passed through the Valley enroute to Franklin Sunday.

§   D. E. Hogsed, Toccoa, GA. I am headquarters for McCormick[?] harvesting machienry [*sic*], engines, saw mills, thrashers, shingle mills, all kinds of harrows, cultivators, plows, hallock weeders and in fact all kinds of latest[?] improved farmers implents [*sic*] and everything kept in an up-to-date hardware store. You will save money by writing or seeing me.

April 3, 1902
Volume 5, Number 11

§ The People's Choice For Ratification at the Democratic Primary For Govenor [*sic*] Jno. H. Estill. Estill. Col. J. H. Estill, of Savannah, South Georgia's candidate for governor, spent a couple of days in Blairsville this week. He did not make a speech here, but he met a great many of our people, and he certainly won the heart of every man he talked to. The Herald takes a great deal of pride in the fact that it was among the first papers in Georgia to champion the cause of Col. Estill in his race for governor...—The Blairsville Herald.

§ The newspapers of this Judicial Circuit are saying some nice things and deservedly so of Judge J. J. Kimsey. We reproduce an article from the Gainesville Eagle which shows, along with other honored gentlemen, the high esteem in which Judge Kimsey is held: The Judgeship. The candidacy for the wearing of the judicial ermine seems to have narrowed down to ex-Judge J. J. Kimsey of White county. Judge J. B. Estes, whom we all love as a neighbor and fellow-citizen, and who now adorns the judgeship with the rarest order of legal accomplisements [*sic*], has, because of failing health, declined to enter the arena for re-election. Judge J. B. Jones of Toccoa, who has been favorably mentioned for the place, has positively declined to run, as has our own Henry Perry, a man who would do credit to the Supreme bench of the United States...

§ Grove
Corn planting time here.
Mr. J. M. Clark, of Spartanburg, S. C., was at Grove selling fruit trees for a Tennesee [*sic*] nursery.

Mr. J. A. Carter, of Stonepile, passed Grove Tuesday on his way to Clayton.

Mr. Thomas Allen, of Tiger, made M. O. Watts a pleasant call Thursday.

Mr. D. P. LaCounte is doing some nice work on Bridge Creek this week.

Mr. Milton Evans, of Creede, was at Grove Wednesday and Thursday.

Aunt Elizabeth Smith, one of our oldest and most respected citizens, died at her home Friday evening at 6 o'clock her relations have the sympathy of the general community in their bereavement.

§   Wild Land Sales. Georgia—Rabun County. Will be sold, on the first Tuesday in July next, at public outcry, at the court house in said county within the legal hours of sale, to the highest bidder for cash, the following lot of wild land to-wit: No. 79 in the 3rd land district of Rabun county, Ga., said property levied on to satisfy a fi fa issued against said lot by Joseph L. Dickerson, T. C. of said county, for taxes due the state and county for the years 1900 and 1901. This March 4th 1902.

Also at the same time and place, lot of wild land to-wit: No. 61 in the 5th land district of Rabun county, Ga , said property levied on to satisfy a tax fi fa issued against said lot by Joseph L. Dickerson, T. C. of said county for taxes due the state and county for the years 1900 and 1901. This March 4th 1902.

Also at the same time and place, lot of wild land to wit: No. 65 in the 3rd land district of Rabun County, Ga., said property levied on to satisfy a tax fi fa issued against said lot by Joseph L. Dickerson, T. C. of said county, for taxes due the state and county for the years 1900 and 1901. This March 4th 1902.

Also at the same time and place, lot of wild land to wit: No. 77 in the 3rd land district of Rabun County, Ga., said property levied on to satisfy a tax fi fa issued against said lot by Joseph L. Dickerson, T. C. of said county, for taxes due the state and county for the years 1900 and 1901. This March 4th 1902.

Also at the same time and place, lot of wild land to wit: No. 77 in the 4th land district of Rabun County, Ga., said property levied on to satisfy a tax fi fa issued against said lot by Joseph L. Dickerson, T. C. of said county, for taxes due the state and county for the years 1900 and 1901. This March 4th 1902.

Also at the same time and place, lot of wild land to wit: No. 98 in the 3rd land district of Rabun County, Ga., said property levied on to satisfy a tax fi fa issued against said lot by Joseph L. Dickerson, T. C. of said county, for taxes due the state and county for the years 1900 and 1901. This March 4th 1902. J. R. Ritchie, Sheriff.

§ Burton

We had a very severe storm Saturday night.

The little infant child of Mr. and Mrs. G. H. King died Friday night.

Mr. Cicero Kerby and wife were visiting [relatives] here Saturday and Sunday.

Mr. H. C. Blalock went to Atlanta last week.

John Laprade and wife are visiting their parents near Mt. Airy.

Mr. John Arrendale and J. E. McClain went to Clarkesville last Friday.

Mr. F. A. Powell visited relatives here Sunday.

Mr. T. W. Jackson passed through this [community] Saturday enroute to Clayton.

Miss Della Blalock visited Mrs. W. R. Wood Sunday evening.

Miss Callie Wood returned home Saturday after spending a few days with her sister and brother.

Mr. Graves Daniel and sister Miss Jennie spent Saturday night with Mr. and Mrs. Felton FinCannon.

§ Sheriff's Sales. Georgia—Rabun County. Will be sold, on the first Tuesday in April next, at public outcry at the court house in Clayton, said county, within the legal hours of sale, to the highest bidder for cash, certain property of which the following is a full and complete description: All mineral and mining priveleges in 90 acres and on lots of land Nox. 104 and 105 in the fifth land district of said county and more fully described in a deed from A. W. Irvin, trustee, to the Alladdain Mining and Milling Co., dated March 27 1899, and recorded in Record of deeds Book M, page 399 and 400. Levied on as the property of Alladdain Mining and Milling Co., to satisfy the state and county tax for the year 1901, written notice given in terms of the law. This Jan. 31st 1902. J. R. Ritchie Sheriff.

§ Notice. To the tax payers of Rabun Co.: I will be a the following named places for the purpose of receiving the tax returns of the Rabun Co., for the year 1902. Valley, Monday, April 7th; Persimmon, Tuesday, April 8th; Tallulah, Wednesday, April 9th; Stonepile, Thursday, April 10th; Tiger, Friday, April 11th; Chechero, Sunday, April 12th; Warwoman, Friday, April 18th; Mocason, Saturday, April 19th; Clayton, Monday, May 5th[?]. John M. Marsingale, R. T. R.

§ Stonepile

Henry Dockins and wife visited Mrs. Hepsey Dockins Sunday.

Mr. H. C. Ramey and Balor[?] Taylor prove very destructive to the briars in the fields of M. B. Ellard.

Aunt Mary Ellard visited Mrs. Lucie[?] Taylor Sunday.

Mr. Lonia[?] Gipson[?] is about to be the [illegible] in the 1275th district and we think he will give full satisfaction, as he has a large mouth. Mr. Gipson will have to make the race for Sheriff or move out of this district. The people are pushing at him from most every side. They all think he will make a good sheriff.

The people are not in favor of a primary for county officers. We would like to hear from all the correspondents on the question of a primary for the county officers. It might be probable that Stonepile will have two candidates this time, one married and one single, so the girls will not be left out.

§   J. F. Earl is setting out apple trees.

§   The court house is now newly covered.

§   John H. Dotson is at Anderson S. C.

§   Dr. Green was professionally at Turnerville Sunday.

§   J. F. Earl is suffering from a mild attack of rheumatism.

§   Sheriff J. R. Ritchie has about regained his usual health.

§   Miss Lucy Duncan of Chechero was shopping in town yesterday.

§   Any one wanting to purchase shingles and lumber call on J. F. Earl.

§   Lee Ritchie salesman for the Deering Harvester Co. was here Tuesday.

§   Mrs. J. M. Long spent Saturday and Sunday with her mother on Tiger.

§   J. A. Wall went to Walhalla on business Tuesday and returned yesterday.

§   It is reported that the mother of W. B. Watts, of Tiger, is dangerously ill.

§   Bring your locust pins to W. C. Donaldson and receive the cash for same.

§   Sheriff Ritchie has three prisoners in jail. Lucky for others they are not there.

§   W. C. Donaldson is engaged in building an addition to the house of Mrs. C. C. Wall.

§   Sanford and Virgil Taylor and Jim Dockins have quit school and returned to their home in Stonepile.

§   Miss Fannie Donaldson, of the Valley, is the guest of Mr. and Mrs. W. C. Donaldson for a few days.

§   Rev. Brown occupied the pulpit in the Baptist church here Sunday morning with much credit to himself.

§   John Dotson returned home from Tallulah Falls Saturday, where he has been at work in a black-smith shop.

§   The State Democratic Executive Committee has set June 5th as the day for holding the primary election.

§   Charlie Ritchie was happily married to Miss Ada Dotson last Sunday night. We wish Charlie and his bride much happiness.

§   Col. Hamby and W. S. Long went up to their amethyst mine near John Hollifield's yesterday. It is said they have found an extremely rich vein.

§   John Donaldson, of town, and Waller Dickson, of Chechero, have moved to S. C. to enter the saw mill business. W. C. Donaldson [says] they will be in Clayton [illegible] month.

§   Tuesday was salesday.

§   Everybody planting gardens in Clayton.

§   Julius Pickett butchered a fine hog Tuesday.

§   The primary is set for June 5th. Watch Estill!

§   J. M. Long went to Tiger on a hunt yesterday.

§   Horace McCurry is up and walking on crutches.

§   Jerry Vickers slaughted [*sic*] a fine porker Monday.

§   A man or boy is judged by the company he keeps.

§   A. S. Allen, of Tiger, was in this village yesterday.

§   C. W. McDade has returned from Ashville, N. C.

§   Candidate Will F. Holden has entered school here.

§   John Marsingale is in South Carolina for a few days.

§   D. L. Parker's children entered school here Monday.

§   Miss Glenn Adams, our music teacher, has received a fine piano.

§   Miss Carrie Grist spent Saturday and Sunday with home folk in the Valley.

§   We are forced to leave out communications from Wolffork and Tiger this issue.

§   Mrs. E. Wall slaughtered a hog yesterday that weighed one hundred pounds dressed.

§   The editor spent Monday and Tuesday with home folk and returned to Cornelia yesterday.

§   Dred Wall has stopped going to school here and went to Ducktown, Tennesee [*sic*], to work in the mines.

§   Harve Penland and Harrison Greenwood, colored, are at Tallulah Falls working on the rail road.

§   Four hundred kegs of powder and two hundred cases of dynamite were brought up to the Falls Monday.

§   W. B. Everhart, traveling salesman for Michall[?] Brothers, of Atlanta, Ga., was drumming in town yesterday.

§   We are requested to say there will be services at the Ridge, three miles from here, on the Valley road, next Saturday and Sunday.

§   D. L. Parker has moved to town and occupies the Barrow block. Mrs. Parker will keep boarders and invites her friends to call on her.

§   For a short time you can get The Tribune, The Semi-Weekly Journal and The Home and Farm all for $1.75. This is 13 papers a month.

§ We received a communication from Chechero last week about preachers, but as no name was signed to the article we are compelled to leave it out.

§ The County Board of Education at their regular meeting Tuesday, elected W. H. Cobb, of Carnesville, Ga., to conduct the next Teacher's Institute here. Mr. Cobb is State Senator of the 31st Senatorial district, a fine orator and has been successful as a teacher.

§ We call your attention to the announcement of J. R. Ritchie for sheriff. It is needless for us to say anything commendatory of Mr. Ritchie. He is our neighbor, a good man and several years' direct dealings with him have been one of pleasantness. His candidacy is the result of many solicitations.

§ Mrs. Sarah York, wife of John C. York, died at her home near town Saturday evening at about 6 o'clock, after being confined to her room for nearly two years. Mrs. York leaves a husband, son and many other relatives and warm friends to mourn her loss. We extend sympathy to the bereaved. She[?] was buried in the cemetery lot here Monday.

§ Cicero Blalock was at the meeting of the Board of education Tuesday.

§ Wesley M. Lee, of Tallulah Falls, was a most pleasant caller at our office Tuesday. It is always cheering to us to have such good men call on us.

§ J. A. Almon and wife were in this city yesterday.

§ J. N. Justus, of Wolffork, was in this city yesterday.

§ Dept. Marshall Hughes has a new duty [assigned] him. It is to keep order in the post-office.

§ Cols. W. S. Paris and James R. Grant are having their property north of town fenced this week.

§ We are ashamed to publish some things happening in this community recently, but want to say some persons have, in our opinion, been unjustly accused.

§ We heard a certain person remark the other day that Mr. H. K. Cannon will have to make a wider road to his house to accomodate the young man.

§   For the accomodation of the public, we will say that a money order cannot be obtained at this post-office except between the hours of 9 a. m. and 5 p. m.

§   Mr. J. F. Earl showed us yesterday evening a pump running from his house to the stables, which comes in very handy in watering stock and washing mud off the stock, buggies, wagons, etc. The pump is quite an improvement.

§   To the Democratic Executive committee of Rabun county: You are hereby requested to convene at the court house in Clayton at 12 m [*sic*], April 12, 1902. Each and every member is earnestly urged to [be] present, since there is important business to transacted by the committee. Respectfully Yours, M. W. Swofford, Chairman.

§   To The Public: I will have my books open at the court-house in Clayton during court week begining on the first Monday in May, for the purpose of allowing all to register all who wish to vote in the primary on June the 5th must request under the rules lately adopted by the State Democratic Executive Committee before they are allowed to vote. Jos. L. Dickerson T. C.

§   Notice to trespassers. All persons are hereby warned against cutting timber, "moonshining," or in any manner whatever trespassing on the land embraced in lot No. 6 in the first district of Rabun County, Ga., under penalty of prosecution. Take notice and govern yourselves accordingly. T. A. Chatham, Macon, Ga., March 27, 1902.

§   Mr. Jno. M. York, an Aged and Respected Citizen, Held Up and Robed [*sic*] of About $1000. About seven o'clock Tuesday night three men called at the residence of Jno. M. York, Sr., an aged and respected citizen of this county, who carries a libe [*sic*] of general merchandise (or commonly known as the "country store",) purporting to want some canned goods. York went from his residence to supply the demands of these [highwaymen.] Upon entering the store one of them held him up with a double-barrel shot gun, the other with a large pistol, and demanded that he open his safe; not having his spectacles with him he was unable to do so. The culprits holding him at the point of their guns demanded axes and other tools and securing a pick finally battered the safe door open and secured some $600 in cash in addition to about $1,000 in notes. The third man, who was keeping watch on the out side of the store, met Mrs. York, who, in response to the calls of her husband for help, had started to his assistance and she was prevented. She then called to a young lady who lived with them to go to a neighbor's for assistance. The man on the out side shot at her and several of the shot penetrated her face. Mrs. York was subjected to a lot of abuse from the said highwaymen which was very vulgar and demands that every man in Rabun County should rise up in arms in defence [*sic*] of our wifes, our homes, and our fair name, county and state. These men not being content with what they had gleamed from the safe made Mr. York hand over his purse. Below is a reward of $175 for these highwaymen.

§ $175 Reward! On the night of April 1st, 1902, I was held up and robbed in my store of about $600 in cash. Now for the apprehension and delivery of these[?] parties to the Sheriff of Rabun County with evidence to convict I will pay one hundred dollars in cash. Descriptions: One was a young man, I think about 5 ten to 6 feet tall, weight about 150 pounds, no beard. The other was a tall man, coarse voice, beard on his face. One out of doors I couldn't describe. A spotted dog in the crowd. J. M. York, Sr.

§   In addition to the above and on the behalf of the heirs to-wit: W. Hillyer York, J. Lee York, M. C. York and my self I hereby offer $50 more as a reward, the payment of which I hereby guarantee. This April 3rd 1902. H. C. Blalock, Burton, Ga.

§   In addition to the above reward I hereby offer a reward of $25 for any information that will lead to the arrest and conviction of the guilty parties or either of them. Said amount to be prorated to each man. This April 4th 1902. J. R. Ritchie, Sheriff Rabun Co.

§   Quartz

Farming is a standstill again, on account of rain.

There was several wagons went to the R. R. this week. Among them was G. F. York, J. C. York, H. A. Kilby and A. M. Keener.

Mr. H. A. Parker died Thursday; he was one of our good men and one we will miss at the church. He suffered a great deal, but bore it with all christian fortitude. We sympathize with the bereaved in the loss of a husband and father and we are one of his many friends to mourn his loss.

The child of M. F. Welborne is very sick.

John Frady is some better.

Charlie Littleton is off to Atlanta to answer a call by the revenue authorities.

The mocking bird and other spring birds say by their singing that spring is near, which fills the old farmer full of cheer for it is time to "haw" to the horse, and "G" to the steer.

The cry with most of us is behind with our work and we would be glad to see clear weather a few weeks.

Nancy Dillingham has the measles and is at the Lee Teem's house until she gets well.

§   Germany

There was a preaching at Germany by the Rev. R. L. Whitmire Sunday. There was a large congregation present.

J. C. Justus says he can't leave home—it's another girl to feed.

Mr. Norman Carnes was visiting relatives here Sunday.

The public roads are in very good condition now.

Mr. Eugene Mozely and wife are visiting friends in Germany.

Mr. Hillier was in town [Saturday] night for the first time in a week.

Our Sunday school is still on a boom at Germany. We have had Sunday school for about two years without missing a quarter. The young folks of this community met at the church and had a lively singing Sunday evening.

§   Dillard

N. S. Thomas, of Franklin, N. C., has rented the A. L. Dillard store room and expects to open up a new line of general merchandise soon.

Rev. Brown, of Gainesville, Ga., after spending a few weeks in the Valley returned home. He will move to the Parsonage near the Baptist church soon.

J. H. Dillard, of Gainesville, Ga., was in the Valley a few days last week.

There are three distinguished timber men in our midst looking after timber. They know the R. R. is coming.

Misses Eula and Mattie Dillard visited relatives and friends in N. C. Saturday and Sunday.

We heard of one of our best citizens hauling hay on last Sunday. I suppose he had not yet found out it was Sunday. I know he was not out of hay for he hauled all the day before.

§   One Cent a Mile to Texas. On account of the Confederate Veteran Reunion, April 22nd to 25th round trip tickets will be sold to Dallas, via the Cotton Belt as a very low rate of one cent a mile. This rate is open to everybody. Tickets will be sold April 18th, 19th and 20th and will be limited to May 2nd for return, but will be extended to May 15th if desired. Stop overs will be allowed at any points in Arkansas or Texas on either going or returning trip. Low rate side trip tickets will be sold from Dallas to all parts of Texas, Oklahoma and Indian Territory. The round trip rate from Atlanta will be $17.75. If you ever expect to visit Texas this will be the chance of your life to od so. For rate and schedule from your home town and for handsomely illustrated pamphlets describing Arkansas and Texas write to N. B. Baird, T. P. A.

§   There will be a special convocation of Tallulah Chapter No. 68 R. A. M. in the hall at Clayton on Saturday, April 5th, beginning at 10 o'clock a. m. sharp. Work in the degrees. By order of R. E. A. Hamby, H. P. W. S. Long, Sec'y.

April 10, 1902
Volume 5, Number 12

§   IMPORTANT! To the Citizens of Rabun County: Every citizen in said county who is opposed to the alternative road law will meet in mass meeting at the court house in Clayton on Monday April 14th, not later than 10 o'clock a. m. The road case will be heard at Cleveland on April 14th. We want your presence and your support if you are opposed to the law. Let every citizen turn out and give their support. Respectfully, W. C. Kerby.

§   Old Tiger

Mr. Steve Gambol has moved to Mr. R. F. McCurry's. What made Mr. McCurry in such a hurry to move him? Of course, Mr. Gambol has two pretty girls.

While Mrs. Sarah Hunnicutt was holding a yearling to treat it for poison last week, it fell on her ankle and crippled her badly.

Mr. Willard Taylor has sold his machinery to Smith and Rochester and is now engaged in the mercantile and meat business.

Mr. Sam Foster's father died at Tallulah Falls last week and was buried in Franklin county. Mr. Foster was about eighty-four years old.

Mr. Henry O'Shieds [sic], it is reported, was married last week to a daughter of Mr. Allen Williams.

We were not shooting at the middle man any way but softly poked our candid apologies at a corner man and hit him, it seems, from the way he kicked, for our apologies were not accepted in the spirit in which they were offered, so we feel fat after all. He is too big to accept apologies and too small to rebuke, but we are big enough to offer no more apologies to one who cannot see farther than to think that a marble ring is a government survey. We decline to thresh where wheat grows only a head at a time for we own a right to buy the R. and D. railroad.

The people were disappointed of preaching at Tiger last Sunday.

Intended for last week.

§ Mud Creek

Messrs. Tom and Frank Kelley spent last Saturday night with Mr. Homer and Miller Grist.

Miss Ida Martin, who has been spending a few days with her sister Mrs. Laura Grist has returned home.

Mr. and Mrs. George Grist visited Mr. R. B. Ritchie Sunday.

Mr. Judge Garland, of the Flats, was in this community last Thursday.

Mr. A. J. and Charlie Grist went to the Flats last Tuesday on business.

Mr. Pat White, of N. C., was in the Valley one day last week.

Mr. B. F. Grist, who has been spending some time with his sister Mrs. Wash Berrong, has returned home.

Little Oscar Brown is spending a few days with his grandfather, Mr. W. A. Martin.

§ Glassy

Corn planting time here.

Jerry Vicker, of Clayton, was visiting friends here Saturday and Sunday.

D. F. Hogsed, of Toccoa, spent Monday night with W. B. Watts.

Aunt Mary Watts is still in very feeble health.

There was preaching at Liberty Saturday by Rev. L. L. Free but no preaching Sunday on account of bad weather.

Joe Love, of Black's Creek, was visiting relatives here Saturday night.

W. B. Watts slaughtered a fine porker Monday.

Roney Arrendale and wife were visiting friends and relatives here Sunday.

M. O. Watts was on the creek Saturday.

Bud Singleton and wife spent Sunday with Aunt Mary Watts.

§ John Marsingale is out on his rounds receiving tax returns.

§ Ed Marsingale is behind the counter at Tilley's.

§ Sheriff's Sales. Georgia—Rabun County... Also at the same time and place, the following described real estate to-wit: Part of lot of land No. 4 in the first land district of said county, there being two tracts, and the same being more fully described in two deeds made by J. R. Ritchie, Sheriff of said county, to J. C. Pickett and recorded in Record of Deeds of Rabun County in Book N, pages 209, 210, 211, 212 and 213, the places whereon G. W. Benfield and J. L. Dickson now reside, containing 200[?] acres, more or less. Said property levied on under and by virtue of and to satisfy a fi fa issued from the Justice's Court of the 509th District, G. M., in favor of L. N. Shirley and against N. V. Benfield and J. F. Benfield. Said property levied on as the property of the defendant, N. V. Benfield. Said property pointed out to me by plaintiff. Written notice given the tenants in possession in terms of the law.

Also at the same time and place, the following described property to-wit: One Peerless engine, four to six horse power engine, also one Kentucky shingle mill. Said mill and engine sold to me by J. S. Carter. Said property levied on and to be sold as the property of defendants M. B. Ramey and J. D. Woodall under and by virtue of a mortgage fi fa issued from the Superior Court of said county in favor of said J. S. Carter and against M. B. Ramey and J. D. Woodall. Said property pointed out to me by plaintiff. J. R. Ritchie, Sheriff.

§ John L. Perkins, Attorney at Law. Cornelia, GA. Will practice both in State and Federal Courts. Office first room up stairs in Bank Building.

§ We are having a nice spell of weather.

§ Mrs. R. E. A. Hamby is critically ill.

§ Jess McCurry is moving to the Simmons house.

§ Howell C. Blalock, of Burton, was in town Friday.

§ J. M. York, of Persimmon, was in town a few days ago.

§ Nelson Tilley went to Tallulah Falls on business yesterday.

§ Mr. J. L. Henson has been doing dental work in town this week.

§ D. E. Hogsed, of Toccoa, Ga., was in town the first of the week.

§ M. C. York and Mr. Fuller, of Clarkesville, Ga., were in town last Friday.

§ Mrs. Lula York, of Tiger, is spending a few days with Mrs. L. C. Hollifield.

§ Sheriff Ritchie went down to Tallulah on official business Tuesday morning.

§ Loma Gipson, of Stonepile district, was a pleasant visitor to our office Tuesday.

§ J. R. Grant spent Monday and Tuesday in Tiger district, working in the interest of the alternative road law.

§   Jim Dockins, of Stonepile, returned to Clayton Tuesday to enter school again. He says they have graded two miles of the proposed extension of the Tallulah Falls Railway.

§   J. W. Almon, of Germany, came in yesterday and greased our palm with some of the oil of commerce. Mr. Almon has not been in town for about four months which shows that he belongs to that class known as the salt of the earth.

§   All parties having good timbered lands to sell can sell same by writing to Chas. H[?]. Brown, 944 N. 5th Avenue, Knoxville, Tennessee.

§   I have just received a new line of millinery and am now ready to accommodate[?] my friends to any thing in this line. Mrs. D. L. Garland, Rabun Gap, Ga.

§   Bart Paris received a pair of belgian hares Monday night.

§   Misses Ada, Leila, and Carrie Cannon attended services at old Tiger Sunday.

§   J. C. Howard gave us a pleasant call Tuesday and gave us a wheel on The Tribune. This is the fifth for J. C.

§   I will not be at Antioch church, on Warwoman creek, the second Sunday at four p. m. but will be there the fourth Sunday at 11 a. m. and Saturday before. N. H. Jay.

§   We call your attention to the announcement of Willie Smith for tax collector, which you will find elsewhere. Mr. Smith is a young man of ability and would doubtless make the county an able officer. He will likely run a close race.

§   Mr. J. C. Howard, one of Rabun county's brightest young men, has returned to his home on Persimmon, after teaching a term of school at Epps Ga. Mr. Howard contemplates entering the normal school at Cornelia, Ga., soon.

§   The Tribune acknowledges favors from the following persons this week: J. C. Howard, Persimmon Ga. John M. York, Quartz Ga. A. J. Ritchie, Waco Texas. Mrs. C. C. Wall, City. J. L. Perkins, Cornelia Ga. H. W. Cleveland, Mt. Airy Ga.

§   School is lively.

§   Educate your children.

§   Judge Long is busy planting his garden.

§   Mrs. J. M. Long is spending the week on Tiger.

§   E. D. Swofford[?] is improved as we go to press.

§   Marion Long is hunting on Black-rock to-day.

§   Gus Hunter, from Glassy Mt., was in the city Tuesday.

§   Justice's court was held here yesterday. Two cases were tried.

§   Mrs. J. C. Langston will join her husband in Oklahoma Teritory [*sic*] next week.

§   Mrs. Lula Wall, of Pine Mountain, has been spending several days with Mrs. C. C. Wall.

§   The Sunday School met Sunday and a liberal amount of money was collected to buy literature for the next quarter.

§   D. T. Duncan went hunting yesterday evening. This is the first time we have seen him go hunting since we came here four years ago.

§   E. M. Manley passed through here to-day enroute to Tennesee [*sic*] Valley to hunt negroes to work on the railroad for Mr. Redmond. He is trying to get one hundred or more.

§   Dillard
   Mr. J. A. Martin is off to S. C. this week.
   Mrs. Mollie Norris is very sick at this writing.
   Sallie Darnell went to Clayton Saturday.
   Mr. and Mrs. Amos Glaspy have returned from Toccoa, where they have been visiting relatives.
   Misses Beulah Green and Ethel Powell spent Saturday and Sunday with home folk.
   Mr. and Mrs. A. P. Turpen are at Turnerville.
   Lizzie Dillard and Carrie Grist were with home folks the latter part of last week.
   Guess what young merchant presented a lady with a small weeding hoe when she called for ladies' hose, saying that that must be a ladie's hoe as it was the smallest he had.

I will agree with the correspondent from Stonepile; I am not in the favor of primary election for county officers. Let all run the race through that wants to.

Frank Godfrey is with his grandpa and grandma, on Chechero.

§   Germany

Written for last week.

New neighbors moved in.

A. F. Welborne has moved to the J. N. Justus mill. Mill days Tuesdays and Saturdays. The gates are moved so laziness can pass with all ease.

New lanes are being built in this section.

The railroad is coming.

The stock law is needed.

If laziness was money we would still have some.

When you want to go to the Falls don't forget to walk, for you can't wagon. We have a good set of officers. It is a disgrace to Rabun county. We never will vote for a Tiger man.

§   Old Tiger

Disappointed again of preaching at Tiger church last Sunday.

We understand Mr. Farret Taylor has killed our favorite calf.

A lot of neighbors went out last Sunday to view the railroad, mules and negroes.

Last Sunday Farret Taylor cut a fellow out, but the defeated applicant got on his mule and went with them. Ask a young lady of Clayton who they were.

Mr. John S. Hunnicutt, of Chattanooga, Tenn., passed through this section last week, looking for timbered lands.

There will be another wedding in this community soon if anybody can get anybody.

Mrs. Henry Dockins and Miss Susie Taylor went to a rail road blasting the other day. They would make pretty bosses.

Misses Emma and Maud Dockins visited their brother, Mr. Henry Dockins, last Saturday.

The rail road hands have been blowing storms of rock across the river and for hundreds of yards around, obstructing the[?] public road, mangling the lands and imperilling the lives of people and stock.

§   Germany

Meeting at Mt. Grove Saturday and Sunday. Preaching by James Holcomb.

The young folks of Germany had the privilege of enjoying a quilting at Mr. A. E. Dickerson's Saturday.

Mr. Frank Welborne, of Gilmer county, had the pleasure of meeting his wife, who has been spending the last six months with her brother J. N. Justus.

Mr. Nelson Tilley and the two sheriffs, Ritchie and McConnell, were in this community Sunday, looking after the burglers that broke into J. M. York's store last week.

Mrs. Marietta Colenback was the guest of J. C. Justus Sunday.

Miss Lillie Moore, of Wolffork, has been the guest of her sister Laura Justus a few days.

M. C. York, of Clarkesville, passed through this community en route to Clayton last week.

Mr. J. B. Powell and daughter Connie went to Clayton last week.

Mrs. Nancy Mozely is spending a few days with her daughter Lula Justus.

The home of Mr. D. L. Justus was brightened by the arrival of a boy last week.

Mr. Anderson Coffee's health is worse than it has been for several weeks.

§ Warwoman

Intended for last week.

The Dicks Creek road hands have been at work the past week. The people say the roads are in the best fix they have been in years.

Miss Leila, Ray, and Ralph Cannon, spent Saturday night with Miss Mary Green.

E. D. Swofford's health is improving slowly.

Miss Maud Holden is spending a few days in S. C.

Mr. J. M. Swofford was in this section Sunday.

Frank Wall went to Clayton Sunday.

Ask Sam Holden what kind of a present he got the other day.

§ Quartz

The weather is fine at this writing and farming is going on.

John M. York had the misfortune to get robbed last Tuesday night. He was called to the store by some unknown person, pretending to want some crackers and canned goods. On entering the house, another man appeared at the door and threw a gun on him and told him to throw his hands up. The young man who first entered drew a pistol on him, and demanded his money. After getting what he had in his pockets they ordered the safe unlocked. Mr. York having no spectacles, he told them he could not see to do it. So they secured a pick and succeeded in getting it open, taking from it the rise of five hundred dollars. All effort was made to get help but failed. The girl that was living with them was shot at by a guard somewhere about the house while trying to get help. One shot, she says, glancing her face. The robbers escaped.

Rev. J. S. Dickson will preach at the Baptist church on the first Sunday and Saturday before in each month through this year.

Miss Ada Justus came home from school on a short visit.

T. M. Justus, and wife, also J. C. York went to the rail road the other day, returning home Thursday.

M. C. York, of Clarkesville, with Mr. Fuller, was on the creek the third inst.

The child of M. F. Welborne died last Tuesday night.

§   Burton

We have had some nice weather for farming.

The little infant daughter of Mr. and Mrs. Byrant Hill has been very sick for a few days.

Rev. Warlick preached an interesting sermon at the Academy Sunday evening.

Mr. J. I. FinCannon and wife visited Mr. H. C. Blalock's Saturday night.

Prof. Mart Free and Graves Daniel were at preaching Sunday eve.

Mr. Guss Arrendale and sisters have gone to Clarkesville to meet their brother and sister, Dr. J. L. Jackson and wife, who have been in Atlanta for some time.

Mr. Will Holden was at Burton Sunday.

The school closed here last Friday until the fall term.

We are [very] sorry to hear of Mr. York's misfortune.

§   Grove

Mr. Loma Gipson and Oliver Harkins, of Stonepile, were at Grove Thursday.

Mrs. Marion Lovell is moving to Mrs. Basha Arrendale's.

Mr. J. M. Arrendale made a hasty trip to Clayton Monday.

Mr. Elisha Johnson has a mole hide stuffed that is quite the curiosity as it is perfectly white.

Mr. Robert Lovell, of Stonepile, made a pleasant call at Grove Thursday.

Mr. L. W. Cathey, of Burton, was in this community Wednesday.

Mr. J. M. Arrendale is gone to Clarkesville with a load of produce this week.

§   If you want a Deven bull go to J. N. Justus, Wolffork, Ga.

April 17, 1902
Volume 5, Number 13

§   Editor J. A. Reynolds of the Clayton Tribune was in Toccoa Tuesday. John A. is not only a facile quill driver, but also has an eye for the compass and his mission in the city was to meet Judge Franklin, who has engaged him to survey the route for the change in the Clarkesville road at city limits, this side of the first crossing of the Toccoa creek. Editor Reynolds is very much enthused over the contemplated railroad from Tallulah Falls to Franklin, N. C. He says the grading of the road bed is progressing nicely and he thinks there is no doubt but the shrill whistle of the steam engine will awaken the echoes around Screamer mountain in the near future.—Toccoa Anagraph

§   Our Railroad. As we came up from the Falls Monday we walked up the new road and we tried to see every man connected with the work. We had the pleasure of our companionable friend, C. L. Hughlett, on our way, and the only objections we can find to him he is a bachelor which we regard next to criminal... We have gone over the line of work before quietly, and it was then we learned that in a camp of about two hundred colored people that quiet reigned almost as it does in a cemetery... The contract to the mouth of Tiger was let about a month ago to Mr. Fred Wagoner... The next man you meet is Mr. Majors, who...superintends... We met Mr. Leonard, an experienced man in blasting... We were informed by Mr. Thomas Fain, who attends the drilling machine, that the machine would go through solid rock at the rate of two feet in about six minutes. We met our old Habersham county friend W. E. Cook who is the engineer, and Morgan Woodall, who sharpens the spider drills. We passed up to Mr. Redmond's[?] camp... It is here you see the colored laborers perfectly ordered and we commend Mr. Redmond for it... [W]e do not hesitate to say that the engineering of the road up Tallulah river is not excelled in the United States, and justly commends Capt. A. R. Gilchrist, who is chief engineer, and Captain W. W. Phillips, who is assistant engineer, as being among the highest in the engineering world... We saw new cross ties all along the line, tressle timber scattered and being shaped and placed under the superintendency of Mr. M. C. Watson...

§   Quartz

The weather is fine and the farmers are taking advantage of it.

We feel encouraged when we can hear the blasts on the railroad and us here on Persimmon farming. It makes us feel that old Rabun is on a boom.

Lester York and sister and V. L. Moore and brother came back from the railroad last week.

A. M. Keener had a log rolling the other day but failed to get done.

John Frady is doing all right since Dr. Garland performed a surgical operation on him.

John Teems and wife are bad off the Grip.

We don't think we ever saw the small grain look as bad as it does this year. The severe winter has almost killed it out.

Sunday school was very good last[?] Sunday evening.

Give us railroad news for we like to hear something that speaks prosperity.

§   J. R. Ritchie spent Tuesday on Burton.

§   J. B[?]. Grant has moved to the Wall house.

§   F. A. Taylor, of Tallulah Falls, was to town Saturday.

§   F. A. Bell left Wednesday morning for Knoxville, Tenn., where he will take a course in railroad engineering.

§   F. A. Taylor will begin an active canvass over the county soon hunting poplar timber for Benbe[?] and Stone.

§   Prof. M. B. York came up from Cornelia Friday night and returned Monday. His many friends were glad to see him.

§   The alternative road law case which was to have been tried at Cleveland, Ga., Tuesday was postponed until Rabun Superior court convenes at the request of the attorneys.

§   Mrs. R. E. A. Hamby is much improved.

§   The prospect for a good fruit crop is flattering.

§   Miss Blanche Wall has a new departure in business and it is burning.

§   W. C. Donaldson and his brother Sine, are building a house for Everett Earl in the eastern part of town.

§   Soloman McKinney, W. H. Greenwood and Thad Hughlett three of the liveliest knights of the grip, were the guests of the Blue Ridge hotel Tuesday.

§   Mrs. J. C. Langston and children with Miss Amanda Earl, left for Oklahoma to-day where Mrs. Langston will join her husband who has been there several weeks. May success crown them in their western home. Miss Amanda expects to return some time during the coming summer.

§   W. P. Ellenburger, D. V. S., with United States Dept. Agriculture is the guest of the Wall house for a few days. He requests us to say to the people that at no time of the year will the Dept. permit cattle to cross the Quarantine line and they must observe it and get rid of the cattle tick and not until they do this will they get rid of the nuisance of this line.

§   The prisoners in jail request us to say that a mouse has broken into their bank and carried away their money, and they would like for some one to catch the mouse.

§   All persons wishing to buy fruit trees for fall delivery will do well to see J. F. Earl.

§   The F. C. Tate Debating and Declaining[?] Society will discuss the question, "Resolved that environment has more to do with the forming of character than heredity," at the court house Saturday night. The speakers are: Affirmative: F. D. Singleton, J. M. Bleckley, James Green. Negative: Nin Ramey, A. A. O'Kelley, John Jenkins. The public is cordially invited to attend, and we assure you you'll hear some fine speaking.

§   Grove
  Farmers are all busy and taking a big interest in preparing their crops.
  Mr. A. J. Meece was at Grove Monday.
  Mrs. R. W. Bramblett's health is improving some at this writing.
  Mr. J. R. Grant, of Clayton, made a pleasant call at Grove Tuesday.

Mr. J. W. Smith, of Stonepile, was in this community Wednesday.

Dr. J. C. Dover was in this community Thursday on professional business.

Constable J. B. Jones, of Burton, was on Bridge Creek Thursday attending to business officially.

Tom Gable says if it makes men's mouths any bigger to kiss women Loma Gipson had better not run for Sheriff as it might spoil him to kiss so many.

§   Stonepile

Fine weather for farming.

Flat Creek mine has resumed work again. Mr. Sam Bugle has brought his brother with him, so lookout for the yellow stuff soon.

It is a continual blast above and below. It seems as if Tiger and Stonepile district will get their rock mixed up as the rail road is blowing them so far.

We were not so large as not to receive the apologies, but the apologies were so large we could not receive them all at a time, but take them as fast as we can. We did not ask for any and will not feel disappointed. No one has ever said he did not own a right to eat railway dumplings. I suppose that is what R. & D. means.

We saw some of the Clayton school students. They look real fine. Clayton ought to have a college of five hundred boys and girls who are scattered throughout the county in it.

The Germany man ought not to talk so harsh for we cannot even walk to the Falls without leaving the road where the river has taken possession and you must go to the woods, but the candidates are not to blame. Some one has posted a notice not to go in there except at your own risk, so you see we have to go back or risk it. The overseer has only 6 or 7 hands and has got four miles of road and the river got one fourth of it. We have a candidate but he can't help it, so don't fret him, for they are awful scarce anyway.

§   Dillard

Mrs. B. R. Dillard is with her father and mother at Turnerville.

Mr. D. E. Hogshed is up from Toccoa on business.

Miss Icy Martin is very sick at this writing.

Mr. Sine Donaldson is at Clayton this week.

Mr. A. L. Dillard, of Westminster, S. C., was in the Valley last week.

Major York is off to Toccoa.

Little Fannie Powell is very sick at this writing.

Miss Fannie[?] Donaldson was with home folk Sunday.

Mrs. J. W. Green, of Turnerville, is visiting relatives in the Valley this week.

Mr. and Mrs. John Ritchie were with Miss Laura Kelley Sunday.

Mr. Lonny Russell was here Sunday.

Mr. Clark, of Spartanberg, S. C., representing the East [Tennessee] Nursery, is in the Valley.

Ask Mage Scruggs if he expects to make a good crop on what he planted last week.

Mr. B. R. Dillard has purchased a new organ.

§   Upper Tiger

Rev. Jay preached at Ivy Hill Sunday.

Mr. and Mrs. S. W. Dover visited their sister Mrs. Thursie Kerby Sunday.

Rev. Warlick will preach at Ivy Hill next Sunday at eleven o'clock.

Mr. Jable Cannon visited home folk Saturday and Sunday.

Mr. Jesse Green and family visited their father and mother on Warwoman Saturday and Sunday.

Mrs. Thursie Kerby spent Friday with Mrs. E. B. Norton.

Miss Brama Sams and Mr. Dutch Henson were at preaching Sunday.

Mr. E. B. Norton was in town Monday.

Mrs. Jay is on the sick list.

Mr. J. H. Derrick was in this community Monday.

The home of Mr. and Mrs. E. B. Norton was brightened by the arrival of a girl Thursday morning.

§   Burton

Pretty weather for farming.

Rev. Jay preached at the Academy Sunday evening.

Mr. L. M. Chastain and H. C. Blalock went to Clayton last Saturday.

Dr. J. L. Jackson, wife and little Irma Sue, of Atlanta, are spending a few days with the family of Mrs. W. L. Arrendale.

Misses Lizzie Blalock and Sallie Smith have gone to Clayton to enter school.

Mr. and Mrs. Bryant Hill visited Mr. Jeff Hill and wife Sunday.

Mr. and Mrs. J. H. Fuller visited the latter's mother Thursday night and Friday.

T. M. Wood and son Frank went to Mt. Airy last week.

Bob Powell and wife spent Sunday with Mr. and Mrs. V. T. Stonecypher.

Mr. J. F. Arrendale went to Clayton Saturday.

§   Mr. Editor:

As you have never heard from us in your paper, we will give you a little sketch or two for a starter.

Peace and good order reign at Tallulah Falls.

The rail road is progressing nicely.

Everything lovely here.

We notice some jackass from Germany trying to poke his nose in our business down here. We think he will have enough to look after his own affairs, if he has any. We are running ours down here.

He says the rail road is coming. We say he would not know one if he saw it. He says the stock law is needed. We say they can build a pen up there to put him in. He says if laziness was money we all would have some. We say if laziness was money he would be a millionaire. He says when you go to the Falls be sure to walk, for you can't wagon. We say he has no other way but to walk. He says it is a disgrace to the county. We say he has disgraced himself. He says he will never vote for a Tiger man. We say we don't want his vote for jackasses are not eligible to vote.

And now Mr. Jackass, take a little bit of advice and don't be poking your nose into other people's business.

B. H. Atkins

§   Notice. The Democratic executive committee of Rabun county are hereby requested to meet at the court house in Clayton by 10 o'clock a. m. on Saturday the 26th inst. for the purpose of transacting important business. You and each of you are earnestly urged to be present, since for lack of a quorum at our last meeting it was impossible to transact any business whatever. This is by order of the committee at [its] last meeting on April 12th 1902. Will F. Holden, [Secretary].

The following are the names of the committeeman. Clayton, W. S. Long and J. L. Hamby. Valley, W. E. Powell and D. W. Rickman. Persimmon, A. B. Forester and T. E. King. Tallulah, H. C. Blalock and L. M. Chastain. Stonepile, J. B. Bramblett and S. T. Taylor. Tiger, J. E. Bleckley and T. A. Robinson. Chechero, M. W. Swofford and J. H. Taylor. Warwoman, J. A. Turpen and S. M. Beck. Moccasin, W. F. Holden and M. M. Kell.

May 1, 1902
Volume 5, Number 15

§   Sheriff's Sales. Georgia—Rabun County. Will be sold, on the first Tuesday in May next, at public outcry at the court house in Clayton, said county, within the legal hours of sale, to the highest bidder for cash, certain property of which the following is a full and complete description: All mineral and mining priveleges in 90 acres and on lots of land Nos. 104 and 105 in the fifth land district of said county and more fully described in a deed from A. W. Irvin, trustee, to the Alladain Mining and Milling Co., dated March 27, 1899, and recorded in Record of deeds Book M, page 399 and 400. Levied on as the property of the Alladdain Mining and Milling Co., to satisfy the state and county tax for the year 1901. Written notice given in terms of the law. This Jan. 31st 1902. J. R. Ritchie, Sheriff...

§   Court next week.

§   Col. Hamby is in Atlanta.

§   Col. Paris was at the Falls yesterday.

§   Mrs. J. M. Long is spending the week on Tiger.

§   Nelson Tilley returned from market to-day.

§   Mrs. W. J. McCurry is dangerously ill.

§   You must register 10 days before the primary election June 5th.

§   Thanks to Mr. C. C. York for a bushel of corn on subscription.

§   There has been quite a crowd of "drummers" in town this week.

§   Miss Stella Langston and Miss Glenn Adams visited Tallulah Falls Tuesday.

§   There will be services at the Ridge next Sunday.

§   Misses Ethel Powell and Beulah Green have returned to Clayton to enter school again.

§   Owing to the general demoralization among our force several letters are left out this week.

§   Mr. Nin Ramey of Tiger will act as his brother's secretary[?] next week.

§   Col. J. H. Estill, candidate for governor, will be here next week.

§   Miss Elsie Ramey spent [Saturday] with John W. Green's family on Warwoman.

§   Gus Wall and wife, of Warwoman, spent Wednesday with Mr. and Mrs. J. S. Ramey.

§   W. S. Long and Spart Ramey went turkey hunting to-day. We wish them much luck.

§   W. S. Long wife and children spent Sunday in the mountains.

§   Dr. Henson is in town to-day.

§   Miss Mary Arrendale spent Saturday night and Sunday on Chechero, the guest of Miss Mattie Price.

§   Miss Fannie Donaldson is visiting Mrs. W. C. Donalson here at [illegible].

§   All the pupils of cabin No. 3 are on Bridge Creek.

§   Mr. and Mrs. David Parker will keep boarders court week.

§   James E. Bleckley will be in Gainesville for a few days.

§   Miss Lizzie Dillard is with home folks for Saturday and Sunday.

§   There are many humilting [*sic*] things in life. Have they come your way yet?

§   Col. Hamby is attending the convocation of Royal Arch Masons in Macon this week.

§   The wild flowers are more abundant, beautiful, brilliant and fragrant than usual this spring.

§   Misses Mattie and Zelma Price are with home folks for Saturday and Sunday.

§   Miss Beulah Green accompanied the Misses Bynum to their home on Warwoman this week.

§   P. T. Gains witnessed for the first time yesterday a tree splintered by a stroke of lightning.

§   Dr. Green, Dr. Dover and Mr. Robins took a day off down at the fishery on Warwoman creek one day last week.

§   Report fine sport and plenty of fish.

§   We are authorized to say that J. W. Peyton cashier of the Cornelia Bank will be here sometime during court and will be pleased to meet the people.

§   Jailer C. D. Comstock of Atlanta is sojourning in our community for the benefit of his health.
    Mr. Comstock is well and favorably known to many of our boys.

§   A. A. O'Kelley returned to Clayton Sunday from Harmony Grove, where he spent a few days last week at the bedside of his mother, who is dangerously ill.

§   Speaking of the candidates in Rabun county the Franklin Press remarks that "the people of Rabun county know a good thing when they see it, as there are fourteen announcements of candidates in the Clayton Tribune."

§   Its reported our good friend W. B. Watts has the most perfect apple and peach parer in the county. When fruit is in it would be our pleasure to test it personally.

§   We had the pleasure of meeting Mr. Geo. L. Prentiss president of the Blue Ridge and Atlantic railroad last week and he told us that he would let the contract to Franklin the first of June. The [contract] will be let at once some distance up Tiger creek.

§   Grove
The farmers are all busy.
The people are all backward about planting corn on the account of cold weather.
Mr. Isaac Cragg was at Grove Monday.
E. H. Baker made a hasty trip to Soque Monday.
Meaks Arrendale made a hasty trip to Clayton Thursday.
C. W. Derrick, of Tiger, passed Grove on his way to Burton Friday.
William Watts and wife, of Tiger, were among relatives on Bridge Creek Friday.

§   Blue Hights [*sic*]
Rev. Landrum preached a good sermon here Sunday.
Miss Sallie Cathey spent Saturday on Tiger.
Ed Holden and John Holt of the Valley attended services here Sunday.
Mrs. H. B. Dotson is in very feeble health.
Rev. Landrum and wife spent Sunday night with Mr. and Mrs. Charley Rogers.
Mrs. Swetman spent some time with Mrs. Clemy Rogers last week.
Mrs. Alex Roane and family spent Saturday and Sunday with parents on Tiger.

§   Upper Tiger
Quite a crowd from this place went to Spring Hill to preaching Sunday.
Mr. Ed Marsingale was in this community Sunday on "special business."
Messrs. John Cannon and John Moore spent Sunday night with Mrs. and Mrs. [*sic*] W. C. Kerby.
Mr. Tom Bleckley went to the Falls Sunday.
Mr. R. E. Cannon and daughters visited Mr. C. C. York and family Sunday.
Jable Cannon visited home folks Saturday and Sunday.

§   Judge Bleckley to Come to Rabun. Judge Logan E. Bleckley intends to make his home in Rabun first as soon as the Railroad is completed. He owns 1250 acres of land bordering on the incorporate limits of Clayton. This land includes the famous Screamer mountain made so because up to a year or so ago there on the towering mountain a three story building built by the Judge and here he spent one summer while he was chief justice of the Supreme court of Georgia. A good big block of the Pinecle [*sic*] mountain and about all of Hogback mountain, belong to this track. It is the Judge's purpose to rebuild on Screamer and settle a colony on the old historical mountain. Among them will be Judge Simmons, his old associate on the Supreme bench. The news of the intention of Judge Bleckley to return to the home of his birth will be received with much delight by all Rabun people.

§   Dillard

Intended for last week.

Miss Bessie Cannon, of Tallulah Falls, and Miss Effie Duncan, of Clayton, were in the Valley Sunday.

Miss Lula Hogsed, of Toccoa, is with her Uncle and Aunt, Mr. and Mrs. J. A. Martin.

Icy Martin is no better.

Little Fannie Powell who has Scarlet fever is improving slowly.

Miss Beulah Green is with home folks for a few days.

We wonder if Tom Bagle has ever been a candidate for Sheriff to enlarge his mouth if not. I would like for him to before we have our pictures made for Tallulah Falls fair.

John Turpen, of Warwoman, was in the Valley the first of the week on business.

Miss Laura Kelley went to Clayton Friday.

Rev. Brown is off to Gainesville after his wife.

Miss Fannie Donaldson is at Clayton again.

R. B. Dillard and family spent Sunday with Captain Beavert and wife.

Rev. Landrum preached to a large congregation Sunday.

§   Notice to Tax-Payers. Last Round. I will be at the following named places: Bridge Creek, Monday, May 12th, 1902, Stonepile 13th, Tallulah Falls 14th, Tiger 15th, Chechero the 16th, Wolffork 24th until 12 m [*sic*], Germany 24th at 3 p.m., Valley 26th, Betty's Creek 27th at 11 a.m., Persimmon 28th, Cross Roads 19th until 12 m. [*sic*], Dicks's Creek 30th until 12 m [*sic*], Kerbytown, same day, 3 p.m., Warwoman June 11th, Moccasin the 12th, Hail [*sic*] Ridge 13th, Darnell's mill 14th at 12 m [*sic*], Clayton, close out, June 16th, 17th and 18th. John M. Marsingale, R. T. R.

§   Quartz

John Teem and wife are getting along very well with the fever.

Mrs. J. C. York is [doing] as well as can expect.

Virgil Justus is severely sick.

A. M. Keener is off with his wagon to Cornelia.

I. P. Coleman carried a load of corn to J. H. Derrick Friday.

M. V. York had a small log rolling Friday.

Dr. Garland is making professional trips every few days on Persimmon. He has wonderful success.

§ The Thomas locust pin factory seems to be fast shaping[?] for active[?] work. Arthur Addington and a Mr. Campbell of North Carolina are engaged at the work.

May 8, 1902
Volume 5, Number 16

§   Resolutions of Democratic Executive Committee.

Be it resolved by the Democratic Executive Committee of Rabun County, now in session,

That, a primary election shall be held on the 5th day of June next at the several election precincts of said Rabun County, at which primary election all white Democratic voters of said county, who are qualified and who register in 1901, or within ten days before said primary election, shall be given an opportunity to cast their votes for the following officers, to wit:

Governor, Secretary of State, Att'y General, Comptroller General, Treasurer, Commissioner of Agriculture, State School Commissioner, Two Justices of the Peace, One Prison Commissioner, Judge of the Superior Courts of the North-eastern Judicial circuit and [Solicitor] General...

10th. That said primary shall be held and managed by the following well-known, active democrats (or by democrats selected by them on the day of said primary,) one of which said managers shall convey and deliver to the County Democratic Executive Committee by 12 oclock m. [sic] on the following day the returns of said primary election: Clayton: J. C. Pickett, W. S. Long, J. R. Grant; Valley: B. R. Dillard, J. F. Ritchie, D. W. Rickman; Persimmon: M. H. James, M. B. Forrester, W. B. Parker; Tallulah: J. F. Philyaw, J. W. Haney, Jas. F. Smith; Stonepile: F. A. Taylor, I. J. H. Hunnicut, S. B[?]. Wilbanks; Tiger: H. B. Cannon, H. J. Ramey, W. M. Lee; Checheroe: W. S. Price, A. J. Duncan, M. W. Swofford; Warwoman: S. M. Beck, M. M. Kell, J. M. Swafford; Moccasin: A. Whitmire, F. G. Holden, J. P. Billingsley...

§   To the voters of Rabun county: After having been solicited by many friends from different parts of the county, I hereby announce myself a candidate for the office of Sheriff, subject to the rules of the Democratic party. I confess I have had no experience in the office, but if I should be elected I will strive to be just and kind to all and to discharge my duty in such a manner that no one will ever be sorry I was elected. Thanking the people for any support, given me. Your friend, Thomas E. Carver.

§   All persons tresspassing on lots of land Nos. 44 and 45 in the 4th land district of Rabun county, Ga., will be prosecuted to the full extent of the law. G. W. M. Chappell. May 6th 1902.

§   All persons are hereby warned against tresspassing under fence on lots of land Nos. 69, 71 and 72 in the 2nd district and 49 in the first district. J. B. Powell.

§   Sheriff's Sales.

Georgia—Rabun County. Will be sold, on the first Tuesday in June next, at public outcry at the court house in Clayton, said county, within the legal hours of sale, to the highest bidder for cash, certain property of which the following is a full and complete description: A part of land lot No. 192 in the 13th land district of Rabun county, Ga., containing 200 acres more or less, and levied on as the property of H. P. Ditzel[?], to satisfy a tax fi fa issued against said H. F. Ditzel and said property by Joseph L. Dickerson, T. C. of said county, for taxes due the state and county for the year 1899. This May 8th 1902. J. R. Ritchie, Sheriff.

Georgia Rabun County. Will be sold, on the first Tuesday in September next, at public outcry, at the court-house in said county, within the legal hours of sale, to the highest bidder for cash, the following lot of wild land to wit: A portion of No. 175 in the 13th land district of Rabun County, Ga., containing 225 acres, more or less. Said property levied on as the property of Draper Moore, Administrator, to satisfy a tax fi fa issued against said lot by Joseph L. Dickerson, T. C. of said county, for taxes due the state and county for the year 1899. This May 7th 1902.

Also at the same time and place, lot of wild land to-wit: No. 50 in the 5th land district of Rabun county, Ga., containing 490 acres more or less. Said property levied on as the property of A. W. Merck, to satisfy a tax fi fa issued against said lot by Joseph L. Dickerson, T. C. of said county, for taxes due the state and county for the year 1899. This May 7th, 1902. J. R. Ritchie, Sheriff.

§   J. C. Cannon, of Atlanta, is visiting in Rabun.

§   Jesse Page leaves Tuesday for Boise[?] City Idaho.

§   Dr[?]. Clifton McCrackin, of Cornelia, is in the city.

§   J. C. Dickson, of Cornelia, is meeting old friends here.

§   William Wall, of Clarkesville, is among his friends here.

§   Mrs. David Parker visited her father at Soque[?] last week.

§   Cashier of Cornelia Bank, J. W. Peyton, was here this week.

§   Dr. D. R. Belt is being warmly greeted by his many old friends.

§   Noah Garland and Dan Hogsed, of Toccoa, were in town this week.

§   Henry Long of Whetstone S. C. was with his children here Saturday.

§   Thanks to Turner Page for two subscriptions to his children in the west.

§   Alvin Moore showed us this week a penny piece that dates back to 1814.

§   See Tom Ritchie if you want to sell your timber. He is still in the market.

§   At noon last Monday the thermometer registered 90 degrees in Clayton.

§   The many friends of Judge F. A. Bleckley are glad to see him in Rabun again.

§   J. I. Langston has planted 1700 apples this season[?]. So the good work good on.

§   The officers of the Tallulah Falls Ry. Co. have moved their offices to Cornelia.

§   We are obliged to Henry F. Watts for all back dues and year in advance. Thanks.

§   W. H. Duncan, of Atlanta, is the guest of the Blue Ridge Hotel for a few days.

§   Prof. J. C. Green, who has been spending the winter in South Georgia is in the city.

§   Thanks to W. H. Darnell for paid subscription to Mrs. Sallie Hopper, of Etowah, Oklahoma.

§   Rev. J. J. Kimsey, of Cleveland, Ga., occupied the pulpit in the Baptist church here Monday night.

§   Walter Dickson has had his hair cut.

§   D. L. Parker has averaged fifty boarders daily this week.

§   J. A. Keener, of Wolffork, made us a pleasant call Tuesday and greased our palm with some of the "oil of commerce."

§   We are not throwing flowers on anyone, but we would throw them on the life of Judge Estes for many reasons.

§   George W. Dickson, aged 89 years, and said to be the oldest man in this county, was here this week and as active as a cat, or at least an old cat.

§   Dept. Marshall Dennis Hughes and Thomas Mitchel came in to-day with a large still and had under arrest William Burton who was in the distillery.

§   M. C. Canup, cattle inspector, soon starts on his rounds of inspection. Clean up your cattle of the infection and get rid of the nuisance of the Quarantine Line.

§   We call your attention to the announcement of T. E. Carver for Sheriff. Mr. Carver is a popular young man and well equipped, and has many friends who will rally his support.

§   John H. Davis of [Hiawassee] is attending Rabun Superior Court this week.
    Mr. Davis says the missing link railroad is not dead and he gives his opinion that the railroad will be built.

§   Mr. J. F. Ritchie told us Monday that he has the Royal Limbertwig apples yet. The Royal is a fine apple, a fine bearer, and is proven by Mr. Ritchie to be an excellent apple. Remember this when you order your trees.

§   Judge J. J. Kimsey, of Cleveland, Ga., is meeting the people here and making scores of friends. Judge Kimsey will be elected our next Judge without opposition, and he well deserves the united vote of every county in this Judicial circuit.

§   General Manager W. S. Erwin is here on business for his road.

He reports that 3 ½ miles of the road is graded and that 5 ½ miles of the road will be graded by the first of June and that everything is progressing nicely and as fast as circumstances will permit.

§   Rabun Superior Court convened here Monday morning and the usual routine of business was hurriedly conducted. Judge Estes made a pointed charge to the Grand Jury—one that will likely be remembered for years to come.

No very important cases have been tried yet and we will wait until next week to give the proceedings in full.

The attorneys attending court are: W. F. Findley, H. H. Dean and Hubert Estes, Gainesville, J. C. Edwards and J. J. Bowden, Clarkesville, John H. David, Hiawasse [*sic*].

§   Rev. D. C. Brown is in town going around among old friends and wearing his same home spun clothes he wore to the conference at Rome that the Rome Tribune talked about as follows: Rev. D. C. Brown of Union county, is attending in a home spun suit of brown cloth made in his county. The sheep were raised there, the wool was carded and spun there and the clothes cut and made by two ladies of Union county. This suit is made in Prince Albert style and is very handsome.

§   Stonepile

Wedding bells are ringing. Mr. G. H. Lovell was married to Miss Susie Wilbanks.

Mr. Mart Wall, the famous black smith of the Falls, passed up Tuesday.

Aunt Mary Ellard has been at F. A. Taylor's, very sick, for a few days, but is better now.

We received a letter from M. B. Ellard, of Taylor, Arkansas, stating that he loaded a log that made two thousand feet of lumber. His wife says she liked old Georgia better than any state yet. Hurrah for Lily!

We spent three days in travelling over a part of this county and were made at some point to feel grateful, at others to feel very sad. As we passed from Clayton over the mountains to Persimmon creek, the well prepared fields, the lovely orchards were truly nice. In viewing the mountains all putting on their green we felt like summer was near. From there we went to the Valley at the head of Tennessee river to the Baptist church to hear Rev. Brown preach. We were glad to meet so many of our old friends and hear such a good sermon but were made to feel very sad when we looked over into the cemetery to find the resting place of the remains of our much loved and esteemed friend and brother Rev. Thomas Carter and there was [nothing] to point a stranger to the grave. How lonely we felt to think of his labors and faithfulness as a Baptist preacher and a Mason and no monument to him!

§ Dillard

Fine weather.

Prof. A. A. O'Kelley was in the Valley Sunday.

Mrs. Fannie Kelley is very sick.

Miss Glenn Adams was with Miss Carrie Grist Saturday.

Willie Franks in the Valley this week.

Miss Lula Hogsed and Pearl Martin was with Lula and Bertha Howard Saturday night.

Rev. Brown preached an interesting sermon at the M. E. church Sunday.

Mr. James Ramey passed through here enroute to Clayton Sunday.

Mrs. D. M. Green went to Clay- [sic]

Mr. Will Holden of Pine Mt. was here Sunday.

Miss Mary Neville was with home folks Saturday and Sunday.

Miss Eula Dillard went to N. C. last week.

Dock Parker has [returned] from Turnerville.

§ Blue Hights

Rev. Barrett preached here Sunday.

Miss Sallie Cathey returned home Saturday from Burton where she has been spending some time with her brother.

Mr. Gus Hunter attended services here Sunday.

Miss Dora Mozely spent Saturday with her [sic], Mrs. Charley Rogers.

Quite a number of young folks from the Valley was here Sunday.

Mrs. Johnson has been spending a few days with her daughter, Mrs. James Moore.

Mrs. H. B. Dotson is still on the sick list.

§ All person hunting, fishing, or in any other way tresspassing on the following property will be prosecuted to the full extent of the law: Part of lot No. 40 in the first land district of Rabun county Ga., part of lot No. 70 in the second district and part of lot No. 71 in the second. A. E. Dickerson. May 8 1902.

§ In memory of H. A. Parker... J. C. York

§   Old Tiger

Everybody has gone to court except those who can get to stay at home.

Mr. Nin Ramey is assisting the Clerk of the court. But we suppose that is publicly known, as so many people are at court.

We standunder [*sic*] that Mr. Thos. E. Carver is a candidate for Sheriff. That is alright, as Mr. Carver is an intelligent young man of spotless character and lives in Chechero district.

Mr. Henry Dockins is improving in health. Mrs. Sabrina Worley is thought to be improving.

A young man of Georgia went to Long Creek, S. C., a few days ago and found a girl who was studying hypnotism, which means to charm. Ask Mr. Henry Cannon if she has learned it. It seems [useless] for her to study how to charm, when her very beauty is enough to charm the most heartless fellow.

On the second thought we knew...we offered the apologies in bits too large for his comprehension to chamber, but we gave him time to pulverize and take them in doses to fit the disease—his dictionary.

Tiger was honored last Sunday with a singing by the Wolf Creek choir.

§   Quartz

The farmers have been in a rush, trying to get ready for court, but they are not ready.

Some evenings you would think Dewey's army was turned loose if you could hear the breech-loaders being turned loose on the squirrells.

John Teem and wife are convalescent.

Neighbors went in last Tuesday and painted John Teem's corn for him.

M. L. Hopper, of Wolffork, was on the creek the other day. He bought a cow of M. V. York.

Among the names that sound sweet none sound so sweet to V. L. M. as the name Hattie.

Mr. F. A. Taylor, of Stonepile, was on the creek a few days ago looking after the B. B. and Stone timber.

Rev. J. S. Dickson preached an interesting sermon at the Baptist church Sunday.

J. J. Parker has gone to Tate City, where he will work awhile.

May 15, 1902
Volume 5, Number 17

§   Georgia—Rabun County. To the Honorable Superior Court of said county:

The Grand Jury selected, chosen and sworn for said county for the February adjourned term, 1902, beg leave to submit the following general presentments:

Public Buildings. We have examined the public buildings of the county and find them in very good condition. We recommend that the ordinary have one room in the jail made sufficient to keep prisoners by re-ceiling the north-west room with oak lumber one and one half inches thick, filling it with twenty penny nailes, one inch apart, and provide said room with one iron door and six new locks and one door for closet by side of chimney.

Paupers. We have examined the pauper list of said county and recommend that the following names be added thereto: Sarah Duglass, $5.00 per year. Lizzie Scroggs $10 [per year]. Elijah Chastain $10 [per year]. Aunt Talley $12 per year. Margaret Tow $5 per year.

We recommend that the amounts paid the following be raised: Thomas Cowart, from thirty five to forty eight dollars. Harriet Cannon, from ten to fifteen dollars. Fajan Wall, from five to fifteen dollars.

We recommend that the ordinary pay at once to Emma Willhite the sum of fifteen dollars.

We recommend that the Ordinary pay to James Stancil $15 for taking care of Ruthy Littleton, a pauper who is now dead, in addition to any amount that might be due her as a pauper at this time.

We recommend that the Ordinary pay to Dr. W. J. Green ten dollars for services as an expert in the examination of Mrs. Vig Arrendale for lunacy.

We recommend that the ordinary pay Dr. J. C. Dover $11.25 for medical attention rendered to W. S. Mahaffey, W. E. Williams and Wm. Giles, while confined in the county jail.

County Officers. The committee appointed by the last Grand Jury to examine the various county offices has made report and we have adopted the same except as hereafter stated... In reference to that part of said report touching the affairs of the County School Commissioner concerning the paying out of money to Garland and Edge we wish to say: That said committee rendered a correct report as based on the information they had before them at the time; but we are glad to report that all seeming mistakes of the School Commissioner in paying out money and otherwise have been adjusted with the State School Commissioner.

We find three vacancies in the County School Board occasioned by the expiration of the terms of Dr. W. J. Green, Z. B. Dillard and Cicero Blalock, and we have elected to fill said vacancies Dr. W. J. Keener, James F. Keener and John Howard.

We have examined the dockets of the Justices of the Peace and Notaries Public in the various districts except the 1014th district. They were all found to be correct. It appears that there was no officer in the 1014th district and what became of the old docket we have not been able to ascertain.

We have elected William E[?]. Owens as Notary Public and Ex. Off. Justice of the Peace for said 1014th District G. M.

We recommend that the Supreme Court reports be kept in the offices of the Clerk and Ordinary and that the same be not kept away from said offices.

We recommend that the Ordinary, at the expense of the county, have built a substantial wooden bridge at or near the ford on Betty's Creek on the Rabun Gap and Franklin road—provided the citizens of the Valley District shall have first contributed one hundred dollars in money, labor or material towards the construction of said bridge.

We recommend that the proper authorities build a bridge over Scott's Creek on the road from Clayton to Tallulah Falls.

We recommend that the following pieces of road be considered as private roads and that the gates remain on said roads as formerly to-wit: The Blalock road, beginning at the district line in Clayton district and running Southeast to Julius Taylor's, thence to the public road near the bridge on Tiger creek: and the James Kell road beginning at a top of the hill near Captain Beck's, thence to district line near Hale Ridge.

We find the roads of the county in reasonably good condition.

We append hereto reports made to the body by the Ordinary, Treasurer and County School Commissioner.

We recommend that the Clerk of this body be paid 25 cents per day extra for his services.

We have examined the pension list and make no recommendation in respect thereto, believing the same to be right as it stands.

In taking leave of his honor, J. B. Estes, and Solicitor General W. A. Charters, we commend them as faithful officers and extend them our thanks for courtesies shown us. We also thank our baliff Jeff Swofford for his attention to us.

R. E. Cannon, Foreman. Isaac P. Coleman, Thos. E. King, John H. Dotson, Wm. B. Watts, Joel M. Arrendale, Lafayette Dickson, Andrew M. Holden, Fred G. Holden, James M. Bell, John Howard, Wm. H. York, Andrew J. Kell, Elijah B. Philyaw, Virgil T. Stonecypher, Jeff D. Beck, Balis C. Nicholson, James B. Hicks, Isaac N. Lovell, Peter E. Thompson, Cicero C. York, Ethel D. Swofford, Marion H. James.

§   We are compelled to leave out the grand jury reports and two or three letters this week.

§   L. C. Hollifield is at his farm on Timpson.

§   W. H. Duncan returned to Atlanta Sunday.

§   Quite a crowd went upon Screamer mountain Saturday.

§   Superior court is over but other courting still goes on.

§   Rev. Brown will preach here Sunday, in the Baptist church.

§   Frank McCrankin [*sic*] has been spending the week in town.

§   John Sumpter is up from the railroad camp this morning.

§   Col. W. S. Paris attended city court at Clarkesville this week.

§   A. B. Sams, of Savannah, is visiting his sister, Mrs. Dr. Henson.

§   Several of our people contemplate going to Atlanta Saturday.

§   See J. F. Earl for your fall fruit trees and get them at thousand rates and save money.

§   The locust pin makers can get $7.50 per m for 18 inch pins. J. F. Earl.

§   Miss May Ramey of Tiger spent Wednesday with Mrs. Spart Ramey.

§　Miss Mary Arrendale is unable to be in school this week on account of sickness.

§　The jury here during court brought in a verdict of guilty in every case tried. Not one person was acquitted.

§　Miss Brama Sams left Sunday for Savannah, Ga., where she will remain several months as the guest of her brother, A. B. Sams.

§　Mrs. Mary Ellard of Tallulah Falls is spending a few days with Mr. H. K. Cannon and family.

§　Rev. Landaum said in his sermon Sunday that to enter the "pearly gates" one should be dilligent in business and work six days of the week.

§　Born—To Mr. and Mrs. Nelson Tilly, this morning, an eleven pound girl.

§　There were no [illegible] drawn at this term of court for the August term. The jury commissioner will revise the jury and draw the grand and special jury themselves. This is the order of Judge Estes.

§　John C. Cannon of Atlanta, was among his [illegible] friends and relatives during court.

§　Kinney Kragg was in our office last week and told us that he has green apples yet. We wonder how long apples will keep in Rabun! Well[?] did Commissioner R. T. Nesbitt say that there is no better place on earth to keep apples than Rabun county.

§　The Thomas locust pin factory here is running at full blast. This is not the only pin factory contemplated. The Gilliland factory will soon start up on Mr. Earl's property. Thousands of the rough blocks are being brought in to both places.

§　Judge Estes decided against the alternative road law and now the system is in full force and the ordinary will proceed at once to buy all necessary tools and machinery, stock and so on for J. I. Langston, superintendant, and work will begin in a few days. All responsibility of the roads of the county rests upon the ordinary now. A large majority of the people oppose the law. We hear the matter will go before the Supreme court.

§ Notice. I will reward the parties who will return my shovel and handsaw as I don't remember who I loaned them to. Please return them at once. J. R. Ritchie.

§ Cases Tried Court Week.
T. M. C. Hunnicutt vs. Laura Hunnicutt, libel for divorce. Total divorce granted.
Bud Wall, misdemeanor. Fined ten dollars and costs. Paid.
Samuel Wilbanks, misdemeanor. Twenty dollars and costs. Paid.
Samuel Wilbanks, misdemeanor. (Concealed weapons.) Twenty five dollars and costs. Paid.
Charley Ritchie, misdemeanor. Twenty dollars and costs. Paid.
Rufa[?] Whitmire, convicted of misdemeanor. Appealed for a new trial.
Charley Swofford, larceny from the house. Twenty five dollars and costs or ten months in the chaingang.
Will Martin, forgery. Five years in the penitentiary.
Charley Nichols, misdemeanor. Sixteen dollars and costs, Paid.
Sam Wilborne, rape. Convicted. Twenty years in the penitentiary.
Bill Giles, rape. Twenty years in the penetentiary.
Jeff Hamby, misdemeanor. Ten dollars and costs. Paid.
Lily Wall, misdemeanor. Twenty five dollars and costs. Paid.
John Hamby, misdemeanor. Twenty five dollars and costs. Paid.
Cintha Holcomb, misdemeanor. Twenty five dollars and costs.
Hary Ledford, misdemeanor. Twenty five dollars and costs. Paid.

§ Quartz
Corn planting is not near done yet.
Court is over and the farmers will hustle to their work.
The beef cattle and yearlings are being taken to the mountains where they will get fat by fall.
On the next first Sunday there will be communion meeting at the Baptist church in Persimmon.
J. F. Keener has been acting post master this week, while L. T. Teems was at court.
Mart Justus and son went to the mountains Friday.
G. H. Thompson is hauling corn to Tate City.
The people in general are well.
News scarce.

§ Clayton, Ga., May 6, 1902. The republicans of Rabun county met here to-day, for the purposes of electing a chairman, two secretaries and five committeemen.
The following declaration of principles was adopted: "The present

prosperity of the county is declared the fruit of republican legislation. The death of the late President McKinley is mourned, his services to the nation enlodged and his exalted character extalled[?]. The administrative policy of President Roosevelt is endorsed in every essential...["] John W. Godfrey, Chairman. W. S. Dickson, 1st Secretary. H. A. Keener, 2nd Secretary.

Committee: A. J. Kell, Moccasin. William Metcalf, Tallulah. W. H. Darnell, Valley. Lafayette Dickson, Warwoman. S. S. Whitmire, Clayton.

Meet again the fourth Saturday in July.

§ Dillard

Mr. D. E. Hogshed is in the Valley this week.

Mr. Charlie Hamlim [*sic*] is here on a visit.

Mrs. Lisa Holden is with her daughter, Mrs. Fannie Kelley.

Mr. Drew Smith was in the Valley on Thursday.

Mr. Noah Garland, of Toccoa, is in the Valley this week.

Mr. Poter [*sic*] Green, of Turnerville, was in the Valley the later part of last week.

Ed Angel, of N. C. passed through here en route to Turnerville Sunday.

Mr. and Mrs. Brab Glaspy are visiting in N. C.

John Godfrey is off to Atlanta.

There were several met and cleaned off the Baptist Cemetery Saturday.

R. T. Green was at D. M. Green's Friday night.

Miss Mary Tanner has returned from Athens where she has been attending school.

Miss Beulah Green has quit school and returned home.

§ Miss Mary Arrendale says for the boys to be [illegible] with their hats.

§ Grove

Weather pretty.

The farmers are all busy making up lost time.

We hardly know what to write, as the last two Tribunes have failed to reach Grove.

Mr. Dennis Williams, of Chechero, was in this community last Thursday.

Court is over and everybody in this community seem to be proud of it.

Mr. and Mrs. Pink Wood, of Soque, went visiting relatives in this community Saturday and Sunday.

Mr. D. P. LaCount was at home from the railroad Sunday. He says he thinks they will complete the culvert work in a month to Tiger.

The revenue officials made a raid in this community Thursday and captured a copper and Willie Burton.

§   Atlanta, Ga., April 24th, 1902. Mr. J. L. Dickerson, T. C. Rabun Co., Wolffork, Ga.

Dear Sir:

Your final statement of 1901 taxes and vouchers received.

I enclose receipt for voucher which closes your account for this year.

I desire again to express my appreciation of your uniformly good work as Tax Collector. The small Insolvent list sent in shows that your work was thorough. I thank you for your promptness in making returns and remittances to the state and commend you as a faithful, efficient officer.

Yours truly, Wm. A. Wright, Compt. General

June 12, 1902
Volume 5, Number 21

§   The Election in Rabun.

A very light vote was polled in Rabun in the primary last Thursday. The primary was too soon for many of our citizens. The county went for Estill by 66 majority, after having been conceded in the Terrell column. We are unable to give the correct vote by precincts. Below is the vote for the various state-house officers in Rabun:

Governor. J. M. Terrell 150. Dupont Guerry 21. J. H. Estill 216.

Secretary of State. Phillip Cook 386.

Comptroller General. W. A. Wright 387.

State Treasurer. R. E. Park 387.

Attorney-General. J. C. Hart 387.

State School Commissioner. G. R. Glenn 151. W. B. Merritt 200. Mark Johnson 33.

Commissioner of Agriculture. O. B. Stevens 341. R. T. Nesbitt 63.

Prison Commissioner. Thomas Eason 207. Wiley Williams 72.

Associate Justices of Supreme Court. Samuel Lumpkin 383. A. J. Cobb 376.

United States Senator. A. S. Clay 386.

Congressman, 9th Congressional District. F. C. Tate 385.

Judge Superior Court, Northeastern Circuit. J. J. Kimsey 389.

Solicitor General Northeastern Circuit. W. A. Charters 389.

Executive Committeemen. The following Executive Committeemen for the various districts of Rabun county were elected last Thursday: Clayton, J. R. Grant and J. M. Marsingale. Valley, B. R. Dillard and D. W. Rickman. Persimmon, A. B. Forrester and T. E. King. Tallulah, H. C. Blalock and L. M. Chastain. Stonepile, F. A. Taylor and S. B. Wilbanks. Tiger, Wyly Pitts and J. C. Green. Chechero, J. H. Coffee and W. S. Price.

Warwoman, M. M. Kell and Jeff Swofford. Moccasin, W. F. Holden and G. N. Bynum.

Delegates to the State Convention. J. C. Pickett and L. M. Chastain. Alternates, Z. B. Dillard and R. E. A. Hamby.

Delegates to the Congressional Convention. W. J. Green, J. I. Langston, H. C. Blalock and H. R. Cannon.

§   Several students and teachers will stand examination for teacher's license here Saturday. Such earnestneess as our scholars have shown this term will surely not go unrewarded.

§   Stonepile
Dry weather.
Clean crops.
We had a mess of green beans for dinner the ninth.
Dock Taylor left for Sylvia [*sic*], N. C., the 7th, where he will enter college.
Prof. Ballew will sing at Eden Church Saturday and Sunday.
We had a letter from our friend S. T. Taylor, of Greenville, S. C., a few days ago.
The boys are talking politics lately.
Look out for the rail road!
There is money enough sent up to run it up to North Carolina. We have heard several ask if the road would go on. Some say it will stop at Clayton, others at Tiger, but we say it will go through. See who tells it right. The harder the hog is to tole[?] the more corn he gets. We are bettered, let it stop wherever it will, but the railroad is worsted unless it goes on.

We went to visit our sick friends Sunday. As we were traveling the highway we passed three girls and two small boys, something like ten or twelve years old, the biggest little boy was barefooted and was smoking. We asked him if he was not too small to smoke. His answer was: "Just the right size." So we began to study and concluded it was right, just the right size to make a failure of life, and just the right size to spoil a man and maybe a woman.

We want compulsory school law and a high school at Clayton and we will give twenty-five dollars.

We want one at Tallulah Falls and we will give fifty dollars and as soon as the school gets in good progress we will give fifty more if they will build a department for the orphan and helpless children of this county whose parents are making mistakes and sad ones too.

§   Notice. To Whom It May Concern: It has been decided by the Management of the Cliff House property to charge a small fee admission, in order to keep up much needed repairs in the grounds. The tickets will also "admit bearer" to the handsome, new, cement swimming pool now constructed on the grounds. Respectfully, R. L. Moss, Manager.

§   Real Estate.

We are in the real estate business and want you to list your property with us. No charge for advertising. Any portion of the county wanted. Describe your land and send to J. A. Reynolds, care of Tribune office.

I have for sale the following land. Read the list and buy you a mountain home.

125 acres, 2 ½ miles east of Clayton, on the Warwoman road, 1 mile from the Tallulah Falls Railway, now being constructed, partly improved, 30 bearing fruit trees, mountain cabin, partly timbered. A profit will soon be made on this property. Price $275.

150 acres, partly in the incorporation of Clayton, a good farm cleared and in cultivation. The very best hard wood timber. A fine water power. A fine place for retaining reservoir. Will come in soon as town property. This property lies partly[?] on and at the base of the famous Screamer mountain, also the strouds. All these [illegible] by statistics the best [illegible] in the world. Price $1500[?].

§   The election over the state in the primary last Thursday resulted as follows:

J. M. Terrell carried sufficient counties to nominate him on the [illegible] ballot for Governor.

W. B. Merritt is nominated over Glenn by an overwhelming majority.

O. B. Stevens is the nominee for Commissioner of Agriculture.

Tom Eason carried the State for Prison Commissioner.

It is unnecessary to mention the other Candidates as they were with out opposition.

§   Tresspass Notices. All persons tresspassing on lots of land Nos. 44 and 45 in the 4th land district of Rabun county, Ga., will be prosecuted to the full extent of the law. G. W. M. Chappell. May 6th 1902.

§   Notice to Teachers. The County Teachers' Institute will begin Monday, June the 9th, and will continue the week. The examination for teachers license will be held June 14th. All teachers are required to attend the Institute. A. A. O'Kelley, Co. S. Com.

§   A Key to Examinations. A new book has just been published containing the Questions and Answers of every Public School Examination in Georgia, since 1888. Fourteen years work. Will be sent, post-paid, on receipt of One Dollar. Descriptive circulars sent free. B. S.

Holden, Cashier, Gilmer Co. Bank, Ellijay, Ga.

§   Peach cider at Tilley's.

§   Rev. Landrum preached at the Methodist Church here Sunday.

§   Mr. Marvin Roane returned to Atlanta Monday.

§   Notice the Masonic Festival announced elsewhere.

§   We do not think there ever was an Institute conducted here with more good done than the present one.

§   Warren Dunlap is in Atlanta, where he goes to stand trial in the united States Court for making stills in Arkansas.

§   Ex-Senator Cobb, for Franklin county, has been acting as expert teacher of the Institute here this week.

§   Lafayette Wall, of Atlanta, is up among friends and relatives.

§   Ex-Sheriff John Dockins was in town a few days ago and brought down with him a shoulder and ham of meat he sold to John T. Long for $8.50.

§   Will Martin, colored, was carried off to the penetentiary [*sic*] last Monday. Martin will pick rocks for the state five years for forgery.

§   Mr. G[?]. W. McDade has closed a deal for the forty thousand acres of timbered land which he has held under option here several months.

§   Mrs. John W. Godfrey, of the Valley, who has been dangerously ill the past week is reported to be convalescent.

§   Our locust pin mill is running night and day now.

§   Institute is in session this week. Let the good work go on.

§   Mr. J. R. Hopper, of Rabun Gap, was a pleasant caller at our office to-day. Mr. Hopper says the worms are eating all the forest timber up there, thereby destroying the mast.

§   Mr. D. G. Dover, who lives away up on Black-rock mountain, says he has corn with tassels and "shoots" both. Who can beat this?

§   The Revenue offices made a raid on Burton Thursday but came out at the little end of the horn.

§   Mrs. W. A. Simmons of Acworth, Ga., accompanied by Miss Mary and the little ones arrived in town Tuesday and will be the guests of Mr. and Mrs. S. W. Dover for the summer.

§   Mr. Anderson Coffee, an aged and respected citizen of Germany, passed away to the Great Beyond last Friday night and was buried Saturday. Mr. Coffee leaves a family and a host of friends to mourn his departure.

§   Now that our school is out, we would appreciate a news letter from some of our Clayton scholars in every section of the county.

§   L. T. Mitchell asks us to say in justice to him, that the grand jury did not find a bill of indictment against him for perjury, as we stated in Tribune two weeks ago.

§   Frank Wall of Warwoman, says he had green beans for dinner on June 1st.

§   Owing to a serious case of "pi" in the Tribune office this week, we are some what delayed with The Tribune, but we ask our good readers to excuse us, and we believe they will.

§   Mrs. Susie Burch, of Cornelia, was in town the first of the week.

§   McDade and Turpen will pay nine dollars in case for locust pins delivered on any public road in the county. See them before you buy your pins.

§   Below we give the register of our two principal hotels for this week:
   Hotel Parker Register. Arthur Addington, Franklin N. C.; Bed Penland, Franklin N. C.; Walter Thompson, Sylvia [sic] N. C.; Jim Smith, Burton; Tom Smith, Burton; W. H. York, Burton; T. M. Hopper, Valley; Miss Mattie Holden, Rabun Gap.
   Blue Ridge Register. R. D. Burch, Atlanta; Joe King, Tallulah Falls; F. C. Mills, Hot Dropville Ky.; C. L. Ingram, Franklin N. C.; M. S. Orth, Chicago; Syd Leonard, Cornelia; C. C. Bealer, Greenville S. C.; J. A. Dummon, Virginia; John English, City; Jule Jacobs, Franklin N. C.; Lee Barnard, Franklin N. C.; B. H. Benson, Newman; B. H. Landrum, Rabun Gap; T. N. Howard, Rabun Gap; C. L. Johnson, Franklin N. C.; H. L. Richardson, Gainesville; L. D. Hughes, Atlanta; E. J. Bengiman,

Chattanooga Ten.; Dow Kimsey, Cornelia.

§   Quartz

Dr. Garland and John Dockins were on the creek a few days ago. John says it is too soon to talk politics yet.

Col. Hamby was on the creek trying to trade W. E. Lindsay a buggy the other day.

Miss Texie York is at home from Blue Ridge where she has been teaching.

G. F. York went to the R. R. and carried off some produce.

Did you ever know of every district in the county to have a candidate before?

Corn is growing as fast as we ever saw, considering the need of rain.

The drill worms are still at work and killing a lot of the re-plants.

See robbing time and they are rich too. S. M. Nichols has 19 to rob yet.

Inglass Coffee and Emanuel Nichols had a combat the other day and a trial Friday but the writer don't know what the result is.

§   From the Wall House.

The Wall House guests are rejoicing in the cool shade of the beautiful trees, swinging in the hammocks, and enjoying the delicious fare—cool butter-milk, fresh butter, eggs, fried chicken and all the early vegetables. Mr. and Mrs. Frederick Maxwell, of Anderson, S. C., are the guests of this delightful house, and all they need to complete their happiness is some nice fresh honey, either sour-wood or sweet-wood. Now, who can supply this? They are also fond of huckle-berries.

"Wells" Maxwell is quite an addition to the household. He is enjoying the chicken bones and country hams.

Dr. Dover and Mr. Maxwell drove to Burton to-day. Clayton should feel proud of her handsome doctor.

§   Old Tiger

Farmers are getting along well with their work.

In a few more days they will have an easy time, for the weeks will die without work unless it rains.

Mr. L. N. Taylor has lots two fine hogs.

Mr. Lawrence Worley was married Sunday before last to a Miss Ivester, of Habersham.

Mr. Harrison Shirley is sick and under treatment of Dr. J. C. Dover.

A certain fellow always feels like singing: "All the tune that I can play, is I wish the girl was mine." But alas! So near and yet so far.

The Temperance [illegible] understood, have been volunteering[?] some of the good citizens to trial for dealing a cause of intemperate indications, or have served them with some sort of notice. We do not believe in a favored few.

Something was seen at Tallulah Falls last Saturday whose sweetness and beauty make impressions that would take poets to express. They were beautiful from the positive to the superlative.

Mr. F. A. Taylor has a heifer that was a year old the 31st day of last August. She took the premium at the Tallulah Falls Fair last year as the finest one-year-old. On the 8th of this month, at the age of 21 months and seven days, she brought a fine heifer calf.

Well, the election was managed at Stonepile under an agreement that the one who carried up the returns for consolidation should keep one dollar for taking them up and divide the balance among the three managers. The time is up and we have not received our part of the balance. If one got it all, which ought to be four dollars, he made a right pretty thing of it; if it was divided between the other two it was a pretty good thing anyway, but their time they lost from their work was worth that much—but our time was worth as much as theirs. All this lost and our candidates beat too! Besides, we had paid, I suppose, five cents a name in taxes to get to vote and then did not cash our privilege but privileged our cash, subject to the acts of the Legislature.

A young lady was seen keeping home alone. She ought to get some one to help her.

Mr. F. A. Taylor carried a load of home raised bacon to market this week. He still has almost a house full of best corn. He has beans and many good things.

§ Ordinary's Citations.

Georgia—Rabun County. Arah Bleckley, having made application for twelve months' support out of the estate of J. M. Bleckley, and appraisers duly appointed to set apart the same, having filed their return, all persons concerned are hereby required to show cause before the Court of Ordinary of said county, on the first Monday in July, 1902, why said application should not be granted. This 27th day of May, 1902. W. S. Long, Ordinary.

§ Georgia—Rabun county. To all whom it may concern: H. V. Murray, having made application to me in due form to be appointed permanent administratrix upon the estate of C. J. Crunkleton, late of said county, notice is hereby given that said application will be heard at the regular term of the Court of Ordinary for said county to be held on the first Monday in July, 1902. Witness my hand and office signature, this 28th day of May, 1902. W. S. Long, Ordinary.

§   State of Georgia, Rabun County.

L. Bloom vs. P. A. Crane } In Superior Court, February adjourned term, 1902.

It being represented to the court by the petition of L. Bloom that by Mortgage dated the 1st day of Nov. 1901.

P. A. Crane executed and delivered to the said L. Bloom a mortgage on certain real estate lying in said county described as follows: Situated, lying and being in the county of Rabun, state of Georgia, containing three hundred acres more or less in the third land district of the said county on both sides of the Chatooga river adjoining lands of W. J. Burrell, J. A. Nix and A. A. Billingsby [*sic*], being the same tract of land bought by me several years ago from W. P. Burrell for the purpose of securing the payment of a certain promisory note made by the said P. A. Crane as aforesaid to the said L. Bloom, due on the 5th day of Nov. 1901, for the sum of three hundred and five dollars and sixtysix cents, which note is now due and unpaid.

It is ordered that the said P. A. Crane do pay into this court by the first day of the next term the principal, interest and costs due on said note, or show cause, if any he has to the contrary, or that in default thereof foreclosure be granted to the said L. Bloom of said mortgage, and the equity of redemption of the said P. A. Crane therein be forever barred, and that service of this rule be perfected on said P. A. Crane according to law.

J. B. Estes, J. S. C.

A true copy from the minutes of this court.

J. S. Ramey, Clerk.

§   Sheriff's Sales

Georgia—Rabun County. Will be sold on the first Tuesday in July next, at public outcry at the court house in Clayton, said county, within the legal hours of sale, to the highest bidder for cash, certain property of which the following is a full and complete description:

Part of lot of land No. 8 in the 5th land district of Rabun county, Ga., containing one hundred acres, more or less, and bounded as follows: On the east by lands of F. A. Bleckley, on the north by lands of John McCrackin, on the south by lands of A. J. Williams and on the west by land of Adaline Knowell.

Levied on as the property of W. E. Stancil to satisfy a fi fa issued from the justice's court of the 597th district G. M. of said county in favor of Taylor and Sweet against the said W. E. Stancil. Property pointed out by plaintiffs in fi fa. Levy made and returned to me by E. M. Manley, L. C. This May 26th 1902.

J. R. Ritchie, Sheriff.

§   Masonic. Notice.

There will be a festival communication of Rabun Gap Lodge No. 265 F. and A. M. to be held in Clayton beginning at 10 o'clock a. m. on Saturday, June 21, 1902, to which the public is cordially invited.

The objects of this communication are feastings, amusements and instructions.

All will be fed and amused and none wearied.

Program.

Music.

Prayer by Rev. R. L. Whitmire, Chaplain.

Address by Rev. W. A. Simmons, of Acworth, Ga.

Music.

Benediction by Rev. J. M. Wall.

Dinner.

By the Program Committee.

June 19, 1902
Volume V, Number 22

§   Mr. Editor:

The amount of school funds and the length of our public school term being called to my attention by the report of the C. S. C. to the last Grand Jury, and after getting the following information I believe we school patrons of Rabun county should have a five months public school term for the present year.

In 1897 Rabun county had $3,707.00 with which our schools were run five months. In 1901 our public school funds had increased to $4591.00, and increase of nearly $900, or one fourth, and our schools were run only four months, (a decrease of one month or one fifth.) Why is it necessary that an increase of one fourth in school funds should make a decrease of one fifth in the length of term...

The school of which I am a patron has 140 pupils and each receives $2.50, making $350 for the term, or $70 per month for five months. Now I think $70.00 is sufficient amount to pay two teachers for one month's teaching and as every child receives the same, I see no reason, with an economical admistration [*sic*] and a small appropriation for certain schools, why we should not have a five months term. Towns, White and Habersham have always had a 5 months public school since 1897, and why can't Rabun?

I will suggest a few changes which I think necessary in our public schools:

1st. The salary of the C. S. C. be two dollars per day instead of three dollars, and the members of the Board one dollar per day instead of two, thereby reducing the expense of the administration one half nearly.

Second. Certain sub-districts should be re-districted, that the pupils may be more evenly divided...

Third. A few schools where the number of children will not draw a sufficient amount to justify a teacher to teach five months, a certain amount should be set aside to meet this deficiency.

What I have said has not been to cast reflection on any one, but are my own ideas, and I hope the Board of Education may devise some method to enable Rabun county to have a five months public school as does Towns, White and Habersham, our adjoining counties.

Observer.

§   We learn from the Clarkesville Advertiser that our old friend and college mate Paul F. Grant was nominated for Sheriff of Habersham County in the June 5th primary...

§   Stonepile.

We had a very nice rain Sunday and failed to have any preaching as there was no preacher on hand.

Mr. James York, of Persimmon, had the class as Mr. Bellew was sick.

Mr. J. M. Chasteen and wife were at preaching Saturday.

Mr. F. D. Singleton past up yesterday nominating the school children in this district. He says they had a fine institute.

The Tiger man says they failed to devide with him I made a fat thing of it. He can call it fat if he wants to, but it was as poor as a summer o'possum.

We met the executive committee twice at Clayton, made one trip to Tallulah Falls, one day to manage the election and one to consolidate and got one dollar for all five days' work, man and mule, and furnished our own wear and tear and were working for men who get from two thousand to five thousand dollars a year.

I don't think Stonepile will ever do it again. We will roost on another limb or go to the deaf and dumb asylum.

I have stood by the Democrats for thirty years and never got but one dollar and that was this time. No if you call that good things I do not want any more of it.

Cromer Shirley is going into the Taylor business.

§   There was a universal expression of delight when it was learned that Judge Bleckley had abandoned his idea of leaving Clarkesville, but would rebuild here. When a great tree falls in our groves or the ruthless ax lays it low there is a feeling of loss but when from the forest of friendship a great oak is withdrawn, against whose sturdy side we have so leaned for support and counsel, and beneath the shade of whose companionship we have found so many happy hours, then truly there are hours of sadness. And it was therefore with great delight that we learn he will remain with us.—Clarkesville Advertiser.

§ We never saw a more civil, gentlemanly bunch of boys than those who were here from Burton last week. If Clayton had one boy of good moral character,—well we suppose the "rowdies" would run him out of town.

§ Notice.
It has been decided by the Management of the Cliff House property to charge a small fee admission, in order to keep up much needed repairs in the grounds.
The tickets will also "admit bearer" to the handsome, new, cement swimming pool now constructed on the grounds.
Respectfully, R. L. Moss, Manager.

§ Lula McClain vs. Frank McClain } Lible for Divorce.
To Frank McClain. You are hereby notified to be or appear either personally or by an Attorney at the next Superior Court of Rabun county to be held on the fourth Monday in August 1902 next, to answer the complaint of Lula McClain in an action for total divorce. In default thereof the court will proceed as to justice shall appertain. Witness the Hon. J. B. Estes Judge of said court. This 17th day of June 1902.
J. S. Ramey, C. S. C.
Jas. R. Grant, Libelants Att'y.

§ Clayton is unusually dull this week.

§ J. Marion Long has purchased a wheel.

§ Nelson Tilley left Monday for Athens and Atlanta.

§ The editor is at Cornelia surveying for the Southern Railway Co.

§ Mr. J. F. Earl is suffering with a cold, which has settled in his eyes. Mr. Earl says we can almost call him blind.

§ Mrs. C. C. Wall requests us to say that since she has quit dealing in intoxicating liquors, drinking and shooting still goes on.

§ Rev. W. A. Simmons, of Acworth, Ga., arrived in town Monday evening and will be the guest of Mr. and Mrs. S. W. Dover for some time.

§ Owing to sickness we are delayed in getting out The Tribune. As our home readers know we could not hire any help as there are no typos in Rabun.

§   The Rabun County Teacher's Association was re-organized here last Thursday evening, and, we suppose, will meet again soon. We would be pleased to publish the program for the first meeting.

§   The old-fashioned smoke-house of the Blue Ridge Hotel, which has been standing at the rear end of the hotel for over thirty years, has been removed in order to build a diary [*sic*], well and smoke-house all in one.

§   Rev. Brown, of Rabun Gap, preached to an attentive audience in the Baptist church here Sunday morning. Mr. Brown said that he would take up collection here on his next meeting day for the benefit of the orphans and helpless children of Georgia.

§   Mr. J. T. Long went down to the Falls Monday. Mr. Long, when we asked him how the railroad was getting along, replied that it was "dead as the devil."

§   Tuesday, however, it was rumored that Mr. Wagener received a telegram Monday evening that the money was waiting with which to pay the laborers, and that the contract would soon be let to build the road[?] on to Franklin, N. C.

§   Mrs. Mary Norris, who has been suffering for some time with rheumatism, is said to be almost entirely recovered.

§   We erred in saying three weeks ago, that the grand jury brought in a bill of indictment for L. T. Mitchell for perjury in the case of the State vs. Miss Lillie Wall. The matter was not brought before the grand jury.

§   We called on Squire and Mrs. Derrick yesterday evening. Squire took us out in the garden and showed us his onion patch. We guess there are fifty rows of onions with not the difference of two inches in the height of every top. We were then shown two or three grape vines and were carried away at the simple beauty of them, with their full, round bunches, and the vines running all over apple trees, with young apples on. It was indeed a lovely scene. We noticed the flowers in the yard, the cedar bushes and running vines on the veranda, all of which help to make his home one of the most pleasant places in town.

§   Below we give the register of the Hotel Parker for the past week: Miss Mattie Holden, Dillard; Marsh Hopper, Dillard; Lige King, Burton; Hanon King, Burton; Tom Carver, Chechero; E. B. McConnell, Mt. Airy; Miles C. Cannup, Burton; W. H. York, Burton; Dude Speed, City; Arthur Addington, Franklin, N. C.; C. W. McDade, Ashville, N. C.; Bell Penland,

Franklin, N. C.; N. S. Thomas, Sylvia, N. C.; A. B. Forester, Persimmon; J. M. Bleckley, Warwoman.

§ A real entertainment was given by the institute here, in the courthouse, last Thursday night. A good crowd turned out and all who attended expressed themselves as being highly pleased with the program, which was as follows:

Music; Lecture by Expert W. H. Cobb; Music; Lecture by Prof. J. S. Burrel; Lecture by Col. R. E. A. Hamby; Music; Recitation by Miss Mary Green; Music; Recitation by Miss Belle York.

Profs. Burrell and Cobb and Col. Hamby all made excellent speeches and the music was grand.

All in all, our Institute was a success, and we believe much and lasting good was done toward furthering educational work in this county.

§ From the Wall House.

All serene and peaceful at "The Wall House" this week. This place is delightful. No flies[?] come to worry your slumber, for gauze windows and doors prevent them. Here one has all the early fruits. "Have fruits?" Huckle-berries, dew-berries and June apples are always plentiful on the delightful and appetizing table, besides the most substantial things of life.

Fresh flowers greet the eye when you partake of this delicious food, "Trailing Arbutus" always in great profusion.

If you seek health, a most superb climate, good, pure water and a delightful abode, for your summer vacation, come to Clayton and there you will find all of these.

There is also published in this little village a bright and sparkling newspaper, namely, "The Tribune." Subscribe for it and find out all about this mountain resort.

Several distinguished guests are expected at "The Wall House" soon, the DeEsteshaxys'[?] and others.

This week we have two cultured young men with us, Mr. Joseph Irwin, Clerk of the Court at Clarksville, and Mr. Thomas, of Franklin, who is president of the...pin factory.

§ All persons are warned against gathering fruit, chinquapins, hunting fishing or in any other manner trespassing on part of lot of land No. 96 in the first land district Rabun county. John M. McCurray.

§ Grove

Weather dry and corn looking well considering bad stand on account of drill worms.

John V., Mary and Eliza Arrendale are attending the Institute at Clayton.

Bridge Creek voted the same ticket to a man in the primary election for state-house officers.

Revenue officers made a raid on the river Tuesday.

Mr. W. M. Baker cut a fine bee tree Tuesday that he found recently.

Dr. J. C. Dover made a professional trip on Bridge Creek Friday last.

Tom Gables says if the legislature did go to Brunswick and get drunk and fight he has no idea they made anything off of Bob Hamby.

§   Dillard

Several people of the Valley attended the Institute last week.

John Thomas, of N. C., passed through here en route to Toccoa Thursday.

Misses T. and Lassie Kelley, of Franklin, are with their sister Mrs. Ocia Greenwood.

Miss Eula Dillard is with her Uncle and Aunt, Mr. and Mrs. Terrel Mosely.

Mr. W. H. Greenwood was with home folks the latter part of last week.

Miss Fannie Scruggs is with her sister, Mrs. Brown, at Gillsville.

Mr. Thomas Carver, of Chechero, was talking politics here Saturday.

On last Sunday morning a certain young man started to put on his pants and found a rat in them. You can guess what happened.

Mrs. Fannie Godfrey, who has been very sick, is improving slowly.

John Harkins has returned from Gainesville.

Mr. John Marsingale, our jovial tax receiver, passed through here Saturday on his last rounds taking in tax returns. We think John M. ought to be elected again, as he makes a good tax receiver.

§   Quartz

News scarce.

Everybody busy.

Rain needed badly.

Rev. Warlick preached at Boiling Spring on the last second Sunday. Quite a crowd were present to hear the interesting sermon he delivered.

John Moore and wife, of Burton, were among friends here last Sunday.

It being Institute week at Clayton and examination day on Satday [*sic*], there are some of the boys and girls missing this week.

Prof. John Howard made his way to Clarkesville Friday, where he will enter the examination on Saturday for teacher's license.

Dr. Garland was on the creek a few days ago and took dinner with J. C. York.

Aunt Liz Haney has been the guest of Mr. Philyaw for the last few weeks.

Well, we would be glad to know what has become of Col. Grant, as he is a man of much use to the good people of Rabun. We never know whether he is out on business or in Clayton.

§   Athens Vaugn vs. Frank Vaugn, Libel for Divorce.

To Frank Vaugn: You are hereby notified to be or appear, either personally or by an attorney, at the next Superior Court of Rabun county, to be held on the fourth Monday in August 1902 next, to answer the complaint of Athens Vaugn in an action for total divorce. In default thereof the court will proceed, as to justice shall appertain. Witness the Hon. J. B. Estes, Judge of said Court. This 17th day of June 1902,

J. S. Ramey, C. S. C.

J. R. Grant, Libelant's Attorney.

§   All persons wishing to purchase fruit trees for fall delivery, at thousand rates, will do well to see J. F. Earl before buying elsewhere.

§   We have in our office a brass spur said to belong to our friend F. A. Taylor, of Stonepile. It was found on the streets of our town the day after the primary and we were asked to advertise it. It is said he has owned it for thirty years.

July 10, 1902
Volume V, Number 25

§   Georgia—Rabun County. Julia Coffee, having made application for twelve months support out of the estate of T. J. Coffee, and appraisers duly appointed to set apart the same having filed their return, all persons concerned are hereby required to show cause before the court of Ordinary of said county, on the first Monday in August 1902, why said application should not be granted. This 19th day of July 1902. W. S. Long, Ordinary.

§   This is to warn the public against trespassing on parts of lots of land Nos. 95, 96 and 121, in the second land district by hunting, gathering fruit, chestnuts, chinquapins or in any other way. J. B. Garland.

§   For the lightest draft, longest life, fewest breaks and best work, buy the Deering Harvesting Machinery. For repairs or machines write or call on W. R. L. Ritchie, Dillard, Ga.

§   Mrs. Lee Ritchie, of the valley, has a pig two months old that weighs 48 pounds.

§   M. H. James and J. N. Crunkleton, of Persimmon, were attending Ordinary's court Monday.

§   Prof. A. A. O'Kelley and J. S. Burrell attended the Institute several days last week at Franklin.

§   Tom Mitchell swapped horses four times in one day recently and says he is anxious to swap again.

§   Our friends and patrons, J. N. and B. B. Bleckley, of Anderson, are on a visit to home folks on Chechero.

§   We are requested by Miss Ada Green to say that her school will begin at Tiger school house on Monday the 14th instant.

§   The prisoners in jail, Wm. Gilds and Sam Welborne, request us to thank John H. Derrick for them for a basket dinner July 4th.

§   W. D. Burch and Jack Farnsworth made their usual trip here Tuesday. Mr. Davidson, of Dinline[?] and Davidson, was with them.

§   Mr. T. S. Wilbanks of Soque, Ga., made our office a pleasant call Monday. He was here to make annual return as administrator on his father's estate.

§   We have had good rains around Clayton the past week and the corn crops on bottom land are fine. We are told the present crop is made so far as rain is concerned.

§   The people of Rabun county are anxiously waiting the decision of the Supreme Court in the cases of William Gilds and Sam Welborne and the alternative road law.

§   J. M. Bleckley's school will begin at Boiling Springs Monday of next week. Miss Ada Justus is assistant teacher. All the patrons are requested by Mr. Bleckley to be present.

§   The Clerk's office is besieged of late by non-residents looking up the land records. Some of these land owners who have been making tax returns of about 8 cents per acre are realizing that they have something in Rabun county.

§   Nelson Tilley has all kinds of school books.

§   Several letters are left out this week and will appear next week.

§   Mrs. A. E. Blalock had the misfortune to lose a fine mule here at the celebration on the fourth of July.

§   There has been a singing school going on at Bethel church this week, conducted by Mr. Ballew, of Habersham county.

§   J. A. Alman has a pie plant, or Rhubarb, that has grown seven feet and three inches in height and one stem and leaf is four feet long.

§   Mrs. D. W. Johnson, of Hartwell, and Mrs. Johnson, of Atlanta, Mrs. Vernadoe and children, of Atlanta, Tommy Roane and Mrs. Langston's family are enjoying the day on Black-rock.

§   Major York is minus his middle finger. In some way his gun fired while his middle finger of his right hand was over the muzzle of his double-barrell shot gun. The accident happened last Friday near his home in the Tennessee Valley.

§   About all the school teachers in the county met School Commissioner O'Kelley here Saturday and contracted themselves into a lot trouble for the next few months. We defy any county in Georgia to trot out a brighter set of teachers or any better looking.

§   See announcement of L. C. Hollifield for Treasurer. Mr. Hollifield needs no introduction from us. It is said he has never run a sorry race, but has always received a good vote in the county when before them and has been elected several terms as Clerk of Superior Court.

§   T. J. Ritchie, J. R. Ritchie, Jno [sic] Howard and W. A. Simmons dined with Sidney Bradley on Betty's Creek last Thursday and ate hearty of venison, mountain trout, and such a dinner as would make glad the heart of a king. The hospitality of Mr. Bradley and his wife is proverbial.

§   The Board of Education had a busy session here Tuesday. The meeting brought many of the best citizens of the county to town. It was a day of re-arrangement and so far as the board could do so arranged for the convenience of school patrons. The board was in session until late in the afternoon.

§   There was some talk Tuesday of every malitia [sic] district in the county putting out a full ticket for county officers. This would make, single shot, 68 candidates and would bring to the editor $126, and adding to the candidates already announced, would run the amount up to about $160. We file no objections to the rumor.

§   Mr. A. J. Duncan has a nice crowd of summer boarders. Below we give those he has at present: Mrs. Rosa Barry, Athens; Mrs. W. B. Barnard, Athens; Miss Mary Barry, Athens; Miss Annie Barnard, Athens; Mrs. John Bird, [Athens]; Miss Eula Bird, [Athens]; Miss Lucia Johnson, Macon; Miss Lou Johnson, Macon; Miss Manda Johnson, Macon; Mr. Hugh Bernard, Athens; Mr. Harrp Popa, Athens.

§   The teachers of Rabun county met on Saturday, June 21ˢᵗ, and organized a Teacher's Association.

A. A. O'Kelley was elected temporary chairman and J. S. Burrell temporary secretary, after which the following officers were elected: A. A. O'Kelley, President; Dora Mozeley, Vice President; James Green, Secretary; Ethel Powell, Corresponding Secretary; F. D. Singleton, Treasurer; J. S. Burrell, Chaplain and Mary Neville, Critic. A committee on program for next meeting was appointed as follows: J. S. Burrell, Netherland Bynum and James Green. This committee made the following report for program:...

How to arouse the interest of the people in regard to libraries, by F. D. Singleton and L. M. Chastain...

The importance of regular attendance of school and how secured, by Miss Lena Bleckley and Miss Belle York...

How to secure a more hearty co-operation of patrons and teacher, by J. M. Bleckley and B. H. Landrum...

On motion the president appointed the following committee to draft by-laws and constitution, to report at the next meeting: F. D. Singleton, Ada Green, Virgil Green, Reed Bleckley and Lizzie Dillard.

It was moved that the next meeting be held at Burton Academy on Saturday July 19, which motion was carried and the association adjourned until that time.

A. A. O'Kelley, Pres. James Green, Sec'y.

§   The Fourth

In response to a notice in the Tribune there was a good crowd out the fourth. No elaborate preparations had been made in the way of a program but on the spur of the moment a committee was selected to prepare a programme, which they did, but owing to the threatening storm the exercises were cut short. The following part of the progamme was carried out:

March by the confederate veterans from court house to the grove back of the Parker House.

Song by the choir.

Invocation by Rev. W. A. Simmonf [*sic*], of Acworth, Ga.

Song.

Declaration of independence was read by Dr. J. C. Dover.

Address by J. R. Grant and W. A. Simmons.

During Mr. Simmons' address an approaching storm caused the people to disperse and seek shelter. The people seem to enjoy the occasion greatly and a general good time prevailed. Many brought the basket dinner but no public table was set. There was no drinking and everything went off nicely.

§   Burton

School will begin at Burton Monday and Prof. Burrell as teacher, Miss Sallie Smith assistant. We anticipate a lively school.

Rev. Frank Loyd preached an interesting sermon to a large attentive audience.

Little Eva FinCannon, aged 14 years, daughter of Mr. and Mrs. J. I. FinCannon, died last Sunday morning. Little Eva was a bright little girl. She had a smile for every one she knew. The bereaved family have the sympathy of the community.

Several of our Burton people went to Clayton Friday. They report a pleasant time.

Mr. John McClain is very sick this week.

Mr. T. A. Arrendale and sister, Miss Viola, attended the all-day singing at Clarkesville last Sunday.

Mr. L. M. Chastain has been on the sick list for a few days.

§   Grove

We are having some showers and crops are looking well.

Mr. L. P. Wall and son Jess, of Chechero, passed Grove Monday.

Mr. Hendrix, of Stonewall, passed Grove Monday enroute to Gainesville to move his family to Stonewall.

Mr. William Thompson is putting up a saw mill near William FinCannon's.

Mr. J. M. Arrendale made a hasty trip to Gainesville this week.

Mr. L. M. Chastain and J. V. Arrendale went to Clayton Tuesday.

Tom Gable says he was going to vote for [B]ob Hamby if he run any more, but if he has went to Atlanta and voted for Estill he will have to vote for the other fellow.

§   Quartz

The health of the community is good at this writing.

Mr. Guss Arrendale and Mr. Horley Thompson, with two of Mr. Justus' girls, went to Towns county Friday. They returned Saturday.

Mr. Lex Darnell and Asbury Darnell were among friends here Sunday.

There was communion at Persimmon Baptist Church Sunday. Rev. J. S. Dickson, the pastor, preached an interesting sermon.

Mr. Thomas, the pin man, has his engine at Mr. G. H. Thompson's where he will soon start up his pin factory.

Mr. H. M. Nichols says[?] the wild cats have been catching his lambs and it is so dry his dogs can't run them.

H. A. Parker killed a large rattlesnake within ten steps of the house a few days ago. That was enough to make any one dream of snakes.

Corn crops looking fine not withstanding rain would do good.

Rev. Hoyl Baker passed through here the other day enroute to Smyrna, to preach to the people there.

We are not bothered with the cattle inspector for he knows that we have no ticks but politics and that don't hurt the cattle.

§   Ordinary's Citations.

Georgia—Rabun County. L. C. Whitmire, guardian of Mary C. Whitmire, having applied to me to be discharged from such guardianship, let all persons concerned show cause before me at the court house in said county, on the 4th day of August next, why such application for discharge should not be granted witness my official signature. This 2nd day of July, 1902. W. S. Long, Ordinary.

§   Georgia—Rabun County. Nettie Conley, having made application for twelve months' support out of the estate of Cal Conley, and appraisers duly appointed to set apart the same, all persons concerned are hereby required to show cause before the Court of Ordinary of said county, on the first Monday in August, 1902, why said application should not be granted. This 30th day of June 1902. W. S. Long, Ordinary.

§   Mrs. Annie Clore vs. James D. Clore. Lible for Divorce.

To James D. Clore. You are hereby notified to be or appear either personally or by an Attorney at the next Superior court of Rabun county to be held on the fourth Monday in August 1902 next, to answer the complaint of Mrs. Annie Clore in an an [sic] action for total divorce. In default thereof the court will proceed as to justice shall appertain. Witness the Hon. J. B. Estes Judge of said court. This 9th day of July.

J. S. Ramey, C. S. C.

Jas. R. Grant, Libelants Att'y.

§   Sheriff's Sales. Georgia—Rabun County. Will be sold on the first Tuesday in August next, at public outcry at the court house in Clayton, said county, within the legal hours of sale, to the highest bidder for cash, certain property of which the following is a full and complete description: One seventh undivided interest in part of lot of land No. 191 in the second land district of said county to satisfy an execution issued by the Justice's court of the 556th District G. M. of said county in favor of Penland Co., against Hade Dillingham, defendant in fi fa. Written notice given tenant in possession. Levy made and returned to me by J. [illegible]. McCurry, L. C. This 30th day of June, 1902. J. R. Ritchie, Sheriff.

July 24, 1902
Volume V, Number 27

§   We spent several days of last week on lower Chechero. Our mission there was to settle a disputed land line. Like a number of other places the people are careless about their land lines and corners. Sixty years ago men would call for certain trees and running from these corners to other tress a half mile or more away, never making the lines nor giving any intelligent courses. All these lines are void after verbal information is dead and cannot be run. A tract of land of this description cannot be sold to a thinking and intelligent purchaser. We are not hunting jobs in the surveying line, but we would advise those who have not a clearly defined and well established line to have it put in shape as soon as possible. You will avoid trouble in the future as well as expensive law suits.

There are people in Rabun county claiming land under titles with the description so vague that a surveyor cannot establish the lines and in some cases makes this title void. We would advise all purchasers of land to have lines well defined and avoid future trouble. We worried over such lines last week on lower Chechero, while the thermometer was ranging in the 90s, among the chigars [*sic*] and snakes, and failed, with the help of the community, to find a line because of no intelligent description in any deed, and all old settlers being dead. After all the worry we had a nice time. How could we do otherwise, since we made our stay with Uncle "Ellick" Williams? In all our travels we never spent time more pleasantly than at his hospitable[?] home. It was our first visit in that section and we found more bachelors there in two miles square than any place in the county we ever saw. For instance the fair ladies have failed to win the hearts of Dennis Williams, Will McWhorter, Abel Williams, John Williams, Hood Smith and Thomas Carver.

During our stay with Mr. Williams we visited a cemetery in which lies a Revolutionary soldier, a drum major, a great-grandfather of Mr. Williams. He was 107 years old at the time of his death. The only mark to distinguish the resting place of the old soldier is a rough stone, not even dressed, with the initials "E. W.," which letters stand for Edward Williams. By his side lies his wife, whose life, no doubt, was one of privations and hardships. The soldier was a drum major in the Revolutionary and the war of 1812. We were told that Mr. Williams was drafted in England to fight the colonies, but joined the side of the Revolutionists when he landed on American soil. Uncle "Ellick["] is nearing the eighty year mark and was born on the farm he lives on. He told us an interesting story of a mound near his residence. On the top of this mound is, or was, a circle thrown up and for many years people of the neighborhood got all the lead they used. This is evidence of heavy fought battles, presumably between tribes of Indians. The mound and surroundings is an ideal place for a fort. Mr. Williams has a fine farm and an exceedingly good crop. He has a large apple orchard laden with fine fruit.

We called on our friend J. F. Godfrey for a few minutes and found him a successful farmer, merchant and fruit grower. We counted 67 fully developed apples on a little limb less than an inch in diameter. Mr. Godfrey begged us to spend the night with him and he told us he had something to eat and he has it in abundance. When we go into the country we find clever people, well doing, and they are the happiest people we ever saw and we believe the happiest people on earth. The crops on Chechero are as good as can be grown.

Our next trip is lower down the Chattooga to fix lines in the burning July sun and the armies of chigars.

§   Notice to Debtors and creditors.

All persons having demands against the estate of T. J. Coffee late of Rabun county, deceased are hereby notified to render in their demands to the undersigned according to law; and all persons indebted to said estate are required to make immediate payment. This 14th day of July 1902. J. S. Ramey. Administrator T. J. Coffee deceased.

§   Trespass Notices. The public are warned not to trespass on land lot No. 46 in the second land district of Rabun county by carting timber or any other way. Alvin Moore. July 21st 1902.

§   Lafayette Wall is up from Atlanta.

§   Suits for men, boys and youths at Ritchie's.

§   Clayton will be an Asheville some day. Mark this saying.

§   Drummer John Bell was drumming the merchants here this week.

§   Everything in the produce line bought at Ritchie's.

§   L. C. Varnadoe, of the fire department of Atlanta, is spending this week with Mr. W. F. Roane.

§   See professional card of H. H. Gardner. Mr. Gardner is thinking of locating in Clayton and practicing law. He is a sober and worthy young man.

§   There has been a writing school going on in the court house since Tuesday. Prof. Self is the teacher and his specimens of penmanship show him to be a master of the art.

§   John J. Strickland, one of the most prominent lawyers in the state, and well known in Rabun county, was married to Miss Elinor Anderson, of Annlston, Ala., last Tuesday.

§   A protracted meeting is being conducted at Rabun Gap by Bros. Williams and Landrum. The attendance is very large.

§   Sheriff J. R. Ritchie, Ed Ritchie, J. R. Grant, Webb Johnson and P. T. Shore spent a few days this week in the noted Nantahalas.

§   A. H. McCallister, of Toccoa, was at the Wall House the past week. He leaves to-day for Franklin, N. C.

§   There is a protracted meeting going on up in Germany, conducted by Rev. R. L. Whitmire.

§   On a piece of land 60 by 70 feet square, J. E. Derrick raised, this year, $20 worth of onion buttons and seven dollars' worth of onions and on the little plot he estimates he will make[?] ten dollars' worth of tobacco and can still make a crop of turnips.

§   A number of our citizens took in the Teachers' Institute at Burton Saturday and Sunday.

§   W. F. Roane has 13 boarders for the month and more to come.

§   Hustling Clinton Taylor was in town Monday.

§   J. H. Coffee had last year's sweet potatoes to the fourth of July and new potatoes on the 17th of July. Only eleven days between the old and the new. Beat this if you can.

§   Miss Mary Neville will not teach school at Locust Field as was announced but will teach at the Glades. Miss Eulah Dillard passed the examination here last Thursday and began the school at Locust Field Monday.

§   Mr. and Mrs. H. J. Canup, of Soque, visited their daughter, Mrs. D. L. Parker here Sunday. Mr. Canup is 72 years old and the father of 21 children, 17 of them living, all married but one, the youngest and he is 18 years old.

§   A general line of everything kept in the up-to-date country store, on hand and coming at Ritchie's.

§   We are told, and reliably so, that the largest gathering ever seen in this county was at Burton at the Teachers' Association and the all day singing last Saturday and Sunday. Perhaps the time when Prof. Leon walked the rope across the grand chasm at Tallulah Falls, about the year 1885, there were more people assembled. The whole-souled people at Burton spread a dinner table about fifty yards long. The people of Burton never entertain by halves.

§   We acknowledge, with thanks, the receipt of a beautiful apple from Mr. A. J. Duncan. His derisive smile told something translucently. This is to tell you, Mr. Duncan, and you may so communicate, that, as the apple hung out on the limb, fully ripe and ready to be pulled, so is the recipient of the favor.

§   Messrs. R. J. and E. D. Stivers left Monday and will go direct to their home at Mason City, Iowa. It is locally known that these gentlemen bought the farm, stock and growing crop of J. C. Pickett, for which they paid the sum of five thousand and five hundred dollars. This farm consists of 500 acres within the incorporate limits of town and is one of the best farms in Rabun county. Mr. Stivers will return to Clayton in a few weeks with his family and will make their home among us in the future. We are told Mr. Pickett reserved 50 acres of land and will build and still be one of us.

§   Mose [*sic*] Shirley says it tires him to go all over his crop and he dreads gathering it, and says for all to come down and look at it. Mr. Shirley has 75 acres of bottom land and 500 acres of land.

§ $1,000 worth of ready-made clothing at Ritchie's.

§   Dr. J. C. Dover and Prof. A. A. O'Kelley spent the first part of this week in Franklin, N. C. They took in the Old Maid's Convention and report it a success.

§   Jas. E. Bleckley is in Atlanta at the bedside of his father, who is seriously ill.

§   Rev. Brown filled his regular appointment at the Baptist church here last Sunday.

§   Chief Engineer A. R. Gilchrist, of the Tallulah Falls Railway came up yesterday in the interest of the road.

§   Every piece of our leather as a brand and guaranteed No. 1. Whitmire.

§   Mrs. Clara Dickson and Master Harold, of Cornelia, are with parents, Mr. and J. B. Murray [*sic*].

§   D. L. Parker leaves to-day for Tallulah Falls to meet a crowd of boarders. They will be the guest of Mr. and Mrs. W. T. York.

§   The latest information from Judge F. A. Bleckley is that his condition is somewhat improved.

§   Whitmire's harness is hand made and of the best made material.

§   Mell Crisp and Lafayette Dockins, of Cornpen, Ga., were here yesterday.

§   A good stock of harness at S. S. Whitmir'e [*sic*].

§   Secretary of State Cook granted an amendment to the charter of the Tallulah Falls Railway Company yesterday by which the capital stock of the company is increased from $300,000 to $500,000. One half of the increase will be in preferred stock and on-half in [co]mmon stock. The proceeds from the sale of this stock are to be used in extending the road from Tallulah Falls to Franklin, N. C.—Atlanta Constitution.

§   I will be in my shop till court and invite you to see our stock of harness. S. S. Whitmire.

§   Burton

Well, we come again to tell you of the news at Burton. We can only tell you of the Institute. We certainly had a nice time. Everybody seemed to enjoy it. We had plenty to eat, but Steve missed his dinner. We had some very fine music on Saturday and a lot of lively speeches. Prof. Green and Wood, of Hiawassee, were with us and gave some very high compliments and a few encouraging words. Miss Belle York recited for us. Her recitation was very fine, and the music rendered by Miss Ethell Powell was beyond comparison. Everyody seemed to enjoy themselves. Then on Sunday Rev. Frank Loyd, of Hiawassee, Ga., preached a grand sermon and took up a collection for the painting of the school building and received $43.00 to the surprise of everybody. The next Institute will be held at Rabun Gap on Saturday before the fifth Sunday in August. The folowing program was arranged:

Music.

What does it take to make a true man? Bentley York and Prof. Landrum.

How would you teach nature studies? Prof. A. A. O'Kelley and Miss Lena Bleckley.

Music.

What do we mean by teaching? J. C. Hard and Miss Beulah Green.

Music.

General discussion by all.

Everybody seemed enthused over the good work of education.

§   Dillard

Dry weather.

Crops looking fine.

Mr. Bud Martin and family are off to S. C. on a visit.

Miss T. Kelley spent Friday night with Misses Beulah and Sallie Grist on Mud Creek.

Lizzie Darnell was all smiles Sunday week.

Marsh Hopper went to the Falls Tuesday.

M. L. Scruggs has returned from Toccoa.

Mr. G. H. Darnell is up from Clarkesville on a visit.

Mr. Bentley York went home Saturday to attend the Teachers Association.

Mr. John Holden and Miss Lula Howard went to Burton Friday.

Mr. John Bell is in the Valley.

Mr. Willie Grist and sister Carrie attended the Teachers' Association at Burton Saturday.

Revs. Landrum and Williams are running a protracted meeting at the M. E. Church South.

Ben Thomas went to the Falls Friday evening.

Mr. Jack Holden and sister are with Mr. and Mrs. George Kelley.

John Hunter was with parents on Tiger Saturday and Sunday.

Tennessee Valley is improving as we have two colored schools and good attendance.

Miss Ethel Powell has gone to her school on Dick's Creek.

Mr. and Mrs. Amos Glaspy went to Clayton Saturday.

Rev. Brown and wife were at Clayton the latter part of last week.

§   Quartz

The most severe storm that has visited Persimmon this summer came[?] last Monday.

Prof. Bleckley has been seeing his school patrons this week, getting the census of the children.

Mrs. Mary Russum, from near Toccoa, Ga., is spending a few days with J. C. York and wife.

Miss Docia Colenback is thought to have a fever.

Messrs. John Holden and Charley Grist and Misses Carrie Grist and Lula Howard stayed with Mr. M. V. York Friday night.

Miss Ethel Powell and her two brothers stayed with Mr. Mart Justus Friday night.

The singing at M. V. York's Friday night was enjoyed by all present.

Quite a crowd attended the teachers' meeting at Burton.

Prof. Bleckley will open his school here Monday, the 21st inst.

Corn crops is looking fine on the creek this year.

§   Upper Tiger

Hauling rye straw and locust pins seems to be the order of the day at our little burg now.

Mr. R. N. Dover began school at Ivy Hill the 14th inst. with a good attendance.

We are very much in need of rain. It seems that we will not make anything if it don't rain in a few days as corn is taking the round stalk and drying upon the stalk.

Ballenge and Mathey Dockins, the two oldest sons of H. D. Dockins, and Lester Stancil, who have been in Cherokee county, Ga., returned home a few days ago on a visit to their parents.

Mr. and Mrs. Ed Norton visited their parent [*sic*], Mr. and Mrs. R. E. Cannon, Sunday.

Some one killed a fine young cow for Mr. Julius Taylor last week. We should have better fences and less cow killing.

Mr. Elbert Jones is getting all the work he can do in the blacksmith shop at present.

Emory Blalock killed a large rattlesnake in the chimney corner of Mr. Albert Lovell's house Monday.

J. R. Hunter has a very sick horse.

H. B. Sonecypher [*sic*], James and Walter Kerby went to Burton Saturday and returned Sunday.

We are glad to learn that W. R. Cannon's health is improving.

Sutton Atkins, of Tallulah Falls passed through Monday enroute to Clayton.

Mr. Geo. Oliver, of Franklin, N. C., visited C. E. Cannon and family this week.

Jas. M. Ramey visited his mother who is very feeble this week.

V. C. Taylor attended the singing school at Eden church last week.

§ In another column will be found the advertisement of The Massachusetts Mutual Life Insurance Co., [*sic*] This company is seeking, through its managers, Mess. Harty & Apple of Savannah Ga., to establish an agency in this section. This Company was organised in 1851, and its best friends are its policyholders. The Company now has a large number of policies on citizens of our State and are seeking to place their plans before the public in our section. Here is a fine opportunity which is well worth investigating.

§ For Sale. 10,000 apple trees to go at $8.00 per hundred delivered in Clayton or $5.00 per hundred delivered at Hartwell, Ga. See J. I. Langston at Clayton, or D. W. Johnson, at Hartwell, Ga.

§ H. H. Gardner. Attorney at Law, Cornelia, Ga. Will practice in all courts in the Northeastern and adjoining circuits.

§ Real Estate.

We are in the real estate business...

Lot No. 64 in the second land district, one and a half miles from Clayton, ¾ miles from Tallulah Falls Ry. All is original forest and well timbered. There is on the lot an epidate mine. Many fine gems [illegible] been obtained from this mine. There is good land for farming [illegible]. Man wants to sell and want a bid. You can get a bargain.

One hundred acres of fine farm, one mile from [C]layton, 15 acres of bottom land, other well timbered on public road. Part cash banance [*sic*] at time. Price made know [*sic*] upon application.

Sixty acres of land ½ mile from town, 12 acres of bottom, balance timber, 3 room house and outbuildings, good apple orchard bearing. Terms of sale, part cash and balance on time. Price made known to purchaser.

§   A Good Business Opportunity.

One of the very best old line, life insurane companies wants a representative in this County. The company writes attractive policies, free from all tricks, and makes friends wherever introduced. To the right man an excellent contract will be made, under which a good business can be established. Only those who are willing to give the business active attention and who can furnish satisfactory references need apply. No previous knowledge of the business is necessary. Apply with references to Harty & Apple, managers for Georgia. The Massachusetts Mutual Life Insurance Co., 117 Bay street east, Savannah, Ga.

§   The McNeel Mable [sic] Co. Vaults and Statuary. Gainesville, Ga. John C. Bell makes territory every 60 days.

July 31, 1902
Volume V, Number 28

§   To the Citizens of Rabun County:

Out of my love for my native county and my sincere desire to see every boy in Rabun county have a fair chance to win the success of which he is capable, I beg to say that upon coming among you again for a short vacation I find myself profoundly interested in the upbuilding of your common schools. I have thought about interests of Rabun County a great deal; so much that I have presented the great need, both of a high school in the county and of better schools in every community, to friends of education who have money fro schools. One of these men, whom I happen to know, has offered to endow a high school at Clayton, but I regret to say, upon such conditions as would involve greater sacrifices than I can afford to make. I wish to say, however, that large and generous aid for both a high school and the common schools of Rabun county is easily within the reach of the people of the county if they will only exert themselves to obtain it. I beg to say that while I am in the county, deeply imbued as I am with the love of my own people and the sincere and unselfish desire to do something to build up my native county, I should like to advise with as many of the citizens and friends of education as have this matter on their hearts. If the people so desire, I will come[?] to to [sic] any community at any time to talk and advise with them on the subject of education.

In conclusion, I wish to say that I am rejoiced[?] to be among the people of Rabun again; that I rejoice with them at seeing their long hopes of a railroad so nearly realized—which, I have no doubt will readily come—and that I rejoice to see the people of this God-favored country contented, healthy and happy.

A. J. Ritchie.

§ The republicans met at Clayton July the 26th. The house was called to order by J. W. Godfrey. It was moved and second that the chairman appoint one man in each district for the purpose of enlisting names of the republicans of respective districts to represent us in our next meeting at the court house on Saturday, August 28.

The following people were appointed: Clayton, S. S. Whitmire, Aug. 9; Valley, A. A. Darnell, Saturday, August 16, 2 p. m.; Moccasin, A. J. Kell, Saturday, August 16, 10 a. m.; Tiger, J. S. Watts, Friday, August 22[?], 2 p. m.; Chechero, Walter Dickson, August 9, 10 a. m.; Warwoman, Lafayette Dickson, August 21, 10 a. m.; Tallulah, A. K. Allen, August 9th by ten a. m.; Persimmon, J. J. Parker, August 9th, 10 a. m.

All republicans are requested to meet at Burton August the ninth by two o'clock p. m.

J. W. Godfrey, Chairman. D. G. Dover, Secretary Protem.

§ Ordinary Citations. Georgia—Rabun county. To whom it may concern: Jim Conley, having made application to me in due form to be appointed permanent administrator upon the estate of Cal Conley, late of said county, notice is hereby given that said application will be heard at the regular term of the court of Ordinary for said county, to be held on the first Monday in September, 1902. Witness my hand and official signature. This 29th of July, 1902. W. S. Long, Ordinary.

§ Notice to Debtors and Creditors.

All persons having demands against the estate of C. J. Crunkleton late of Rabun County, deceased are hereby notified to render in their demands to the undersigned according to law; and all persons indebted to said estate are required to make immediate payment. This the 26[?] day of July, 1901 [*sic*]. J. N. Crunkleton, Administrator C. J. Crunkleton deceased.

§ L. C. Whitmire, guardian of Mary C. Whitmire, having applied to me to be discharged frm such guardianship, let all persons concerned show cause before me at the court house in said county, on the 4th day of August next, why such application for discharge should not be granted witness my official signature. This 2nd day of July, 1902. W. S. Long, Ordinary.

§ We are obligated to Miss Leila Earl for a basket of fine apples.

§ A prize was offered last week by Prof. Self to the student who made the best progress in penmanship. The prize was awarded to Miss Maud Coffee.

§   Miss Annie Crisp is visiting Katie and Daisy Robins.

§   Priece [*sic*] Bradley, of Rabun Gap, has located a blacksmith shop at the Thompson old shop and asks the public to call on him. He does good work.

§   New clothing at Tilley's, at a cheap price, cash or credit.

§   W. R. Ritchie is with a corps of engineers surveying a rail-road through Oklahoma and Indian Territory for the Missouri, Kansas & Texas Railway Company. He receives The Tribune at Tulsa, Indian Territory.

§   Squire Derrick has some gooseberry bushes that have been full this season.

§   One of the prettiest hats we have ever seen was worn out in town by Little Maud Earl last Saturday. The hat was made by Little Leila Earl, of paper and corn husks.

§   J. D. Cooley, a prominent merchant and farmer of White county, was in Clayton Saturday.

§   S. S. Burnett was on his usual rounds here Saturday.

§   Mr. and Mrs. Webb Johnson returned to their home in Hartwell Wednesday, after spending several weeks here. They were guests of Mr. and Mrs. J. I. Langston.

§   Miss Mary Simmons has returned to Acworth.

§   The infant child of Mr. and Mrs. J. M. Wilkerson was buried here last Saturday. Trouble is added to the family by the serious sickness of Mrs. Wilkerson.

§   The rooms of the Wall House have been re-papered the past week. Miss Blanche did the work herself and nicely too.

§   The supreme court will not reach the alternative road case, we are told, till some time in August.

§   Ira Holden, of the Valley, has 20 head of fine beef cattle.

§   Irvin J. Price, of Birmingham, Ala., is with home folks on Chechero.

Irvin is a model young man and numbers his friends by his acquaintances.

§   Judge F. A. Bleckley is slightly improved, but his condition is still critical.

§   Mrs. [sic] and Mrs. J. F. Smith, of Burton, were in town yesterday. Mr. and Mrs. Smith are the same age—78. They have been mearried nearly sixty years. Mr. Smith is active and bids fair to live many years yet.

§   During a thunder storm about noon Tuesday a bolt of lightning struck the large barn of J. F. Earl, shattering a number of the posts of the building. The bolt struck the top of the building where four valleys come to-gether. The lightning ran down all four of the valleys and down the walls at the foot of the valleys to the ground. Mr. John Dotson and his little boy were in the building at the time grinding an ax and were badly shocked. One of Mr. Earl's horses was in the stable but was not hurt. The building is badly shattered at the four points of the valleys. It tore some of the posts into splinters and melted the nail heads in one of the doors. Fortunately the building was not set on fire.

§   Ritchie's clothing is suitable for fall and winter, and knobly styles.

§   Prof. A. A. O'Kelley is visiting home folks in Jackson Co.

§   F. A. Taylor, of Stonepile, was here on business yesterday.

§   Mrs. Paris is in feeble health.

§   Sugar at 18 pounds to the dollar at Ritchie's.

§   Ritchie pays $1.00 for rye.

§   Mrs. S. W. Dover spent yesterday with sisters, Mrs. John M. York and Mrs. Laprade, at the residence of J. M. York, on Persimmon.

§   Mr. J. F. Earl and his daughter, Miss Nora, are at Bryson City, N. C.

§   Mr. and Mrs. J. N. Peacock, of Waynesville N. C., and Mr. and Mrs. J. W. Derrick, of Georgia Wise county Virginia [sic], returned homeward Tuesday morning after several days visit with their parents, Mr. and Mrs. J. E. Derrick. Mr. J. W. Derrick had the misfortune to lose one hundred and fifty dollars on the trip down here which to some extent marred the pleasure of his stay here.

§ "Webb" Johnson the popular ex-sheriff of Hart County purchased what is locally known as Blue heights farm of J. I. Langston this week. This farm will be known as the "Passover farm," a name very appropriate as the farm lies in the famous Rabun Gap, the lowest gap in the Blue Ridge mountains. Mr. Johnson has already 2000 apple trees set out on this farm and it is his purpose to increase the number to 5000 this fall. The Tallulah Falls R'y right of way belts the land on east and in many ways this farm is a most desirable one. In point of coolness it may be called the iceberg of Rabun. We are told there is never a day nor an hour but what there is a breeze through the gap. It is here the famous Tennessee River heads, a fact not generally known but nevertheless true. The Tennessee river heads in Georgia. The farm is well adapted to fruit growing, fully demonstrated by the bearing trees, they being laden so much as to be propped now and trees many years old seemingly perfectly healthy.

§ Tom McCombs, colored, of Franklin, N. C., who has been around Clayton for the past three months, was landed in jail Thursday of last week, charged with stealing clothes from Aunt Harriet Bleckley's. Aunt Harriet does washing for a number of people in town, among them Clerk of Court J. S. Ramey, D. L. Parker and others. Mr. Ramey recognized his shirt while McCombs was wearing it on the streets and after McComb's arrest a shirt of Mr. Thomas' and a small dress belonging to Little Gertrude Parker, were found in the darkey's valise. McCombs acknowledged to taking the clothing and there will be very little to do at court, in his case, until Judge Estes pronounces sentence on him.

§ Jugware at Ritchie's, suitable for canning.

§ That clothing at Ritchie's is going. Get you a suit now.

§ A. J. Ritchie, Professor English Language and Literature in Baylor University in Waco, Texas, is spending a few days with relatives in Rabun. Mr. Ritchie, an old Rabun boy, is bound to make his mark in the world. He has been teaching in the State University of Texas this summer, but is among a corps of thirty two teachers in the Baylor University, a school with an enrollment of about one thousand students.

Professor Ritchie's success shows what a Rabun boy can do with ance and determination to win. Receiving his early education at the old Rabun Gap Institute, tak [sic] his high school course at Hiawassee teaching in that school and in this county, and gradually working his way through colleges at different institutions, graduating first at the University of Georgia and then from the Harward [sic], the oldest and the largest University in the country, he now stands at the top of his profession, at the head of the English Department in one of the leading Universities of the South. This is an example worthy of emutation [*sic*] and shows what a Rabun boy can do, and should be an inspiration to them.

§ Dillard.

News scarce.

Miss Texie York was in the Valley Saturday.

Prof. O'Kelley and Mr. Dennis Hughes attended preaching here Sunday.

Miss Julia Penland, of N. C., is with her sister, Mrs. Homer Penland.

Mrs. Liza Kelley and cook were with Mrs. Octa Greenwood Sunday.

Mr. Rush Grist and wife were down from the Flats Sunday.

Our school at Fort Hill is progressing nicely.

Mrs. W. T. York has eight boarders from Apopka, Florida.

Mr. and Mrs. B. R. Dillard are off to Westminister, S. C., this week.

Mrs. Lee Ritchie is off to Toccoa to see her brother.

Miss Mary Norris is still visiting in the valley.

Mr. Oscar Scroggs is on a business trip at Toccoa.

Harry Duncan was in the valley Sunday.

Mr. Berry Brown and daughter, Miss Fay, were with Rev. Brown and wifv [*sic*] the latter part of last week.

§ Quartz.

Rev. Jay and Alman ran a few days' meeting at Boiling Spring this week.

Miss Docia Colenback has Typhoid fever.

There are several kinds of fever, and Mr. V. L. M. has one that seems to be taking a strong hold[?] on him. We could not say it was contagious, but there is a girl that is likely to catch it.

While I was traveling along the road the road [*sic*] tha [*sic*] other day I saw a girl standing though as charmed, and on nearing I found that Mr. Marshall Moore was making the banjo strings ring with all the fingers he had, seemingly.

Mr. V. L. Moore made a trip to the rail-road and returned Thursday.

Mr. J. M. Bleckley, with Miss Ada Justus, opened up a school at Boiling Springs with the attendance of about seventy pupils, and is still growing.

Litsle [*sic*] Octa Philyaw, the little girl of E. B. Philyaw, is very sick.

A debatig [*sic*] society was organized at Boiling Spring Friday night.

Mr. J. A. Burrell has a sheey [*sic*] that has five perfect feet.

§   Burton.

We have one hundred and eight students in school.

Mr. Lucian McClain died at his home last Thursday morning. The bereaved parents and relatives have our sympathy.

Dr. Dover made a professional call [here] last week.

Ethel Powell spent Saturday night with the family of Jas. F. Smith's.

Mrs. J. F. Arrendale and Mrs. Frank Wood spent last Monday with Mrs. J. R. Stonecypher.

Dr. Green made a professional trip here last Monday.

After a weeks meeting at Zion there were seven baptised on last Sunday morning preaching at eleven by Prof. Burrell to a large audience.

Mr. and Mrs. Henry Burrell visited Mr. and Mrs. J. R. Stonecypher.

§   Bethel.

Our school at Bethel is progressing nicely.

There was an interesting sermon preached at Bethel Sunday and a large crowd attended.

Mr. Henry Taylor, from Tallulah Falls, was at Bethel Sunday.

Miss Hannie Whitmire is very ill with Typhoed[?] fever.

Ask Willie Watts and James Kerby who got beat Sunday. Come again Henry.

Miss Laura Wall was all smiles Sunday evening.

§   Grove.

Weather dry, and the crops are beginning to need rain.—J. M. Canup, of Popcorn, was in this community Wednesday.—J. N. Justus, of Germany, made a pleasant call at Grove Tuesday.—A. J[?]. Carter, of Creed was at Grove Thursday.—Meaks Arrendale made a hasty trip to Clayton Friday.—D. L. McClain died at his home near this place Thursday morning with typhoid fever.—He leaves a family and a lot of relatives.— The family has the sympathy of the community.

§   Entertaining.

A small crowd of young people gathered at L. T. Mitchell's last Friday evening for a royal good time and reports say they had it.

Saturday evening Misses Vinnie and Florence Marsingale entertained a large number of young people. Games of all kinds were played, followed by a candy drawing. The young people were up a late hour, and all that happened to mar the pleasure of the evening was one of the fair sex getting her fore-head bumped but at last accounts she was [illegible].

§   Old Tiger.

Esq. M. M. Hunnicutt took dinner with Mrs. Allen Turpen on July 22nd, which was his 75th birthday.

We performed the sad duty of conveying to Wolf Creek cemetery, last weeek, Harrison, little son of Mr. and Mrs. Walter Smith. He was a bright, beautiful child.

Mr. Sidney Heaton accidentally struck a little negro in the head with an eight pound hammer, while driving steel on the rail road at the Falls last week. It is thought the boy will die. Mr. Heaton says he was an innocent boy and he regrets the misfortune.

Last week the citizens of Tiger community met and placed a good foot-log across Tiger creek just below the church-house.

After another dry spell we are having a little rain.

Gambling is a Sunday occupation among Mr. Redmond's negroes.

One of Mr. W. R. Sweet's houses at Tallulah Falls was torn up with a blast last week.

J. C. Rochester and family were among the excursionists to Atlanta last Saturday.

We are offered ten cents per thousand in cash for rail road checks at the R. R. commissary at Tallulah Falls. It must be an indication of the flourishing condition of the country from the effects of rail-road.

Mr. Redmond worked a squad of hands on the rail-road last Sunday.

August 14, 1902
Volume 5, Number 30

§   Educational by A. J. Ritchie.

To the citizens of Rabun county.

I wish to put before the people of Rabun county a plan that has occurred to me for building and maintaining in Rabun a first class high school.

The plan as it presents itself to me is first, to state it briefly, to build in the vicinity of Clayton, on suitable, spacious grounds with available supply of water, a modern, up-to-date, well furnished building to cost not less that $2500 or $3000.

Second, to put in charge of the school a corps of the best teachers that can be had at reasonable salaries.

Third, to maintain a school that will give the average pupil a practical, comprehensive, bread-and-butter education, and prepare advanced students for college.

Fourth, to secure, in addition to the reasonable tuition fees, a fund for permanent support by means of endowment.

These, it seems to me, are the essential features of any plan for the building of a high school that is to be efficient and permanent; and I believe that such a school can be had by the people of Rabun county. I am sure it can if the people really want such school in their midst. It is with the people, however, to determine whether or not they will undertake such an enterprise. I am clear in my mind that such a school can be built and maintained if the enterprise is taken hold of with the proper interest and vigor...

§   Stecoa Creek.

Rain needed very badly. Corn, beans and such are suffering very much for the want of rain.

Mr. Hendricks, wife, son and daughter, Mr. Murray Hendricks and three or four others visited the Stecoa Falls last Friday.

Little Miss Ola Taylor, who has been sick for some time is improving slowly.

A very large crowd of Mr. W. F. Roane's boarders and Mrs. Roane visited Stecoa Falls last Friday. The falls is a beautiful place that most people enjoy visiting.

Mrs. Matilda Taylor is visiting the family of V. C. Taylor this week.

Mrs. H. Cannon is with her parents and sisters on the creek this week.

Mr. Marcus Taylor spent Saturday and Sunday with his brother, V. C. Taylor.

Miss Amanda Taylor visited friends and relatives in this community last week.

Mrs. Bud Lovell and son, Dalton, visited the family of Thomas A. Ramey Saturday.

Miss May Price attended Sunday school at Bethel Sunday afternoon.

Miss Maube [sic] Dockens visited Mi [sic] Ella Ramey Saturday and Sunday.

§   Hot.

§   This is sure August.

§   Court next Monday week.

§   The chestnut crop is good.

§   See county treasurer's report.

§   Marion Long is nursing a lame foot.

§   James Robins of S. C. was here Tuesday.

§   We are having all kinds of courts now-a-days.

§   James Green was with home folks Sunday.

§   Remember the Confederate Veteran's day.

§   W. T. York is crowded with summer boarders.

§   Some of our citizens are anxious about a school.

§   Virgil Green visited James Collenback Saturday.

§   Drs. Green and Dover are quite busy professionally.

§   Rain is badly needed in many places in the county.

§   We will take wood on subscription and want it now.

§   Bottom land corn is exceptionally good in this county.

§   Mrs. W. F. Roane has 30[?] boarders and turning others away.

§   Jesse W. Green has been up among relatives for several days.

§   J. Marcus Bleckley went down home from Persimmon Saturday.

§   We say hurrah for the Tallulah Falls railway and Rabun county.

§   Hundreds of low landers are visiting the mountains this summer.

§   Goods are being sold cheaper in Clayton than they are in Atlanta.

§   Everywhere in Rabun you see the apple trees bending with apples.

§   There is over four thousand feet difference in altitude in Rabun county.

§   Cabbage will grow and head nicely on broom sage fields in this county.

§   Drew Turpen and family have been visiting home folks in the Valley.

§   Mrs. J. I. Langston and Miss Stella visited Walhalla the past week.

§   Miss Janie Kell, of Moccason, is visiting Miss Ida Ford.

§   There has been more lightning this year and more timber killed than usual.

§   Remember the meeting of the Confederate veterans, September the fourth.

§   The railroad news is now encouraging to some who have disputed its being built.

§   We have seen some of the finest Irish potatoes that grows in our travels over the county.

§   The county is out of debt and over one thousand dolars in the treasury.

§   Sine Donaldson will move down from the Valley. He has rented the Wall property on Warwoman street.

§   The south-east corner of Rabun county, on Chattooga river, is lower than Atlanta and equally as hot. We have tried it this year.

§   More rattlesnakes this year than any year since we have known Rabun. The dry weather has brought them off the mountains to the low lands.

§   Chance Vickers is studying very seriously over the matter of having to give up his mail contract since some people believe the railroad will be built.

§   G. W. Allison of Penrose, S. C., made us a pleasant call Thursday of last week. Mr. and Mrs. Allison are visiting[?] Drewy M. Smith on Wolfcreek. Mr. Allison is among our subscribers in South Carolina.

§   Capt. S. M. Beck happened to a serious accident yesterday by falling in front of his saw, cutting and sawing his right hand from his fore finger to his wrist, losing a part of three leaders and two bones of his hand and arm.

§   J. J. Huly of Oakway, S. C., and family and S. C. George and family of Anderson, who attended a reunion of the family of Hoey[?] Parker, their uncle, passed through this place on their way to Highlands and Horse Cove Saturday last.

§   Prof. A. J. Ritchie will address the people of Burton on the 18th day of August and at Wolffork Aug. 22, on the subject of education. Prof. Ritchie has something of interest for the people of Rabun and all lovers of education should avail themselves of this opportunity to hear him.

§   Col. Claude Estes, his good wife and little daughters, Nannie, Evelyn and Claude, of Macon, Ga., are registered at the Blue Ridge hotel. Col.

Estes is on his tenth annual outing in this mountainous section, and his affability has won for him much popularity among the people, not only here but all over the state.

§   Grove.

And still dry weather.

A ten days meeting closed at Rocksgrove Sunday with several conversions.

Mr. J. M. and Meeks Arrendale went to Tallulah Monday.

Mr. Murry Hendricks, of Stonewall, was at Grove Tuesday.

Three candidates went down the road Wednesday.

E. L. Canup, of Soque made a pleasant call at Grove Wednesday.

Mr. Thomas Carver of Chechero was among voters in this community Wednesday.

Mr. William Jones, of Chechero passed Grove Wednesday.

§   The alternative road law which has been the absorbing interest by large majority of the people of the county for nearly a year is at last decided by the Supreme Court which confirmed the court below. Now the alternative road law is effective and tools ordered and in a few days the Superintendant will make his programe known. The new system will require a great deal of care and though on the post of the Ordinary and Superintendant and the people will watch the proceedings of the new system with much interest. The only point decided by by [sic] the Supreme Court was the legality of the [illegible] grand jurymen who voted for the pasage [sic] of the law.

§   Old Tiger.

F. A. Taylor was at Tiger preaching last Sunday and visited his sister Sarah Hunnicutt.

Rev. D. D. Taylor, pastor of Tiger church, resigned the pastorage because of the church's negligence. We regret to give him up. He is a devoted and earnest christian.

When we meet the few who are left of the old christian about Tiger it reminds us of former days days [sic] the good old preachers such as old father Robert Dickson, Thomas Carter, J. S. Dickson and father James Ellard used to preach as often at Tiger and at the dwellings of the citizens and almost every home in the community was a house of prayer and everything was a solemn lovliness [sic]. These were bright days and memory accasionally calls them back and we are sad that they are passed for ever.

Allen Turpen visited I. J. H. Hunnicutt Sunday.

Why is that a lawyer can rule a thing off a paper as easy as a school boy can off of a slate?

§   Stonepile.

Some nice rains but not enough yet.

Mr. Ramey Arrendale passed en route to the Falls to day.

W. S. Paris, J. R. Grant and our old friend Crate Hollifield attended justice's court Saturday. While one was watching the game at the gap the other one was driving over the mountain cracking his whip.

Some of the boys left the Falls in a hurry Saturday.

The new railroad is getting up a hussel[?] [illegible] the wagon will soon roll.

Mr. F. D. Singleton attended the funeral of Hon. F. A. Bleckley.

Mr. Harrison Shirley is in feeble health.

The Oklahoma crowd will leave in a week from to-day.

We have in one row of corn ten feet long twenty-five silks. If any doubts this let him come and see for himself.

§   North Chechero.

Miss Ada Cannon was visiting on Chechero Sunday.

Misses Florence and Winney Marsingale spent Saturday night and Sunday on Chechero.

W. B[?]. Coffee and daughter Miss Maybell passed through here en route to Westminster S. C.

Mrs. Frank Cannon and little ones were visiting their grandmother, Mrs. F. A. Bleckley, Sunday and Monday.

Miss Leila Cannon was all smiles Saturday evening.

Jeff Ramey has gone to the Falls on business.

Rev. Landrum is holding a protracted meeting at Chechero this week.

Callie York had special company Sunday evening.

A. J. Duncan is expecting some more boarders this week.

Mrs. F. A. Bleckley is in feeble health.

Mrs. Leila Earl was on Chechero Wednesday.

Ola Taylor is dangerously ill.

Minnie Smith is absent from school on account of sickness.

C. B. Singleton is off to Toccoa with a load of produce.

J. L. York has returned from N. C.

§   Your Gems.

There are minerals and precious gems in this county in abundance. This county is known all over the United States as having the finest corundum and amethyst in the world. Some of our people have been gulled lately by gem seekers. Men who make it a business to go over the county and take options on land, and say if the mine prove satisfactory they will buy the land after getting up a crowd of men and getting a supply of gems, leave with thousands of dollars worth and the owner left without a cent. The thing for the people to do is to tell these gem hunters that they may hunt for the gems and when they find a sample to stop or pay for the land or gems and not let them get out all they want or, all that are easily gotten and leave without paying a cent. A sample is all they should ask for. These men are usually experts and they take the advantage of the people's ignorance and generosity. We mean of course their ignorance in minerals. We heard a man of ability and experience say few days ago that one man had lost five thousand dollars of these gems that were taken out under the old plea "option." It is a shame for the people to be gulled in any such a way. So we advise you to not let a sharper get the uper [sic] hand of you by the smooth word "option," a word in many instance to cover a fraud. Your gems are valuable and keep them or make them pay for every one of them. If you want to sell your gems we can and will tell you where you can sell them. If they are worth nothing they will cost you nothing to keep them. And you had as well keep them as the sharp gem seekers. If there is any one we detest it is a legal rober [sic].

§   The Confederate Veteran's will appreciate any [illegible] in the way of basket dinner from the people September 4th. The old soldiers will, however, indeavor [sic] to furnish a sumptious repost [sic] for all.

§   Mrs. L. N. Shirley has taken some people for the summer.

§   To the honest and fairminded people of Rabun and adjoining counties:
I take this method of publicy [sic] branding the reports circulated by Rabun and adjoining counties to the effect that Frank Ritchie had any part in the robberies recently committed in this county or had made a confession of the same, or had any knowledge here of, as maliciously false. I defy his accusers to come into court and swear what they have alleged to this effect. I wish also publicly to wage the honorable grand jurors of Rabun county to make the most careful inquiry into the whole matter. I court the most thorough investigation.
A. J. Ritchie.
Friendly papers please copy.

§   Trespass Notice. The public are warned to not trespass on the following in Rabun County in no way: Lots of land 5, 6, 19, 20 and 22 and a part of lot No. 80 in the 4th land disttric [sic], also land lot No. 6 in the 5th land district. This August 18th 1902. Miles Philips.

§   Dillard.
Miss May Donalson was in the Valley Sunday.
Miss Julia Penland has returned to her home at Frankllin.

Mr. W. H. Duncan was in the Valley Saturday and Sunday.

Mrs. Octa Greenwood is at Franklin with her father and mother.

Miss Icy Martin was visiting Mr. Bud Martin and family the latter part of last week.

Mr. Lee Ritchie was with home folks Saturday night.

§ Georgia—Rabun County. Will be sold on the first Tuesday in September next, at public outcry, at the court-house in said county within the legal hours of sale, to the highest bidder for cash, the following lot of land to wit: Part of lot of land No. 168 in the second land district of said county containing 75 acres more or less lying on both sides of Mud Creek adjoining lands of G. W. Greenwood and including the mill and shoal. Known as the Pierson mill and shoal. Said property being in possession [*sic*] of Eli Mason and levied on as the property of L. M. Wall, and Ella Wall defendants in fi fa. Property pointted out by H. P. Garland plaintiff in fi fa. Written notice given in terms of the law. This May 26 1902.

J. R. Ritchie, Sheriff.

§ Annual statement of John W. Green County Treasurer of Rabun county to W. S. Long, Ordinary... Total $3089.15

Leaving yet in treasury subject to the legal indebtedness of said county, Aug. 7th 1902 less treasurer's commission $1142[.]55.

Respectfully submitted, John W. Green, Co. Treas.

August 28, 1902
Volume 5, Number 32

§   The Superior Court met Monday morning promptly. On account of Judge Estes sickness Judge Russel of the easten [*sic*] circuit presided. The grand jury was organized by electing Mr. W. E. Powell foreman, John F. Ritchie clerk, and Jeff D. Swafford bailiff. The docket is a light one.

The visiting attorneys are: Robt. McMillan and J. E. Edwards of Clarkesville, H. H. Dean and W. F. Findley of Gainsvelle [*sic*], M. L. Ledford of Blairsvelle [*sic*], John H. Davis of Hiawasse [*sic*], R. J. Swain and Solicitor General W. A. Charters of Dahlonega, Newt Morris of Marretta [*sic*].

§   In a mass meeting of the citizens in the court house Tuesday. A motion was passed to ask the United States authorities to suspend or move the national Quarantine line to county line on the south and the state line on the east. There seems to be no reason why the line should not be moved as M. C. Caniup reports the county as practically free from the cattle tick.

§   The Hon. M. L. Ledford of Blairsville, demorcratic [*sic*] nominee for senator from the 4th sentional [*sic*] district, was among our people Monday and Tuesday. It affords us much pleasure to say the people of Rabun that Mr. Ledford was unamuously [*sic*] elected by the demorcats [*sic*] of Union County in primary and with out his asking for the office, this not is as good a recommendation as a man need want and it will be the pleasure of the demorcats [*sic*] of Rabun to cast their votes for him.

§ Notice. The Democratic Executive com. of Rabun county Ga., are hereby requested to meet in mass meeting and the citizens generally are invited to meet with the Executive committee of said county, in the court-house, at Clayton, Ga., on Thursday, September the 4th 1902 which is the first Thursday, at 12 o'clock sharp to transact important business. Every Democratic candidate for the various county officers are required and requested to be present. This August 27th 1902. James R. Grant...W. S. Price...

§ In the interest of truth and fairness I authorize the publication of the following statement:

About the first week in June, 1902, one George, a supposed detective, came into the office of Drs. Green and Dover with Frank Ritchie and presented a statement which he had evidently prepared himself for Frank Ritchie to sign. I personally examined the statement and could see nothing in the nature of a confession in it. I could see no harm in Frank Ritchie's signing it.

He said he knew nothing about the robery [sic].

The statement was substantially as follows. "On the night of the 12th of March I passed Rabun Gap Post office between the hours of eleven and twelve o'clock and saw no one. I am familiar with the house in which the Post office was kept having clerked there a year before. I am well acquainted with Son Henson, but do not know John Ledford, I stopped in the blacksmith shop one night out of a shower of rain. I hopened and shut the door. I own a spotted dog. I will abstain from bad company and use of whiskey.

The above is a substatnial [sic] copy of statement but not not remember exactly the date of night. This Aug. 20, 1902.

Jesse C. Dover.

§ Upper Tiger.

Capts. Hampton and Hughlett have moved commissaries and general Railroad business up to Tiger Church. the [sic] have finished clearing the right-of-way on their new contract of the first mile above mouth of Tiger Creek. All the boys of the settlement are working.

Capt. E. V. Henderson and his good wife are among the crew. Mrs. Henderson is the only lady in the new home.

Court week and fodder pulling make hands a little scarce for a while.

Mr. Redmond has stopped people from peddling produce in his camps, in order to keep out whiskey.

Mr. Redmond has two brothers with him. They are nice boys and they with some other railroad men are looking after the protection of the peace while railroading. Mr. Webb, who is with the Redmond boys is also a nice man, in face we never saw a nicer railroad crew than the one now on the Tallulah Falls railroad.

Mrs. Sarah A. Hunnicutt is still in feeble health.

Mr. Walter Smith's son Oscar, is about well.

Mr. R. F. McCurry continues to haul produce to the Falls.

Miss Ada Green is progressing nicely with her school.

§   Warwoman.

Gus Wall killed a fine beef Monday for the court.

Capt. Beck is in Clayton being treated by Dr. Green.

The Walhalla revenue officers were over Tuesday of last week and capture a still, whiskey and beer.

Miss May Ramey visited Miss Ada Green Saturday.

M. V. Beck is off to Anderson with a load of apples and irish potatoes.

John Wilson and wife are in poor health.

John Wilson sold six head of sheep for seventeen dollars.

About 80 head of sheep were sold on the Creek last week. They brought two and half cents gross[?].

John Bell, the tomb stone man, spent Friday night with A. M. Wall.

§   Germany

Mr. Ira Taylor's little two old [sic] child died Saturday of last week with scarlet fever.

D. I. Justus is clearing a large new ground field.

Ed Almon is putting up a saw-mill on Scotts creek.

John Justus Jr. has been sick but is improved.

John Justus Sr. has been nursing a sore hand for some time, but is now able to irrigate his corn.

§   Bettys Creek.

"Bud" Darnell was at Clayton Saturday.

A school started[?] at the head of Bettys Creek on the N. C. line Monday of last week.

Judge Hardeman, of Macon, is with A. A. Darnell. He is up for health.

Bry Darnell is sick though improved.

Crops are fine.

Lafayette Long has moved over the line and is now a North Carolinian.

About ten wild bee trees have been found on the Creek this summer.

J. M. Hopper went to the Ridge Pole Saturday on a hunt.

§   Georgia—Rabun County. To whom it may concern: J. N. Bleckley, B. B. Bleckley and J. E. Bleckley, having made application to me in due form to be appointed administrators upon the estate of F. A. Bleckley, late of said county, notice is hereby given that said application will be heard at the regular term of the court of Ordinary for said county, to be held on the first Monday in October, 1902. Witness my hand and official signature. This 18th[?] day of August, 1902. W. S. Long, Ordinary.

§ Having had solicitations sufficient to lead me to the conclusion that my announcement for Clerk of the Superior Court would meet the approval of a good majority of the people of Rabun county, I hereby announce myself a candidate for the same, thanking you all for the kindness with which you have always treated me, not only while I was on official duties, but on every occasion when an opportunity presented itself. Your friend, Miles C. Canup.

§ To the voters of Rabun county: I hereby announce myself a candidate for the office of Sheriff, subject to the democratic primary if one is held, Promising if elected to serve you honestly and faithfully. Yours truly, W. M. Parker.

§ I hereby announce myself a candidate for re-election for the office of Sheriff, subject to the action of the democratic primary. Thanking my friends for past favors and soliciting your help in the future, I am, Respectfully yours, J. R. Ritchie.

§ To the voters of Rabun County: At the solicitation of friends I have decided to become a candidate for tax collector. I make this announcement subject to the democratic primary or any other action of the democratic party. If elected I promise to serve you to the best of my skill and ability, always looking to the very best interest of Rabun county people. I am respectfully, Willie Smith.

§ To the voters of Rabun county: Having been solicited by friends and to satisfy my own feelings, I have consented to become a candidate for the office of county Treasurer of Rabun county, and if elected, I will execute the duties of said office according [illegible] to the best of my ability. L. C. Hollifield.

§ Rain at last.

§ Thanks to Horace McCurray for a load of wood on subscription.

§ L. N. Robins, went to Walhalla S. C. Friday.

§ The usual sport shooting bulbats [sic] has started up in town.

§ A nice letter from Persimmon or Quartz signed "Friend," consequently it goes to the wastebasket.

§   Treasurer John W[.] Green was painfully hurt as he went from town Monday, caused by his mule running away down the Saddle hill.

§   The friends of W. R. Ritchie will regret to learn that he has fever in Tulso [*sic*] I. T.

§   The Hon. F. C. Tate addressed the citizens in the court house at the noon hour yesterday.

§   Prof. A. J. Ritchie made an educational address yesterday at the noon hour.

§   The Parker hotel has a new sign, it is very neat and speaks well for Judge Long who painted it.

§   Hon. H. H. Perry, of Hall County was nominated State senator in the recent primary by about twelve hundred majority.
He is one of the ablest lawyers in the state and will be among the leaders for state senate.

§   Prof. A. J. Ritchie with his brother Frank leaves tomorrow for Baylor University. Frank goes to attend his brother in Indian Territory where he has Typhoid fever. Frank will enter the Baylor University later.

§   Mr. A. F. Holden is attending court. He has not been here since he was pardoned by President Roosevelt. He was charged with violating the internal revenue law.

§   I. J. H. Hunnicutt is assistant clerk this week.

§   Andy Holden sold a sheep last Friday that weighed 165 pounds gross and brought $350.

§   We had a refreshing rain Saturday the first in weeks.

§   Tom Gains who lives 4 miles N. E. of town has not been in Clayton in 15 years. He is an intelegent [*sic*] hard working man and has plenty at his home but it is remarkably strange he has not been in town in 15 years.

§   William FinCannon of Burton made us a call Monday, and in a conversation told us that twelve of the family had died within the last 12 months, among them his brother in the Indiant [*sic*] Territory and five children in five days.

§   Mr. T. M. Burrell of Brownlee, S. C. formally [*sic*] of this county, was up last week on business[.] Mr. B. of course takes The Tribune.

§   The Harris Locust pin [*sic*] Co. has two hundred thousand locust pins on Mr. Earls premises.

§   The Rabun county singing will commence at lower Chechero, on Friday before the first Sunday in September.

§   The appeal case of William Gilds and Sam Wilborne will not be heard untill [*sic*] October. If the Supreme court confirms the decission [*sic*] of the court below they will go to the penitentiary and if a new trial the case goes to the February court.

§   Grove.
Weather warm and dry.
Mr. John W. Green spent Saturday night with M. L. Arrendale.
The Association at Flat Creek seemed to be a good place for the candidates to work as they were all there but one.
A successful protracted meeting is being held at powel gap [*sic*] this week as there are several commissions.
J. M. Crag, of Stonepile, was at Grove Wednesday.
Mr. J. Arrendale went to Tallulah Falls Thursday.
Miss Fannie Watts of Tallulah Falls is visiting relatives on Bridge Creek.

§   Stonepile.
Mr. Raney Arnold and wife came down Thursday and carried Mrs. Fannie Watts and her little son Andrew back to spent [*sic*] a few days with relatives and friends.
Mr. Clarke the fruit agent is around selling trees and spent the night with F. A. Taylor.
Mrs. A. B. Smith and daughter visited Dial D. Taylor Friday.
Aunt Mary Ellard is visiting Eva Cragg before she leave [*sic*] for Oklahoma.
Fodder will be in next week.
The candidate [*sic*] at the association were numberous [*sic*].

§   Notice. All republicans are earnestly requested to meet at Clayton on Friday Sept. 18th 1902, at 10 o'clock a. m. for the purpose of transacting important business, then we will have speeches from Mr. Geo. W. Johnson, of Hiawassee, Ga., and others everybody is invited. This Aug. 23, 1902. J. W. Godfrey, Chairman. G. W. Darnell, Sect'y.

§   Jim Eal [*sic*] Justus of Germany, a section north of Clayton, beyond the Blue Ridge, not the old Empire as some think, but a locality settled by Germns [*sic*] many years ago, gave us a call Saturday and in a conversation he told us of some home raised products.

He has 50 fine sheep, fat and ready for the market, 9 middlings of meat, also hams to eat on till his 30 hogs and the frost comes so he can kill and save again, 10 head of beef cattle, five fine milch cows, a lot of corn to sell and don't owe a dollar except a small bill to The Tribune and we are not losing any sleep about that bill, as "Jim Eal" is fixed so are many more in Rabun and most any one can get there if they will.

§   The Democratic Executive committee will meet on the fourth, old soldiers day.

§   Do not fail to come Thursday and bring a basket dinner.

§   R. B. Collins, of Fort Madison, S. C., a prominent farmer is attending court. He is registered at the Langston house.

§   Blalock.
Prof. G. N. Bynum went down to Clayton Saturday.
Upland corn short, but bottom corn good.
G. E. Thompson lost one of his milch cows last week. She fell between two logs.
Miss Nora and Lex Justus went to Clayton Saturday.
The Thomas pin factory is on a boom. They are running night and day.
Rollie Lunchford and Sam Littleton went to Clayton Tuesday.

§   Quartz.
The many hearts was made glad this morning to see a good shower of rain, and prospects for more.
The health of the community is as good as usual no sickness at all.
The home of J. F. York was made glad a few days ago by the new advent, it's a girl.
There was quite a crowd at the debate Friday night.
Tom Ritchie passed through with a large drove of sheep the other day. He certainly can handle the stock.
There was several of the youngsters attended the speaking at Wolf Fork Friday, they report a fine time.
Miss Docia Colenback is convelsant [*sic*].
J. C. York done a few days work for Joseph L. Dickerson on his house.

§   Dillard
Mr. D. E. Hogshed, of Toccoa, is in this community this week.

Several people attended the speaking at Wolf Fork Friday.

Misses Texie and Belle York were with us the latter part of last week.

Mr. Oscer [*sic*] Powell of Atlanta is with his parents Mr. and Mrs. Powell.

Miss Carrie Grist is no better with fever.

Oscar Scruggs has returned home.

Mr. and Mrs. G. H. Grist spent Saturday night in the Flatts.

Mr. and Mrs. Berrong are over from Towns County on a visit.

Mr. John Bell was in our berg on last Sunday.

Mr. B. H. Greenwood is here from Oklahoma.

Mr. W. H. Greenwood is with home folks this week.

Sheriff Ritchie was in the valley Sunday.

Ask Homer Grist where he went Sunday. Homer says he is going to Atlanta.

Rev. Brown preached to a large crowd here Sunday.

A nice dinner was enjoyed by a large crowd on last Tuesday at Mr. and Mrs. Rile [*sic*] Ritchie's.

§   The time has come that people want to buy thier [*sic*] groceries cheap and we are going to give you prices that the world cannot beat.

We are selling for cash first patent flour at 4.00, second 3.75, salt, 100 pound for 50 cent, green coffee 12 pounds, arbubkles [*sic*] coffee 10 pounds, standard granulated sugar 20 pounds to the dollar, meat 10 cents per pound, best lard 10 cents per pound. The world cannot beat these prices. Come one come all and buy your groceries at T. N. Carter's. Westminster.

§   Application for Charter. Tennessee, South Carolina, and Georgia Railroad Company.

State of Georgia, Rabun County:

To the Hon. Philip Cook, Secretary of the State...of Georgia.

The petition of the undersigned whose names and addresses are herein after fully set fourth [*sic*], and intend to be made a paat [*sic*] hereof respectfully shows:

1 That they desire to be incorporated as provided in the Acts of 1892 and the acts of 1895 amendatory therof, pages 60 and 61,

2 They desire for themselves, their successors and associates to be incorporated under the name and style of "Tennessee, Georgia, and South Carolina Railroad Company."

3 The railway contemplated under this petition for charter is to be about two hundred (200) miles in length, Beginning at a point upon the Eastern boundary of Rabun County in the State of Georgia and running in a north westernly direction through said Rabun county and through Towns County in said State, north west passing through the town of

Hiawassee, thence to the town of Young Harris, thence in a north west direction Blairsville in Union County, through Union County to Morganton in Fannin County, through Fannin County to or near the State Line of Tennessee at or near Ducktown, Tenn., thence in a north west direction to Charleston, Tenn.

4 The capital stock of said railway company shall not be less than 3,000,000 dollars nor more than 5,000,000 dollars, the same of common stock.

5 They desire the Charters of said Comnpay [*sic*] to continue for and during the term of one hundred (and one 101) years, as allowed by law.

6 The principal office of said Railway Company shall be located in the Town of Blue Ridge, county of Fannin, in the state of Georgia.

7 Your petitioners declare that they do intend in good faith to go forward without delay to secure subscriptions to the capitol [*sic*] stock and to contract, equip, maintain and operate said railroad.

8 Your petitioners further show that they have given four (4) weeks notice of their intention to apply for a charter, by the publication of this petition in[?] the newspaper in which the Sheriffs advertisements are published in each of the counties through which said railroad shall run once a week for four weeks after the filling of this petition.

9 Wherefore your petitioners pray that they may be incorporated under the provisions of the laws and constitution of the State, with all powers and privileges common and incident to said corporations.

10 Your petitioners attach hereto their names and residences respectively, as follows:
William B. Frank, Chicago, Ill.
J. W. Lasure, Chicago, Ill.
George Bancroft, Chicago, Ill.
Merrill Skinner, Blue Ridge, Ga.
C. G. Baugh, Mineral Bluff, Ga.
W. V. Brownlee, Mineral Bluff, Ga.
A. F. Christopher, Mineral Bluff, Ga.
W. L. Hunter, Mineral Bluff, Ga.
W. D. Smith, Morganton, Ga.
J. A. Butt, Blairsville, Ga.
Dated Aug. 25th 1902.

§   Notice to Confederate Veterans
There will be a re-union of the Confederate Soldiers of Rabun county in Clayton on the fourth day of September next. There will be a barbecue for the soldiers and general public, and a social good time for all. Speakers are invited.
Capt. S. M. Beck Commander, L. C, Hollifield Sect'y

§   Real Estate.

We are in the real estate business and want you to list your property with us, No charge for advertising. Any portion of the county wanted. Describe your land and send to J.A. Reynolds, care of Tribune office.

I have for sale the following land[.] Read the list and buy you a mountain home.

125 acres, 2 ½ miles east of Clayton, on the Warwoman road, 1 mile from the Tallulah Falls Railway, now being constructed, partly improved. 80[?] acres bearing fruit tree, mountain cabin, partly timbered. A profit will soon be made on this property. Price $275.

One hundred acres of fine farm, one mile from Clayton. 15 acres of bottom land, other well timbered on public road. Part cash banance [sic] at time. Price made known upon application.

Sixty acres of land ½ mile[?] from town, 12 acres of bottom, ballance [sic] timber, 3 room house and outbuildings, good apple orchard bearing, Terms of sale, part cash and ballance [sic] on time. Price made known to purchaser.

September 4, 1902
Volume 5, Number 34

§   Democratic Ticket.
  For Governor, Joseph M. Terrell.
  For Secretary of State, Philip Cook.
  For Comptroller General, W. A. Wright.
  For State Treasurer, R. E. Park.
  For Attorney General, John C. Hart.
  For State School Commissioner, W. B. Merritt.
  For Commissioner of Agriculture, O. B. Stevens.
  For Prison Commissioner, Thomas Eason.
  For Associate Justices of Supreme Court, Samuel Lumpkin, A. J. Cobb.
  For United States Senator, A S Clay.
  For Congressman, from 9th Congressional District of Ga., F C Tate.
  For Superior Court Judge, Northeastern Circuit, J. J. Kimsey.
  For Solicitor General, Northeastern Circuit, W. A. Charters.

§   Georgia, Rabun County.
  The Grand Jurors selected, chosen and sworn to serve at the August term 1902, of the Superior Court of said county, submit the general presentments.
  County officies [sic]. We have examined through appropriate committees the books and records of the various county officers and justices of the peace and notaries public and ex-officio justices of the peace. Without exception we find said books and records kept according to law and all the offices are in good condition.
  We find that there is on hand in the county treasury the sum of one thousand and seventy dollars and two cents.
  Public property. We have inspected the court house and jail. The court

house is generally in good condition. We recommend that the ordinary supply the court house with two dozen more chairs, and we further recommend the stove pipe flues in the court house be repaired as to avoid danger from fire.

We recommend the following improvements and repairs at the jail: that the fire place and hearth in the front room in north end of the jail be made secure; that a new iron door be made for the southwest cell of the jail; that an extra floor be placed in two back cells, the same to be made of one and one half inch lumber and well spiked.

We have examined the tax digest and suggest no changes therein.

For public information we incorporate in these presentments the pauper list as it now stands as follows:

Names	Am't paid per yr.
G. W. Worley	$25.00
Wm. Turpen	$20.00
Elmina Hidden	$15.00
Clara York	$15.00
Thomas Cowart	$48.00
Charles Turpen	$40.
Arah Littleton	$20.
David Smith	$50.
Harriet Cannon	$15.
Cloey Talley	$15.
Mary Fowler	15.
Lydie Gaines	35.
Nerva Coffee (col)	20.
Fojan Wall	15,
John Wooten	93.
Lula Ramey	5.
Comby Gipson (col)	20
Harriet Bleckly (col)	5.
Lidie Hollifield	20
Lizzie Cook	12
Sarah Frady	15
Sarah Douglas	5
Lizzie Scroggs	10
Elijah Chastain	10
Antony Talley	12
Margaret Tow	5

We recommend the following changes in and additions to said list: that Lidyie [sic] Gaines be increased to forty dollars; that Sara [sic] Douglas be increased to ten dollars and that Elijah Chastain be increased to twenty dollars, and that same be paid to A. J. Kell for him; that Dicey Stubblefield be added to said list at $5 per year; that Nancy Johnson be added at $10 per year to be paid to Bright Burrell; that Alice McCall be added at $10 and John W. Queen be added at $10.

We have examined the pension list and make no recommendation of changes therein. J, C. Scott whose name appears on said list is now deceased.

We recommend that the Ordinary take prompt and immediate action to the end that work on the roads under the new system be speeded.

We recommend the per diem of Jurors and Bailiffs for the ensuing year be fixed at one dollar.

We suggest to the Judge the names of R. L. Whitmire and J. M. Crist as suitable persons to be appointed as Jury Revisers to fill the vacancies on the Board.

We recommend that John F. Ritchie be paid 25 cents per day extra of his per diem as a grand jurors [*sic*] for service as Clerk for this dody [*sic*].

We attach hereto and make part of these presentments the reports made to us by the Ordinary, Clerk, Sheriff and Treasurer.

We have selected W. E. Powell, James F. Smith and R. L. Whitmire as a finance committee to examine into the various county offices and into the affairs of the county and make report to the next grand jury. Said committee to receive the same per diem as jurors during the time devoted by them to said service.

We desire to return our thanks to Hon. R. B. Russell who has been presiding this term of the court for courtisies [*sic*] extended this body. We entertain for him both personally and officially the highest regard and and [*sic*] believe him to be an able and just Judge. We shall always extend to him a most cordial welcome to return to this county.

We commend Solicitor General W. A. Charters for faithful and diligent discharge of duty.

And we return thanks to our Bailiff Jeff D. Swofford for his attention to this body.

We recommend that these presentments be published in The Clayton Tribune and that the publisher be paid five dollars therefor.

J, H. Jones, J. B. Dockins, E. N. Holden, J. N. Billingsley, Joal [*sic*] M. Arrendale, L. N. Shirley, J. M. Crisp, D. W. Smith, Clemmy Rogers, H. B. Stonecypher, John A. Burrell, W. E. Powell, J. C. Green, W. J. Bleckley, H. K. Cannon, Virgil N. Lovell, Horace J. Ramey, C. A. Rogers, I. A. Ramey, James M. Ramey, W. J. McWhorter, R. L. Whitmire, John F. Ritchie.

§   Ordinary's Report.

Georgia—Rabun County.

Office of the Ordinary of said county.

To the Hon. Grand Jury, at this the August Term, 1902 of Rabun Superior Court.

I, W. S. Long, Ordinary of said county, do hereby certify that I have collected the sum of $11.87 county funds, and have turned the same over to the County Treasurer of said county since my last report to your honorable body.

The Records of my office, I beg leave to submit to your Body for inspection and examination.

Your humble servant will take great pleasure in acting upon any reccomendations [*sic*] that you may see fit to make, as to any public improvements.

Respectfully submitted, W. S. Long, Ordinary.

§ Sheriff's Report.

Georgia, Rabun County.

To the Hon. Grand Jury:

I beg leave to submit this, my report to your Hon. body.

I have since last court received the following am't of monty for convict hire.

Charlie Swofford ($42.75) which I have paid over to the County Treasurer and taken receipt for the same.

This Aug. 25th 1901 [*sic*].

Respectfully submitted, J. R. Ritchie, Sheriff.

§ Clerk's Report.

Georgia, Rabun County.

I, J. S. Ramey, Clerk of the Superior Court of Rabun County make this my report[. T]here has been no money come through my hands belonging to the county since last term of this court.

This Aug. 25th 1902.

J. S. Ramey, Clerk.

§ Grand Jurors for Feby. term 1902. M. L. Arrendale, Wm. A. Smith, M. H. James, R. C. Smith, J. E. Neville, M. C. Canup, J. R. Ritchie, H. A. Keener, A. J. Grist, J. A. Martin, A. J. Kell, J. F. Smith, J. H. Derrick Jr., A. J. Duncan, W. C. Kerby, H. M. Burrell, W. S. Price, W. J. Ramey, Sam J. Page, E. H. Williams, A. F. Holden, Thomas Nichols, M. L. Hopper, Lafayette Dockins, W. C. Scruggs, T. E. King, J. S. Bleckley, W. C. Norton, A. J. Billingsley.

§ Twelve Month's Support.

Georgia, Rabun County.

Sarah E. Bleckley, having made application for twelve month's support out of the estate of F. A. Bleckley, and appraisers duly appointed to set apart the same having filed their return, all persons concerned are hereby required to show cause before the court of Ordinary of said county on the first Monday in October, 1902, why said application should not be granted.

This first day of September, 1902. W. S. Long, Ordinary.

§ Pearl grits at Ritchie's.

§ F. D. Singleton has vacated his school for fodder.

§ The Ordinary is having the jail repaired.

§ Prof. I. N. Foster has charge of the school here.

§ Eighteen true bills were found by the last grand jury.

§ Claude Green was up from the Falls several days last week.

§ The last grand jury pulled some blind Tigers in this section.

§ Shered Burnett, the popular drum of Gumbling Shoe Co. was here last week.

§ "Nin" Ramey's school is out at Carnot, Banks County, and is at home.

§ Miss Lola[?] Stonecypher, of Burton, was with Mrs. J. S. Ramey Monday.

§ Schools in the county are generally suspended on account of fodder pulling.

§ Republicans meet on the 19th of Sept.[?] instead of the 18th as given [illegible] notice in our last issue.

§ The friends of Capt. Beck will regret to know he has not been feeling so well the past week.

§ Capt. A. R. Gilchrist was up from the Falls Friday looking after the interest of the railroad.

§ Mrs. E. A. Bell has returned to Walhalla after a weeks stay with her sister Mrs. Emily Wall.

§ All[?] who need lumber will remember[?] that J. F. Earl will cut it [illegible] when called for. Get [illegible] logs ready.

§ [--rett] Earl had the misfortune to very sereously [*sic*] cut his leg in Ledwedge[?] Ark. He will return to Rabun as soon as he can stand the trip.

§ A protracted service conducted by Reverands Brown and Hawkins has been going on at the Baptist church this week.

§ Mrs. L. P. Wall was in town Tuesday for medical treatment. Her injury[?] is a result of a fall from [illegible] near Clarkesville sometime [illegible].

§ Postponed.
The old soldiers day has been postponed till September 26th Inst., on account of Capt. Beck, commander not being able to serve.

§ Mr. and Mrs. J. H. Surber who have been at the Blue Ridge hotel for a week or more returned to Atlanta Tuesday. During their stay they made many friends and Mrs. Surber was cooth [*sic*] to leave.

§ There is a movement on foot for a college building in Clayton, hundreds of dollars are being subscribed by our best citizens. The movement is meeting with much favor and before another year we expect to see a good modern college building in town.

§ Judge Russel said in his remarks while discharging the grand jury Friday morning, that he never knew a more faithful or fairer Soliciter General than Col. W. A. Charters. The remark meets the hearty approval of the good citizens of Rabun and the compliment paid to Col. W. A. Charters is a deserved one.

§ There are a number of young men able bodied and well to do in the county smile at us and say they are not able to take their county paper, but here comes J. O. Freeman, Capt. Beck's miller who is in 70th year, has no property, among our cash subscribers. He has never failed to pay for the paper in advance. He says he wants the paper, and we want every man in Rabun Co. to get down with the same want.

§ Railroad.
A genial railroad party consisting of Geo. L. Prentiss, President of the Tallulah Falls R'y. W. S. Erwin general mag'r, A. R. Gilchrist chief engineer. Albert Fendig of Brunswick and L. Magid of N. Y. spent a portion of Friday and Saturday among citizens here.

§ There was an enthusiastic meeting held in the court house, presided by R. E. A. Hamby. W. S. Erwin was unaimingously [*sic*] elected secretary[.] The purpose of the meeting was to devise means to get up the timber for cross-ties and tressle timber for the road through the county. As a result an organization was instituted for this purpose, by electing a committee of three who were Dr. W. J. Green, R. E. A. Hamby and Dr. J. C. Dover. It was decided to employ a man to canvass the county and solicit donation from the people along the line of road for which there was made the sum of one hundred dollars cash in a few minutes. Mr. Prentiss addressed the citizens and said if the people would even comply in part of their guarantee of last year the road would be built as soon as possible to be done to the N. C. line. There were several of the citizens present who gave timber and we believe the people will rally and give of their timber in order to insure the building of the road, at least we hope they will.

Mr. Fendig, of Brobston Fendig and Co. in Brunswick, Ga., and one of the largest industrial firms of the South, is looking over the field with an eye to the future. He is a wide awake gentleman and any section may be congratulated to have the influence of such a man.

Mr. Magid who has recently came among us is interested in silk culture and can tell you more about the silk worm and the silk culture than any man perhaps in the United States. Mr. Magid is a man of much energy and to be with men and to hear him talk of the industry is a sourc [*sic*] of much pleasure.

The Tribune extends to all such a hearty welcome among us, and trust that prosperity may be theirs.

§ To all who are due me, if not settled by note or otherwise, in two weeks, will find their accounts in the hands of J. C. Picket.

J. T. Long

§ See grand jury presantments [*sic*].

§ Big big bargains at Ritchie's for the next thirty days for cash.

§ Quartz.

The rain is over and the farmers are glad to see sunshine again for seed and fodder time or on hand.

The debate Friday night...was an enteresting [*sic*] one. The subject was "Resolve that the State of Georgia should have prohibition.

The candidate, Mr. Smith, for Tax Collector was among the voters this week.

Prof. Bleckley gave his school a happy repost Friday evening.

The health of this community is good.

§   Dillard.

Bentley York has vacated for fodder and gone home.

Miss Fannie Scruggs has returned from Gillsville where she has been spending some time with her sister Mrs. Brown.

Tom Ritchie is a drove of cattle.

Miss Carrie Grist is improving.

The negroes are running a protracted meeting here now.

Several people from in and around Clayton attended the Teachers meeting on last Saturday.

The next meeting will be at Clayton the first Saturday in Oct.

Miss Ethel Powell has vacated her school for fodder and gone home.

J. A. Turner and Nesby of Turnerville were in the Valley the later part of last week.

Mr. [*sic*] Lizzie Martin and Miss Maggie spent Saturday with Bud Martin and family.

§   Jurors drawn for Feb'y Term 1903. Traverse Jurors. S B Wilbanks, F R Baker, W R Keener, T F Wall, W P Smith, J F Earl, J E Bradshaw Sr, W A Parker, J W Hollifield, Richard McClain, Cicero Blalock, J H Laprade, John Martin, G W Holden, Jerry Burton, H D Pitts, J B Rholetter, Jno L Watts, C T Smith, J F Cathey, J R Stonecypher, M M Marsongale, A P Smith, J Z Ford, John W Almon, A M Holden, John Williams, J H Chastain, J A Alman, F A Taylor, A J M Burrell, J H Taylor, John Shed, John M York Jr, T R Williams, Lewis Owens.

§   Notice to Confederate Veterans. There will be a re-union of the Confederate soldiers of Rabun county in Clayton on the 26th day of September next. There will be a barbecue for the soldiers and the general public, and a social good time for all. Speakers are invited. Capt. S. M. Beck, Commander. L. C. Hollifield, Sect'y.

September 11, 1902

Volume 5, Number 35

§ The Rabun County Singing Convention which was held at the Baptist Church on Chechero, [illegible] Sunday, was a nice one. Some of the boys called it a swinging convention, which is applicable to them perhaps, but there are more popular gatherings in the county than the singing convention and not one more enjoyed by the young as well as the old, and a vile wretch it is who is not moved to nobler thoughts under the sound of voices that wafted[?] from the beautiful little church of lower Chechero. The people of the community stood by it nobly and no one, we think left hungry. These gatherings bring to gather largely, the social element as well [as the?] musical talent of the county [illegible] consequently their popularity for nearly a quarter of a century these conventions have been held in the county and will, in all probability, continue to time immemorial.

§ At a meeting held this day held by the Confederate Soldiers of Rabun County,

T. N. McConnell was elected as temporary chairman. John W. Green as temporary secretary.

On motion it was ordered we have[?] [illegible] and basket dinner and that there be a committee of three to author[?] a program[?] for the day.

Committee: J. C. Dover, John W. Green, R. E. A. Hamby, T. N. McConnell.

Moved that a committee be appointed to solicit subscriptions for the dinner on tenth day of October, Clayton.

Clayton. [illegible name], C. C. Hollifield, [illegible].

Tiger. B. H. Adkins, Boin Cannon.

Chechero. L. T. Wall, J. H. Coffee.

Warwoman. E. D. Swofford, Calvin Speed.

Moccasin. A. J. Kell, George P. Reed.

Persimmon. M. V. York, H. V. Moore.

On motion the day for the meeting was changed from the 10th day of October to 26th day of September.

On motion the following resolution was adopted:

Be it resolved by the Rabun County Confederate Veterans now in session in the court house, that our sincere sumpathy be extended to our worthy commander in cheif [*sic*] Capt. S. M. Beck who is now confined to his sick bed and pray God for his hasty recovery.

On motion the meeting adjourned until 26th day of September. T. N. McConnell, Chairman. John W. Green, Sec'ty.

§   Notice. Everybody is especially invited to bring their tools and dinner Saturday the 20th to help clean off the grave yard at Clayton Ga. Yours truly, George Brown.

§   Georgia—Rabun County.

Will be sold on the first Tuesday of in October next, at public outcry at the court house in said county, within the legal hours of sale, to the highest bidder for cash, certain property, of which this is a full and complete description.

Part of lot of land No. 168 in the second land district, of said county, containing 125 acres, more or less, and bounded as follows: On the north by lands of G. W. Greenwood, on the east by the district line, on the south by the lands of W. J. Green and others, on the west by T. J. Hamby, said property being in possession of Ella Wall, and being levied on as the property of L. M. Wall and Ella Wall defendants in fi fa. Property pointed out by H. P. Garland plaintiff in fi fa. Written notice given in terms of the law, This the second day of September 1002 [*sic*].

Also at the same time and place part of lots of land 18 and 19 situated and being in the 4th land district of Rabun Co. Ga., and bound as follows: North by lands of A. M. James and Drew Smith east by lands of John Denney south by lands of L. V. Cannon and west by lands of Mrs. Canada and also No. 4 in the 4th district of Rabun county bounded by lands of John Smith, Mrs. Canada and the estate of F. A. Bleckley: a certain track [*sic*] in the 4th district adjourning [*sic*] lands of Jim and William Ramey and Mrs. James Mozely; also parts of lots Nos. 19 and 20 in the fourth district and bounded as follows: North and east by lands of Jackson Smith south by lands of J. W. Harvey and west by lands of Allen Turpen containing three hundren [*sic*] acres more or less: Said property levied on as the property of Miles Phillips, J. S. Denney and L. V. Cannon to satisfy mortgage execution issued from the Superior Court of said county in favor of Nathionel Phillips and R. B. Collins against said Miles Phillips, J. S. Denney and L. V. Cannon.

Also at the same time and place, a tract of land situated lying and being in the county of Rabun, State of Ga. containing three hundred acres more or less in third land district on both sides of Chattanooga River adjoining lands of W. J. Burrell[?] J. A. Nix and A. A. Billingsly, being the same tract of land bought by P. A. Crane several years ago from W. J. Burrell, together with all the rights and priveleges [sic] thereunto belonging as the property of the defendent [sic] P. A. Crane. Said property levied on as the of P. A. Crane to satisfy mortgage execution issued from the Superior Court of said county in favor of L. Bloom against said P. A. Crane.

Also at the same time and place part of lot of land No 21 in the 4th land district of Rabun County and State of Georgia and described as follows to wit: Commencing at the east end of the cross fence near the [illegible] running the big road a northeast direction to the gap at the ridge at the foot of the mountain, thence up the mountain a northeast direction to the top of the mountain to a rock, thence down the top of the ridge same direction to the original line west to the corner, thence the original true south to branch to a rock corner, thence down the hollow to a rock, thence up the ridge to the top of a rock corner, thence down the dividing ridge to the starting place, containing one hundred acres more or less together with all the rights and privileges there unto belonging as the property of the defendant M. A. F. Williams. Said property levied on as the property of M. A. F. Williams to satisfy a mortgage execution issued from the Superior court of said county in favor of J. M. Swofford against [said] M. A. F. Williams.

This Sept. 9th 1902. J. R. Ritchie, Sheriff.

§   Trespass Notice. All persons are notified not to trespass on the following part of land lot No 40 in the first part of lots No. 70 and 72 in the second land district. A. E. Dickerson.

§   Mrs. W. S. Long is on the sick list this week.

§   A. L. Beck of Cullasaga [sic] gave us a pleasant call Tuesday.

§   Wednesday and Thursday of last week were ideal days.

§   Dr. Dover has been very busy of late attending patients.

§   Prof. M. B. York spent several days in Clayton the past week.

§   Prof. J. S. Burrell was over from Burton Tuesday of last week.

§   County Treasurer John W. Green has given the R. R. the timber on 50 acres of land near Clayton.

§   Prof. A. A. O'Kelley was elected president and Walter Dickson secretary of the singing convention.

§   Dr. Ellenberger is looking after the cattle tick in the connty [*sic*], but is having poor success in finding them.

§   Waiting for Sheriff and the editor being absent on a survey in the mountains has delayed The Tribune somewhat this week.

§   Col. J. J. Bowden was up representing the T. F. Ry. Co. this week. Col. Bowden is a prominent Atty. of Clarkesville Ga.

§   Judge W. B. Hill of Clarkesville is registered at the Blue Ridge hotel. He is here in the interest of Mr. Prentiss and the Tallulah Falls Ry.

§   We learn from Prof. A. J. Ritchie of Fort Worth, Tex. that his brother, W. R. Ritchie, has[?] fever at Toulon 1[?]. T. is doing very well.

§   The many friends of Dr. Green will be pleased to know that he is after a serious attack of bronchial trouble able now to push [illegible] again.

§   Mr. A. L. Beck wife and daughter, of Cullasga [*sic*] N. C. are at the home of J. I. Langston's to see the last remains of Capt. Beck laid in the tombs at Antioch church on Warwoman Dist.

§   A Card of Thanks. With the very tenderest feelings [illegible] emotion, we thank the kind people of Clayton, and especially Mr. and Mrs. D. L. Parker, for thier [*sic*] kindness shown us during the sickness of our little babe, Harold. We shall cherish you all in our memories. Mr. and Mrs. M. C. Warlick.

§   We learn from Mr. J. B. Rholetter that the three year old child of Wesley M. Lee died of scarlet fever Monday week and that the 18 months old child of Sam Ledford died from a rattle snake bite. The snake bit the child on the back of the right hand and it died the same day. The Tribune extends sympathy.

§   Capt. S. M. Beck, aged 77 years died last Monday night, at 11 o'clock at the home of his daughter, Mrs. J. I. Langston, of a conplication [*sic*] disease. It will be remembered that he got his hand tearfully sawed by falling against his saw. He then took typhoid fever[,] inflamatory rheumatism any one of which was almost sufficient to cause death. He suffered greaty [*sic*]. Capt. Beck was among the most prominent men in this section of Ga. Our symyathy [*sic*] goes [on] to the bereaved.

§   Blalock.
Mr. P. E. Thompson raised a watermelon that weighed sixty nine pounds.
The locust pin factory at Thompson's is still on a boom.
Miss Rosa Thompson says she thinks she can elect the Pine Mt. candidate with a large majority.
Rile Ritchie and Mrs. A. J. Ritchie past [*sic*] through here on thier [*sic*] way to Towns County.
Otto York killed a rattle snake that had eleven rattles and a button.
Mr. G. N. Bynum stopped his school two weeks for fodder.

§   Quartz.
Prof. OKelley with Prof. Singleton attended Prof. Bleckley's school this week.
John H. Derrick was among the voters a few days ago.
Dr. Garland made a professional trip to Jas. F. Keener's the other day.
Prof. Bleckley stopped his school for fodder.
Some of the Persimmon people attended the singing convention at Chechero.
J. C. York is looking out among the voters a few days they have him almost a solid expression.
Candidate Baker was on the creek looking after votes this week.
We can tell you who will be the man the 2nd of October.

§   Dillard.
Fodder pulling time is at hand.
Cloudy with prospects for rain.
Miss Laura Kelley and her brother Thomas attended the Singing Convention at Chechero on last Saturday and Sunday.
Miss Carrie Grist is worse at this writing.
Nopolean Turpen is off to Webster N. C. this week.
Little Fred Grist is dangerously sick with Typhoid fever.
M. L. Sroggs[?] is off to Toccoa with a load of cabbage.
Mr. Tom Ritchie has returned from down in the country where he has been with a drove of cattle.
Mr. D. D. Turpen is from Turnerville on a visit.
The infant child of Mr. and Mrs. G. L. Dorsey died on last Tuesday night. The bereaved family has our sympathy.
Rev. Brown happened to a very painful accident by sticking a nail in his foot while running a protracted meeting at Clayton.

§   One of the most unique arrests was made Friday of last week, by Marshall Dennis Hughes and T. L. Mitchell that has come to us ever.

A distillery was reported to the officers near Burton and they went to it and found two men at work, arrested both but one failed to appear according to promise made by made the officers and the other brought to town and as usual, they trusted him about the town and he too left the officers. All this got a determined look on the Marshel's [*sic*] face, and he was soon on his back track to Burton from whence he had traveled before and a little later was at the place where they had took a still from the furnace the same day.

These moonshiners obtained an other still and was preparing to run out the beer and and [*sic*] just as one of them said it would be h—l if the officers should come and get this one and he no longer spoke the words when Tom Mitchell says "we have got you." One of them were captured and brought to town handcuffed, and was bound over to the United States Court, the other making his escape.

§   Old Tiger.

Hughlett and Co. have thier [*sic*] grade points opened up and are at work.

Col. H. H. Dean made the champion speech at Clayton court. It was in behalf of Tom Mitchell.

Miss Susie Taylor is expected to visit I. J. H. Hunnicutt soon.

Mr. Allen Turpen was elected president of the union singing Sunday.

C. L. Taylor visited Mrs. Sarah Hunnicutt.

§   Program for Rabun County Teachers Association to meet at Clayton on the 1st Saturday in October.

The best plans for building a high school in Rabun Co. by R. E. A. Hamby, A. A. O'Kelley, and F. D. Singleton.

The needs of our public schools by J. C. Howard, L. M. Chastain, and J. M. Bleckley.

Is normal training necessary for successful teaching by J. S. Burrell, Miss Texie York and M. B. York.

How to teach grammar by I. N. Foster, B. H. Landrum, and James Green.

Program committee: B. H. Landrum, James Green, F. D. Singleton, Belle York, Lizzie Dillard.

§   Tallulah Falls Railway Company. Time Table No. 25. In effect Sunday Sept. 7th 1920... Tallulah Falls... Tallulah Lodge... Turnerville... Hollywood... Anandale... Hills... Clarkesville... Demorest... Cornelia... W. S. Erwin, General Manager.

§   Notice. All republicans are earnestly requested to meet at Clayton on Sept. 19th to transact important business. Everybody is invited to come, Ladies and gentleman [*sic*], of all creed and denomination we want you to be present. I want everybody to have a chance at the republicans doctrine. J. W. Godfrey, Chairman.

September 18, 1902
Volume 5, Number 36

§   In our travels over the county we see many things interesting. Tuesday, Wednesday and Thursday of last week we were on a survey near the Rabun Bald mountain, a point only a few feet below the highest point in the State, Mt. Enotah, near Young Harris, the highest point in the State, being only a few feet higher. Our mission there was to run out a large track [*sic*] of land for Geo. L. Prentiss. Our companions were our old Habersham county friends Ex Ordinary W. D. Hill and Col. J. J. Bowden, also our townsman J. I. Langston. Away up in the air nearly a mile above the sea, we spent, and very pleasantly, the time squinting through the telescope of our transit, and viewing some of the grandest scenery on earth. We must not forget that we were the guest of James H. Ramey who for 29 years has lived on this beautiful elevation. We always become highly interested in these genuine mountain homes. These people who have roamed the mountains so many years, have rich hunting stories and many other things to tell you of much interest. Mr. Ramey showed us a large cave in the mountain side, that extends for nearly a quarter of a mile along the mountain side where a man stayed during the civil war and it is so arranged that it would have taken a small army to have captured him and he defied all home guard force. The approach to the immense cave is somewhat difficult and after you get in sight of the cave there is a long open gap so arranged as it would enable one man well armed to kill almost a regiment of men before he could be captured, [and] after surrender it would be a difficult task to have found him after refuge in the main cave. The cave extends a long way along a cliff and has no outlet on the east[?]. This is a fine place for tourists to [illegible] away many leisure hours and will someday be a popular resort. This point is located on the north double, Knob mountain, two mountains of note, locally. We think every apple orchard the prettiest, and Mr. Ramey's among the best we have ever seen. The locality seems perfectly adapted to apples. Mr. Ramey told that he had a plot of ground that took just one hour to work it over and he had cultivated it this year in cabbage and had already sold about one hundred dollars' worth of cabbage and thousands of pounds going to waste now. This sort of statement will not be disputed by the people of Rabun, but may sound like a lie to our northern and western readers. We yet fail to see why some of our readers want to leave and go to the west when fortunes lay at their door in apples alone, in cabbage alone, and in Irish potatoes alone, in Rabun county. A little later on, when we get railroads running through the county, and can put our products in the market before the dew dries on them, there will be people making fortunes raising these products where they are so naturally adapted.

§   The candidates are all busy.

§   Winter goods at Ritchie's.

§   Don't forget the old soldiers day.

§   Mrs. D. L. Parker is on the sick list.

§   [Illegible].

§   There[?] was frost last week in the highlands of Rabun.

§   You can get 12 cents for eggs at Ritchie's.

§   Lee Ritchie was in Athens last week buying goods.

§   Mrs. J. F. Earl is spending a few days in Walhalla, S. C.

§   Born—To Dr. and Mrs. W. J. Green Tuesday night, a girl.

§   Nelson Tilley was in Atlanta last week replenshing [*sic*] his stock of merchandise.

§   Prof. Foster is teaching our school again, after a vacation of a week for fodder.

§   The Harris locust pin factory is running two miles north of Clayton on the Hunnicutt farm.

§   Logan York says they had a frost up on Scotts Creek one night recently that "bit" the fodder. [Illegible] is this for Rabun?

§   M. E. Earl, who has been in the [illegible] for a short while, returned home[?] a few days ago. It will be remembered that Everett had the misfortune to cut his leg badly while out there, and is not over it yet. He is feeling badly.

§   Superintendent J. I. Langston will begin working the public road under the new system in dead earnest Monday morning.

§   The Ordinary and Superintendent has in part appointed overseers [illegible] different parts of the county as follows[?]: Valley, J. N. Fisher and [illegible] Dillard; Warwoman, Lafayette[?] Dickson; Chechero, Jesse [illegible]; Tiger, none; Stonepile, [illegible]; Tallulah, Wm. FinCannon and[?] Virgil Lovell; Persimmon, none and Clayton none. The authorities will make five appointments of overseers this week.

§   New winter goods will be in in about three weeks, and I wish all who are due me as much as five cents to come in and settle or I will sue all who are due me one cent. L. Duncan.

§   Miss Blanch Wall is still in feeble health.

§   Mrs. Jesse W. Green and her son R. T. Green were the guests of Dr. Green Monday.

§   Hon. Howell C. Blalock, of Burton broke the monotony of our quiet town Tuesday by his genial presence.

§   The management of the Southern Inter-State Fair, of Atlanta, has our thanks for a souvenir in the form of a pen holder.

§   Mrs. Ed Carter, of Anderson, S. C., and three children passed town yesterday en route home from Tennessee Valley, where they have been visiting.

§   D. L. Parker and J. I. Langston have been engaged this week as registrars. They report eleven hundred and seventy five, (1175) and all except three are fully qualified voters.

§   We measured a prickly ash while in the mountains last week at John Darnell's mills, which measured 2 feet around it. Also at the same place stands a walnut tree that is 75 feet from tip to tip of the limbs.

§   We are requested to announce that all who are interested in the building of a high school at Clayton, are urgently requested to be present the first Saturday in Oct., Teacher's day. It is desired that every district in the county be well represented.

§   There are four candidates before the people of the state for the position of Judge of the Supreme Court, to fill the vacancy of Judge H. T. Lewis. The candidates are Judge John S. Chandler, of the Stone Mountain circuit; W. R. Hammond, of Atlanta; Judge Russell, of the Western circuit; and John P. Ross, of Macon, Ga. Two of the above named gentlemen, Judge John S. Chandler and Judge R. B. Russell, are generally known to our people, having each held a session of our Superior Court. All the candidates are, so far as we know, competent men and they all have the endorsement of their local bars.

§   Some one played a little trick on our Old Tiger correspondent in our last issue. Sometimes our correspondents send their letters not sealed and some one, just for fun, will add a few lines just to tease the correspondent. This is the case from Old Tiger, in which the correspondent denies that he wrote that Miss Susie Taylor was expecting to visit I. J. H. Hunnicutt and that Allen Turpin was elected President of the Union Singing. The Tribune printed the letter as it came to the office. In a letter of a few weeks ago, a certain gentleman came to our office and told us he had played a trick on our correspondent by adding that "the respondent was mad at this writing." Be sure to seal your letters and do not let them lie around where the funny young people will get them, for they will have fun.

§   We are having delightful weather this week, and the farmers are taking advantage of it.

§   John T. Long is clerking for W. R. L. and T. J. Ritchie the past few days.

§   H. K. Cannon is off to Anderson, S. C., with a load of produce.

§   Prof. A. A. O'Kelley returned Monday evening from a visit to home folks in Jackson county Ga.

§   Miss Carrie Cannon is again at The Pines teaching school, after vacating "for fodder."

§   A Certain Cure for Snake Bite.
    An Indian cure which has been kept a secret for many years I wish to

make known to the people of Rabun county and the people who read The Tribune. First take sweet fern roots and tops what you can grasp in one hand. Second the same amount of of snake root and tops. Third the same amount of salve weed, just the top beat well and boiled in 1 qt. sweet milk; let the patient drink. For poltice, top of devil shoe string one hand full, one hand full of fire weed, one hand full. wild rose Mary one hand full. Beat these and add the boiled weeds together and bind to the bite, do this three times over, then bind salt peter to the bite for a few days. This will cure any snake bite. J. H. Williams.

§   Dr. E. C. Bransom, of The State Normal College, and Dr. Glenn, State School Commissioner, will deliver addresses before the Rabun County Teachers' Assocation on Saturday, Oct. 4th next. Everybody should take advantage of the occasion and hear these gentlemen. They will have something good for all,—teachers, patrons and pupils. Let everybody come to enjoy the biggest educational rally Rabun has ever had, for there are going to be some really good and interesting features connected with this occasion. A. A. O'Kelley, C. S. C.

§   Betty'o Crcck.
The people are busy pulling fodder this week what time it is not raining.
They have organized a new Sunday school at the Last-chance school house. We think Betty's creek is doing well as we have two Sunday schools and two day schools.
There was a large crowd to help A. A. Darnell eat water melons Sunday.
Messrs. James, Emery and Claud Garrett, of Cherokee, N. C., are with A. E. Burrell this week.
Mr. C. F. Garland and wife went to the Flatts Monday night visiting Miss Carrie Grist.
Misses Icy, Della and Bry Darnell visited in the valley Saturday night.
Judge Hardeman accompanied by A. A. Darnell, G. W. Ledford, Preest Bradley, Marsh Hopper and Lex Darnell went to Nantahala Friday morning. When they got to the camp they found Mr Turner Page and his company and report a fine time.
Success to The Tribune.

§   Dillard.
Cool weather.
Mr. Riley Garland and wife of Toccoa visiting in the Valley this week.
Mrs. Lura Ritchie has been spending some time at Dillsboro N. C. with relatives.
John Harkins is off with a load of apples.

Prof. York has returned to his school.

Miss Pearl Martin purchased a new organ.

Mrs. Ida Dorsey is improving slowly.

John Holden and Miss Lula Howard were happily married at the brides home on last Sunday.

We wish the happy couple a long and happy life.

Col. Bowden and W. H. Duncan was in the Valley Friday.

Mr. Bill Parker was talking politics in our berg [*sic*] the latter part of last week.

Mr. Lome[?] Russell was in the valley Saturday and Sunday.

Little Fred Grist is some better at this writing.

§   Mud Creek.

Prof. B. York began his school Monday.

Mr. and Mrs. Powell, with their boarders, went to Mud Creek Falls Thursday and Miss Ethel had Misses Eula Dillard, Lula Hogshed, Mattie Dillard and Mr. Bates with her. They all enjoyed themselves very much.

Mrs. Rush Grist is with her father, Mr. Martin, this week.

Mrs. Scroggs has been with her daughter, Mrs. Turpen, the past week.

Mr. Rush Grist, Homer Grist and George Martin are in Athens wagoning.

Little Fred Grist is very sick with Typhoid fever.

Miss Carrie Grist, who has been desperately ill for some time, is improving.

Mr. Oscar Scruggs is off to Toccoa this week.

Mrs. Will Greenwood, with her brother Ben, was in Franklin Thursday.

Mr. W. A. Martin was in the Flats last week.

Mr. J. J. Greenwood was in N. C. on business last week.

Mr. Charley Page, Cardie Hopper and Willie Moore visited Mr. G. R. Martin Tuesday night.

Miss Icie Martin spent a few days with her sister in the Flats last week.

Miss Lula Hogshed was with Miss Ida Martin Friday night.

Mr. Bob Ritchie went to the Flats last Saturday.

Mrs. Sarah Dillingham and her daughter Mary and Mrs. Maggie Carter returned from Anderson, S. C., one day last week.

Miss May and Ida Dillard spent Saturday night with Icy Martin.

§   Quartz.

Mr. M. B. York has returned to his school in the valley.

Mr. John C. Howard has gone after his mother.

The Sunday School was lively Sunday.

Mr. M. L. York returned home from Tampa, Fla., where he has been spending a few months.

Fodder pulling is the order of the day.

The revenue officers have been paying their respects on this side of the county.

The old lady Justus is very feeble.

§   The friends of Capt. and Mrs. William Berry sympathize with them in the loss of their baby. The little one had been sick some while, but on Sunday was eased from pain and carried to the home above. The interment was at Bethlehem, where the services were conducted by E. M. Vance. –Clarkesville Advertiser.

§   Old Tiger.

Last Saturday was law day at Tiger.

We understand that Mr. J. H. and V. C. Taylor, of Checheroe, are no better of fever.

Rail-roading and fodder-pulling are on hand, and some of the boys want to do both at once but can't.

Capt. Hughlett will come up to Tiger frequently.

Dr. Long and his wife were up at Tiger last Sunday.

There are some mistakes in the letter from Old Tiger last week. The correspondent wrote that Miss Susie Taylor was expecting a visit from her brother V. C. Taylor who is sick on Chechero. And that Mr. Allen Turpin visited I. J. H. Hunnicutt. And that Mr. Allen Williams was elected president of the Union Singing. He did not say that Allen Turpin was elected, nor that Miss Susie was expected to visit I. J. H. Hunnicutt. It is supposed, however, that he would not object to such a visit.

Dr. Dover, of Clayton, is very busy professionally. He was in Tiger Saturday and Sunday. He reports Scarlet fever about Camp Creek.

Mr. Willie Smith's little girl, in Tiger, has fever.

September 25, 1902
Volume 5, Number 37

§   Read the Tribune.

§   The fair in Atlanta opens Oct. 9th.

§   Uncle Jack Keener has an affection of the eye which has caused much suffering. He was able to be out in town Saturday however.

§   T. N. McConnell will serve the people for coroner if elected.

§   W. G. Donaldson has been in declining health for some time.

§   Mrs. Norton is very much improved after a severe illness of a week ago.

§   R. L. Whitmire's family are much improved, after many weeks of Typhoid fever.

§   W. H. Duncan, who has been with home people over a month, was called to Atlanta Friday. "Bud" has many friends in Rabun who would be delighted to have him remain here.

§   W. C. Norton has returned from market.

§   A. J. York, of Westminster, S. C., who has been visiting relatives here, has returned home.

§   Col. Hamby returned from Atlanta Friday.

§   The ticket for the general election is of the secret ballot form. Now we favor going farther and have the Australian system entirely.

§   The State and county tax for the year 1902 is one dollar and thirty three cents on the hundred dollars in this county, two cents less than last year, with the full limit of road tax levy, which, of itself, is twenty mills on the hundred.

§   Send your fine apples, in dozen lots, before the 1st of October.

§   Marion Long killed eighteen squirrells [*sic*] in one day a few days ago.

§   Clayton, it seems now, will have two railroads.

§   Last Saturday was regular court day here and some cases of importance were tried.

§   It is a violation of the laws of Georgia to roll rocks down a mountain.

§   Jeptha Taylor, we are sorry to [hear?], has the Typhoid fever.

§   Barbecue and basket dinner tomorrow.

§   Mrs. D. L. Parker has been very sick this past week.

§   The wagons loaded with mountain produce may be seen every few hours going to market.

§   The chestnut crop is immense in the mountains.

§   The sports report more squirrells [*sic*] [illegible] usual this year.

§   [Capt.?] Collector E. L. Birdstrong [illegible] us to say too the moonshiners[?] that if they will leave an axe [illegible] their distilleries instead of burning them, as they did one on Warwoman last week. The law says they must be destroyed, if [page cut off here].

§   The revenue officers captured two distilleries last week.

§   The Republicans held a meeting here Friday. Owing to the rain or lack of enthusiasm, only a few were out. Mr. Johnson, of Hiawassee, addressed the meeting.

§   M. M. Marsingale has put up thirty eight stacks of fodder. This is a pretty good one man's crop.

§   Superintendent J. I. Langston began working the public roads under the new law Monday.

§   We want for exhibitions in the northern states, specimens of apples. If you will bring a dozen of each variety to our offics [sic], with your name, we will forward them to Washington, where they will go to all points at the northern fairs being held now.

§   V. C. Taylor has a very severe case of Typhoid fever. Clinton is one of our most industrious and enterprising citizens, and we hope soon to announce his recovery.

§   We would like to have your property for sale. List it with us and we will put it before the northern people through the land and industrial agent of the [Southern Railway?], Washington, D. C.
    If you want to sell your land let us have a description. It will cost you nothing if we do not effect a sale.

§   A number of people are out in county soliciting timber for the railroad.

§   Notice. The public are warned not to trespass on my premises in any way, especially by taking fruit or cutting timber. L. W. Colenback.

§   Uncle Jeff Duncan has returned from the Falls after spending the summer months down there as the popular guide. Everybody is glad to see Uncle Jeff. He is in rather poor health.

§   The Association. The following poem on The Association on Flat Creek we publish with apologies to the writer for delay...

§   Railroads! Railroads!
    Just now the railroad prospects for this section are very encouraging and there is no [illegible] that this section has the attention of capitol [sic] and within the next few years. We may be expected to be connected with the outside world by railroads, telegraphs and telephones.
    We clip the following from The Mt. Airy Protectionist:
    Mr. Prentiss is much encouraged by the outlook and from the fact also that his road will have direct connection with East Tennessee from Franklin, N. C., [by?] the Carolina[?] and Tennessee Southern Railway, which was chartered by the State of North Carolina [on?] August 26th,

1902. The distance to be built is 60 miles and the work will be done by the Southern Railway Co. Then the Tennessee, Georgia and South Carolina State Line is to extend from Charleston[?], Tennessee, to Walhalla, S. C. [illegible] connect with the Knoxville [branch?] of the Southern Railway [illegible] Tennessee and with [illegible] Ridge at Walhalla [illegible] will cross [illegible] [Georgia?] and the Tallulah Falls Railway at Clayton, thus giving Clayton two railroad outlets. It will pass through Fannin, Union, Towns and Rabun counties of Georgia and Oconee, S. C.

The Southern, it is stated with authority, will build a road from Maryville, East Tennessee, to Bushnell, N. C. The company has made immense purchases of lands and lots in Knoxville and will tear down or remove over a hundred houses, arch over 2nd creek, an immence [sic] engineering scheme span the Tennessee River with an iron bridge and as the company now owns the Knoxville and Maryville road which is 16 miles, and nine miles more is graded to Montvale Spring, thus will these extensions connect the coal fields of East Tennessee. Coal Creek and Walden Ridge mines of the Cumberland Mountains with the manufacturing districts of North East Georgia, with its hard woods and and inexhaustible mineral resources and lovely gems, and there will be "King Cotton" of the beautiful Southland greet the Black Diamond Queen of the Cumberlands.

We are in receipt of information that the engineers will begin early in October, and that the right of way will be asked for in the near future for the Tennessee, Ga. and South Carolina Railway. We are in receipt of a letter bankers of Atlanta saying that a charter is asked for a trolley line from Atlanta to Roswell, Cummings, Dawsonville, Dahlonega, Cleveland, Tallulah Falls and Cornelia. This line will open up eight counties and prove a great benefit to each, as well as every village and farm, adding to the value of every piece of property in each county.

§   Quartz.

Little Henry Kilby's family has Scarlet fever and Henry is thought [page cut off here].

Ira York is in the community buying stock. The is lot [sic] of good cattle here.

J. C. York has been away from home over a week looking after votes.

Miss Lula Parker is at Clayton.

§   An Appeal to the Voters of Rabun County and to the Democrats of Said State.

We are now confronted in this, the 40th Senatorial District, of which Rabun is one of the counties that constitutes this district, with a problem that the voters of Rabun county must solve at the October election, and it behooves the executive committeemen in each district to earnestly support the nominee of the party and to insist upon each voter at the polls to do so. According to the time-honored custom of Senatorial rotation, it is now Union county's time to furnish the Senator for this district. They have presented to this district by their primary held on June 5th, 1902, one of Union's worthy sons in the person of Hon. M. L. Ledford, whose candidacy was endorsed by their expression on June 5th, and further endorsed by the fact that he had no opponent in the June primary, therefore we can feel assured that he is worthy of the honor that has been placed upon him, and feel assured that in the person of Mr. Ledford we have a gentleman who will be true to his trust and to his constituents.

We are further met with the person of Mc. G. Colwell, of Union county, who aspires to represent this 40th district as Senator. I am informed that Mr. Colwell has no politics; that he neither claims to be a democrat nor republican, but is what is known as an "independent;" or in other words, he is on the fence, and straddles democracy and republicanism, and will fall to one side of the fence or the other, like the persimmon. At the election precincts on Wednesday, October the first, you will find the official ticket with the name of Hon. M. L. Ledford thereon. We, as democrats of Rabun county, must stand true to our colors, and let the standard of democracy continue to waft over what is known of Georgia and all over the state as the banner county in Georgia in democracy. The banner of democracy in Rabun county was raised by our fore-fathers, and has wafted over homes of men who have been true and of men who love liberty, and o'er men who are brave, and will go down in the history of the county as such. Therefore let us, the sons of these brave, true and tried supporters of democracy again unfurl our banner in support of Mr. Ledford, and not let our banner trail the dust. I don't believe that the republicans of Rabun county will support Mr. Colwell, nor do I believe that the democrats will. I do not fall out with a man because he is a republican, nor because he's a democrat, because under our constitution we are given the right to worship according to the dictates of our own conscience. We are a free and liberty loving people and the elective franchise is one of the greatest liberties we have, and ought to be as sacred, and as carefully guarded and exercised, as our religious opinions, and our church affiliations. Therefore I beg all democrats and republicans to guard your elective franchise on October the first, and support a man who has conviction and stands by them as true as steel, and support the man who has the conviction and stands by them [sic]. And I ask you not to support a man who has no party, who has no convictions, and who is neither ruled by the platform and principles of democracy nor republicanism. There fore cast your ballot for the man who stands before you upon an announced principle and does not stand upon the fence.

Jas. R. Grant, Chairman Dem. Ex Com. of Rabun county. Clayton, Ga., Sept. 23rd 1902.

§   Germany.

We are hustling now, gathering chinquapins. J. N. Justus' boys carried about three bushels to Clayton last Saturday. The bushes are bent to the ground.

J. N. Justus says he has a full crop of persimmons. He has bushes not as high as his head full of persimmons, some not knee high from the ground. I can prove all I say if I can get a witness.

Mr. H. A. Keener went through Germany taking subscriptions for the railroad.

Represntative Bleckley went through the valley Monday visiting voters. He is soon aiming to be ready to go down the road. He is one sober man in the field.

J. N. Justus' children gathered one bushel and a peck of chinquapins by 10 o'clock Tuesday and left more on the ground for the hogs.

The Good Book says it will rain on the just. It has come our time at last. Look out for feed to be scarce.

If you want milk cows, come to Germany.

§   Dillard.

Rain with cool weather.

Miss T. Kelley is with her sister Mrs. Greenwood.

Miss Ethel Powell has gone back to her school.

Prof. York went to the Falls Saturday.

B. H. Greenwood has returned to Oklahoma.

Mrs. York's boarders will leave for their home in Apopha, Fla., this week.

Geo. L. Dorsey is off to Gainesville this week.

Prof. Fox delivered an address to the people here Saturday night.

Miss Carrie Grist is convalescent.

Willie Franks is with his sister Mrs. Garland.

§   Court of Ordinary, Rabun County. Sitting for county purposes At Chambers.

It is ordered that, a tax of eighty cents, (.80) on the one hundred dollars of the taxable property of said county as per digest of 1902, be and the same is hereby levied, and that the same [be] collected by the Tax Collector of [said] county, for the following purposes, to wit:

1st To pay all the legal indebtedness of said county, due or to become due, 11 cents on each...

2nd To repair the court house, jail or any other public improvement, 1c on each...

3rd To pay sheriffs, jailers or any other officer that may be entitled, 15 cents on each...

4th To pay coroners all fees that may be due them for holding inquests, etc., 1c on each...

5th To pay bailiffs at courts, non-resident witnesses, fuel, etc., 3c on each...

6th To pay jurors per diem compensation, 17c[?] on each...

7th To pay the expenses of the county in supporting the poor, 12c on each...

8th To pay the salaries, working and improving the public roads of the county, 20c on each...

Making in the aggregate the [missing] sum of eighty cents on the one hundred dollars of the taxable property [missing] said county, for county purposes, [missing] the year 1902. This 20th day of September, 1902.

W. S. Long, Ordinary.

§   Hon. M. L. Ledford, of Blairsville, candidate for senator, is expected to-morrow.

§   Little Beth Long has been sick for a week or more.

§   Vote for the Hon. M. L. Ledford Wednesday.

§   To the delight of the citizens of the town the hogs have about all disappeared from the streets of late.

§   It has been summer weather again.

§   To-morrow is the reunion of the old soldiers. Big preparations are being made to feed the crowd. Hundreds of pounds of meats will be served and a general good time is expected.

§   Everett Earl is "on his feet" again.

§   Come out to the gathering tomorrow.

§   The chinquapin crop in this county is usually good this year. It is feared the squirells [sic] will destroy most of the chestnuts.

§   There will be several sick men after the general election Wednesday.

§   Vote for the best man Wednesday, and do your duty.

§   Mrs. J. S. Ramey spent a few days with her parents on Tiger, Mr. and Mrs. J. M. Ramey, last week.

§   We are having rainy weather this week, which does not go well with people's stacked fodder.

§   If you want to hear some fine music, hunt up and down Main street until you find a certain young lady with blue eyes and brown hair who lives opposite our office, find the banjo and your desire will be granted.

§   Send me the news from every nook and corner of Rabun county. We want it. If it is nothing more than foolishness it will be read with interest by some.

§   Judge Long spent yesterday on Tiger, looking over the public road in that district.

§   J. T. Long went up to his farm on Scott's Creek yesterday and returned with a load of apples for home use.

§   Marion Long killed four squirrells Tuesday evening.

§   Mrs. J. F. Earl has returned home from Walhalla, S. C.

§   Rev. Geo. Brown filled his appointment at the Baptist church here Saturday and Sunday. Rev. Brown is an excellent pastor.

§   A small crowd turned out to clean off the cemetery Saturday, but those present worked faithfully, and as a result our graveyard is much improved in appearance. A larger number is wanted on the second Saturday in October, as the people want to finish the work then.

§   Miss Susie Long and Mrs. J. R. Grant took a pleasant drive out in Tennessee Valley a few evenings ago.

§   Dutch Henson, of Tiger is real sick.

§   Superintendent J. I. Langston is working one hundred hands on the public road between here and Tallulah Falls this week.

§   Miss Blanch Wall, who has been sick for some time, we are glad to report convalescent.

§ Mart Wall has moved his tools from near the Falls back to Clayton, and will shoe horses here for a while.

§ John Burton is not feeling as well as usual.

§ Bailiff Mart Wall butchered a yearling yesterday morning.

§ Sol McKinney, the popular dry goods drummer, was in town this week.

§ Lee Ritchie went to North Carolina yesterday.

§ John Harkins passed through town Tuesday evening with a drove of 60 head of sheep. He is taking them to Lenton Williams, of Athens, Ga.

§ Cannon and Thompson, Tiger's progressing merchants, have bought already 25 bushels of chinquapins. They bought 17 bushels in one day and 12 from one man. This is the biggest chinquapin business we have ever heard of.

§ Mrs. Emily Wall is expecting a visit from her brother, Judge Logan E. Bleckley, of Clarkesville, this month.

§ Harve Penland, colored, returned from a peddling trip to Hartwell, Ga., Saturday night.

§ John McCurry, of Tennessee Valley, passed through town yesterday going to Athens with a load of cabbage, apples, chestnuts and chinquapins.

§ Miss Lula Parker, of Persimmon, who has been here for medical treatment for some time, is about well again, and expects to return home in a few days.

§ J. E. Derrick has some nice looking cabbage and beets in his garden.

§ Asbury Owens, of White county, Ga., is visiting his cousin, D. G. Dover, on Black-rock mountain, for a few days.

§ The revenue officers captured a still, cap and condenser in the Tennessee Valley last Friday. The outfit was unusually new.

§ Dr. Green reports all his patients in the county as doing fairly well.

§   L. T. Mitchell is engaged in putting a coat of paint on his residence one mile south of town.

§   The many friends of Mrs. D. L. Parker will be glad to hear that she is greatly improved.

§   R. H. Parker, of Persimmon, came to town Monday to see his daughter, who is here for medical treatment, and brought with him five bushels of green beans. He sold nearly all of them here.

§   Prof. J. Marcus Bleckley was in town yesterday.

§   Ex-Sheriff Webb Johnson, of Hart county, came up yesterday. He will be on his farm about ten days before he returns. Mr. W. A. Profitt accompanied him and will likely make this county his future home.

§   At this season of the year thousands of butterflies are going in a southwesterly direction. For ten years we have noticed them going this way. They are large and yellow with black and white spots. Where they go and their mission we would like to know. They travel at the rate of about ten miles an hour, and at this rate would go across the state in about three days.

§   Quite a number of boarders from Florida that have spent the summer with W. T. York left for their homes Monday.

§   John Dotson and John Pelfry killed ten squirrells and one groundhog Saturday.

§   Next Wednesday is the general election.

§   Tom and Lee Ritchie went through town Monday with thirty head of cattle and sixty head of sheep for the market.

§   A singular incident happened at the home of Patton Queen Thursday of last week. Mrs. Queen was roasting a gourd for the purposes of making a dipper of it and it exploded, throwing the fire, and burning two of their children, one of them, five years old, was badly burned.

§   As will be seen elsewhere in our columns, the Hon. M. L. Ledford, of Union county, democratic nominee for senator of the fortieth senatorial district, has opposition in the person of Mc G. Colwell, who is an independent candidate for this honorable position. We are informed that Mr. Colwell has been repeatedly honored by the party which he now seeks to demoralize. Union county has stood nobly by our nominees in the past and Rabun democracy will stand by Union now.

§   To the people of Rabun county: Through a desire to remove from its present unfortunate position in the county what is known as the national quarantine line, and my position as local inspector of cattle forcing me to give that subject my undivided attention for the last four weeks, and the further misfortune of the serious sickness with Typhoid fever of my sister-in-law who is now at my house, I am forced to withdraw from the race of clerk of the Superior court. From the depths of my heart I thank my many friends for their kind assurance of support and hope to be placed in a position in the future to return the same. Respectfully, Miles C. Canup.

§   Chechero.
The people are beginning to make up syrup.
Prof. V. A. Green is teaching again, after a vacation of three weeks of fodder.
Mr. J. H. Taylor is very ill at this time.
Miss Hannie Whitmire who has been very sick with Typhoid fever, is convalescent.
Miss Zelma Price began teaching again after vacating for fodder.
The school house at Lower Chechero is about completed.
We hear Miss Mattie Price has toothache very badly.
Miss Ella Ramey entertained a crowd of young folks the 3rd Saturday night.

§   Stonepile.
Rain every few days.
Syrup making and fodder pulling is the order of the day.
We have failed to see any passing lately, as it is done mostly in the night. The people are in a terrible hurry and no one to throw on the brakes. We fear some will runaway up hill with the trucks. Everything is pushing—cane making, sheep shearing, pea picking, rye sowing and the mill to go to. A man hardly has time to pick the beef out of his teeth. When he has it, as a rule he swallows the last bite and leaves the table— and that is about all that is left. I guess we will adopt the McCrackin plan of living, and eat dried apples for breakfast, drink warm water for dinner and pap for supper. That is the way Uncle John McCrackin said to do when in a hurry.
Mr. Ritchie was around shaking up the boys one day last week.
Mr. Wm. Beard killed a large rattlesnake last week.
We wish some correspondent would report up our sick friends on Checheroe and Kerbytown, as we would like to hear from them.

§   Grove.

Rain plenty.

The farmers are very anxious about pulling fodder and seeding.

Mr. J. M. Arrendale is off to market with a load of produce.

John Carter, of Creede, was among relatives in this community Wednesday.

Mr. M. L. Arrendale returned Wednesday from Atlanta, where he has been for treatment, with his health much improved.

Rev. E. H. Baker went to Clayton Thursday.

Sheriff J. R. Ritchie was in this community summoning jurors for the next term of court.

Mr. J. Baker captured a fine fox the other night while it was trying to catch his chickens.

Success to the Tribune.

§   Popcorn.

The Bible says it shall rain on the just and unjust. We are having ours now during fodder time but then we did not say we are the unjust.

Elisha Canup, of Soque, visited his brother Sunday.

Vicey Burton, who has been confined to her room sometime with Typhoid fever, is improving.

M. C. York and family, of Clarkesville, were on the Creek Sunday.

Rev. M. A. Dills has resigned the pastorship of Cross Roads church. Rev. Frank Eller officiating in his stead.

Otto York is contemplating taking Horace Greely's advice ere long.

There is a magnet in the shape of Mollie S. that draws Miles Thompson to Towns county, we fear there will be a contract shortly.

October 2, 1902
Volume 5, Number 38

§ W. J. Burrell, of Pine Mountain, rolled us the wheel on subscription Friday.

§ In the receipt [*sic*] for a snake bite of a few issues ago, we erred when we said snake root. It should have read piney snake root.

§ Our good friend J. A. Walker, of Cornelia, who has for thirty years been a trusted employee of the Southern and Tallulah Falls Railway, was here Wednesday, was here Thursday and Friday of last week in the interest of The Tallulah Falls railroad. Mr. Walker has been superintendent of bridge and trestles for more than nine years for the Tallulah Falls road.

§ W. K. Rhodes will make one thousand pounds of tobacco this year on a three-acre tract of new ground one mile from town. Mr. Rhodes says he will get two hundred and fifty dollars for the crop, leaving enough out for home use, and that he was offered one hundred and fifty dollars for it green. This is the largest crop of tobacco we have ever[?] heard of in this county, but "Kirk" says he is going to [illegible].

§ W. F. Roane left for Atlanta last Friday, and will be the guest of his children there for a month.

§ Sine Donaldson returned from the Flats Friday evening, where he has been at work for five weeks, building houses.

§ Mrs. Jesse McCurry is still in feeble health.

§ Harry Duncan took in the excursion to Atlanta Saturday.

§ The people on Scott's Creek are busy making syrup. It is estimated that W. H. Holcomb will make one hundred gallons, and that Ed Alman will make over two hundred gallons.

§ Jesse Dunlap returned from a trip to Walhalla, S. C., Saturday night.

§ W. S. Erwin, General Manager of the Tallulah Falls Ry., was in town Friday. He was accompanied by J. J. Bowden, a prominent attorney of Clarkesville. They were guests of the Blue Ridge.

§ O[?]. W. McDade, the timber man, is registered at the Parker House.

§ [Prof?]. Foster spent Saturday and Sunday with home folks on Burton.

§ J. [illigeble]. Langston, of Whetstone, S. C., was here at the barbecue Friday.

§ J. M. Atkinson, of Asheville, N. C., was registered at the Parker Hotel last week.

§ Mrs. J. M. York and family, of Scott's Creek, spent Friday night with Mrs. W. S. Long.

§ J. R. Grant went to Checheroe [*sic*] Saturday.

§ [---ford] Taylor and Jim Dockins[?], of Tallulah Falls, were the [illegible] of Mr. H. K. Cannon and [illegible] Friday night.

§ [---nn] Burton is well again.

§ Mr. D. W. Johnson, of Hartwell, Ga., who came up to Rabun last week to look over his farm at the Ridge, left Saturday for his home.

§ Judge Logan E. Bleckley and wife, of Clarkesville, Ga., came up Saturday to spend a few days in his native county.

§ Mr. Dyer, the picture taker, who spent several months in Clayton, is here again, after a tour in S. C.

§ Mr. and Mrs. J. F. Earl, with their charming daughters Miss Nora and Leila, spent Sunday on Chechero.

§ Mrs. Andy Ritchie passed through town Monday morning en route to her home in Waco, Texas. She was accompanied by Mrs. Frank Ritchie, of the Valley, who is going to Texas to join her husband out there.

§ Mr. S. W. Dover has been engaged painting his residence.

§ Money Order Lost.
   Lost—Between Clayton and Tennessee Valley, on the public road last Friday evening the 26th, money order No. 1114, amount thirty dollars. Finder will please return same to D. T. Duncan Clayton, or R. L. Ritchie, Rabun Gap, Ga. It will do no good to keep it.

§ Col. Paris attended justice's court on Chechero on Sunday.

§ Jack Duncan, of Whetstone, S. C., took in the barbecue here Friday.

§ Send us the news and we will assure we will print it.

§ H. K. Cannon is preparing to make up syrup.

§ Always sign your name to your communications.
   Did you ever see anyones [*sic*] name signed to a letter in our paper.

§ "Jimmy," a little rabbit, the companion of Prisoners Sam Welborne and Bill Gilds for five months, got in behind the jail ceiling Sunday and has not been captured up to this day (Monday). "Jimmy" was placed in jail for the offense of stealing cabbage, and as a penalty for desertion the boys say he will be barbecued when caught. We ask for a hind quarter if he is ever captured alive.

§ Seven wagons were seen in a drove here Monday going down the country.

§ Notice to Teachers.
   1 Make out your report in pen and ink.
   2 Make it for the first two months taught.
   3 Have it in my office by the first Tuesday in Oct. next, the 7th.
   4 Be certain to have it signed by an officer authorized to administer an oath.
   A. A. O'Kelley, C. S. Com.

§ Mr. Turner Page, of Wolffork, with his sons Charlie and Jess, each with a load of apples and produce, passed through town Monday en route "down the country."

§   A number of our citizens and young people attended the baptizing on Burton last Sunday. About nineteen were baptized.

§   Hamp Nimmons, one of our colored readers, has been suffering with a severe blood boil on his face for several days.

§   V. C. Taylor, of Tiger, who has been sick with fever, is doing nicely.

§   L. M. Robins left Monday for Atlanta with his daughter Katie, and will put her in a school for the deaf at Cave Springs, Ga., before returning.

§   Mrs. W. C. Norton is still feeling badly.

§   W. E. Long, Eugene Mozely and Carlton York, of Scott's Creek, left with a load of apples and produce Monday, for down the country.

§   D. L. Parker went to Atlanta on the excursion Saturday.

§   Miles Parker and Miss Ida Ford took in the baptizing on Burton Sunday.

§   Trespass Notice. The public are hereby warned not to trespass on land lots Nos. 74, 75 and 94 in the second land district, by gathering chestnuts, chinquapins, fruit and no other way trespassing. Catherine Page.

§   Rabun county land seems to be increasing in value, and is in greater demand now than for many years past. One of our citizens informs us that he has been asked to pick out two or three farms for one man, in one district of Rabun county. The man is expected here any day to purchase.

§   We are in receipt of a letter from G. S. & F. M. Scofield of Atlanta, who contemplate building a Trolley Line from Atlanta, Roswell, Alpharetta, Cummings, Dawsonville, Dahlonega, Cleveland, Tallulah Falls to Cornelia and in all probability an advertisement for application for charter will appear in our columns at an early date.

We do hope this road will be built for the grandeur of our mountain scenery, our rich agricultural landsand our excellent mineral deposits and coal, will then become known to the world, and this very section of Georgia will then be the most noted in the state. All that is required to place us in the front ranks of prosperity is that others know what we have in store.

What encouragement can you give the proposed road? Could you not afford to give one half present value of your property that it might increase its value three times within two years? Most certainly we can, but this will not be asked of us, however, let us each and every one put our shoulders to the wheel at the propert time and this road will be a success, and our very desirable mountain country will become the "Garden spot of the State."

Cleveland Courier

§   Grove.

Rain pleney [*sic*].

News scarce.

A. J. Carter and Bud Gosnell, of Creede, were at Grove Sunday.

J. M. Marsingale was in this community Monday looking after votes.

Candidate W. F. Holden was at Grove Sunday.

Everything brought a good price at the sale Wednesday.

Rev. E. H. Baker went to Clayton Friday.

Success to the Tribune.

§   Warwoman.

Fodder pulling is at hand. The boys are having a jolly old time in it.

The candidates are visiting this creek.

Two boys went coon hunting last night and caught a rabbit in under an old pine tree.

Ask Julius Beck where he went Sunday.

The revenues [*sic*] have done a great deal of damage on Dick's Creek lately.

Miss Gussie Ledford is improving at this writing.

Miss Dovie Williams has a wound on her foot and is not able to teach school.

Mr. T. C. Kell went to Chechero Sunday with one of the candidates.

Miss Lena Bleckley has gone to her school at Germany.

John Turpen was down on the creek Sunday.

A boy caught a fox Saturday morning.

§   For sale. One lot of land, 490 acres more or less, No. 64 in the first land district. Twenty five acres of bottom land on said lot, with one good double room house with two fireplaces. One good grist mill, good barn, corn-crib and stables, all under roof. A good garden and one hundred good bearing fruit trees. All for $850. Come and see it. Thomas Coleman, Quartz, Ga.

§   Georgia Crop Report. Issued by the State Agricultural Department. Comparison of Conditions. Some counties report crops unusually fine, but the great majority say they are considerably below average...

In the Three Sections. The condition of the various crops compared to an average for the various sections is as follows:

Northern Section—Cotton, 62 per cent; corn, 62 per cent; upland rice, 31 per cent; sweet potatoes, 64 per cent; tobacco, 52 per cent; cow peas, 67 per cent; ground peas, 68 per cent; forage crops, such as shredded corn, hay, etc., 63 per cent; number of hogs, 76 per cent; conditions of live stock, 83 per cent; sugar cane, 70 per cent...

§   Whence the Savannah Flows to the Sea. Mountainous Rabun, Its People and Its Prospects—"Old Hickory" and Governor Rabun. By J. H. Estill. From the Morning News, Sept. 21...

Rabun is a county of mountains. Look in any direction and you will see mountains piled upon mountains. And where there are mountains there must be valleys. The valleys of Rabun are the Tennessee, War Woman, Persimmon, Tiger Tail, and Simpson, which correspond in name with the nearby mountains, or the rock bottom streams meandering through their green fields of waving grain. I was there in the spring, when the days were bright and the air crisp, and the nights suggestive of overcoats and blankets.

Rabun county, though it has only a little piece of railroad, a half mile long I believe, is one of the best known sub-divisions of the state, not because of personal visits, but by reason of Rabun Gap in the Tennessee Valley being known as the lowest and best place for a railroad from the northwest to the southeast to cross the Blue Ridge mountains. The Rabun Gap Railroad was a dream of the people of Charleston and Savannah fifty years ago. It was financed in the former city whose merchants and capitalists sunk a million dollars or more in the great undertaking. The abandoned cuts, tunnels and stone viaducts in the mountains and valleys of Rabun county are monuments of their enterprise and memorials to their misfortunes.

The ruins of another great project of the past are seen in Rabun: that of a canal, a hobby of Gen. Miller, which was to unite the waters of the Tennessee with those of the Savannah river, so that boats could come from the Ohio and Mississippi rivers to Savannah, and return the same way. That project was another irridescent [*sic*] dream.

A railroad through Rabun Gap is about to be realized by an extension of the Tallulah Falls Railroad, from Cornelia to Tallulah Falls through Rabun county into North Carolina. The project is to build to Franklin, N. C. via Clayton, the county seat. When it is completed there will doubtless be a rapid development as to agriculture and manufacturing, and a large increase in population in Rabun county.

There is another railroad projected[?] to Clayton. It is called the Tennessee, Georgia and South Carolina. It will begin at the eastern boundary of Rabun county and extend almost due west through the towns of Clayton in Rabun, Hiawassee and Young Harris in Towns county, Blairsville in Union county, and Blue Ridge in Fannin county, and thence to Charleston, Tenn. I don't know of any country where a railroad is more needed than that through which is projected, and I hope to live to see it built.

There are good crop-producing soils in the mountain sides and tops and in the valleys, but no cotton grows in Rabun: it is too high in the air for that. Corn, wheat, rye, oats, potatoes, rice and sugar cane do splendidly. Apples grow to perfection, Bermuda and all grasses, and do well, and there is excellent pasturage for cattle of all kinds.

The farm products according to the last census, for a year, were 300,000 gallons of milk and 70,000 pounds of butter, 50,000 eggs.

There are 37 schools for whites, and 2 for colored children; average attendance at the former 1,100, and the latter, 30.

The Baptist and Methodist churches furnish the religious food for the people, but the former, judging by the number of churches, are in the lead, the Baptist having 22 and the Methodist 10 churches. Other religions are practically unknown.

According to the census of 1900 the population of Rabun county is as follows: Chechero 570; War-Woman 367; Tallulah 1,137; Tennessee Valley 1,143; Clayton, including Clayton town 872; Clayton Town 190; Tiger, including Tallulah Falls town 530; Tallulah Falls town 134; Persimmon 699; Moccasin 525; Stonepile 442. Total 6,285.

The headwaters of the Savannah river are in Rabun. If one will take a canoe at Savannah and keep paddling up stream and meets with no accident in surmounting the cataracts, keeps off the rocks and follows the Savannah to the Tugaloo, and the Tugaloo to the Chatooga, and the latter to the Tallulah, his boat will be well up on top of the Blue Ridge, and by a portage of two or three miles through the Tennessee Valley, he can descend on the other side by way of the Little Tennessee river and paddle his way westward to Sioux City, Iowa, or even further! That would be quite a trip!

Leaving Savannah a hack that didn't come, and a car that was not on schedule, was the cause of my missing the night train on the Central of Georgia. I arrived at the depot in time to see the red lights rapidly disappearing from view towards Lincoln Park. So I did not get away until the next morning. One miss makes many, and at Cornelia I had to charter a locomotive and car to Tallulah Falls, where I spent the night so as to make an early start for Clayton. The road thither skirts the Falls for some distance, and then crosses them by means of an iron bridge. From there onward to Rabun's county seat, it is nothing but mountains, but the roads are good and safe. For a long distance the road lies along Tiger Creek, which at places is a mountain torrent tumbling over rocks and through crevices, and then again where the valley broadens, it is a quiet, meandering riverlet. Along this part of the road there are sites for thousands of picturesque mountain homes, and some day they will be there.

A long climb brought us in sight of the court house in Clayton and a sharp turn to the right from the direction we had been traveling and we were at the Wall House, kept by Mrs. Wall, a sister of that great Georgia jurist, Hon. Logan E. Bleckley, whose mountain home on Mt. Screamer overlooks the town, and of Col. F. A. Bleckley. We were guests of Mrs. Wall during our stay.

Clayton was named after Hon. A. S. Clayton. It was originally called Claytonville, but the people showed their good sense by cutting off the meaningless "ville."

The late Dr. H. V. M. Miller, the "Demosthenes of the Mountains," who was a surgeon of the Eighth Georgia Regiment, C. S. A., and after the war a Republican, and as such was elected U. S. Senator but never took his seat, was a Rabun county man, and I doubt if there was ever an abler man in Georgia than he. Good at everything he undertook, except his politics, he was a power in Upper Georgia. His memory is still kept green by the mountaineers.

Judge Estes presided over the court, [illegible] his permission I addressed the people at the recess hour. I had a large and attentive audience, and from the majority that Rabun gave me I think I must have made an impression upon my mountain friends.

Lounging on a veranda after tea, one of those characters, whom we read about but seldom meet, came up with some friends to see the Judge and the solicitor. After a round-about talk, it transpired that the visitor had a son who was to be tried for playfully shooting at a man who tried to arrest him. He told the judge "there was nothing in it judge, only a boy you know, just 23 years old, and he didn't hit him, just shot so, you know, judge, how boys do." It turned out that the judge knew his caller well. He had been a witness in a case when another party had put a rifle bullet through him. Recalling the incident and trial to the judge's memory, our mountain friend said, "I never blamed Jim for shooting me. He had to do it, judge. He thought I would shoot him, and I guess he might have been right about that, but he was afraid of me judge, and shot me before I had a chance, judge. Jim and I are friendly, judge. I came mighty near shooting him judge, but Jim was too quick. Jim is a right smart man, Judge. Judge, do what you can for my boy, he didn't hit Mr. ----, the ball just scraped his hair. Be easy with him, judge."

This story with variations was repeated over and over again for an hour, but the judge listened patiently to the father pleading for his boy.

I had the pleasure of meeting D. L. Duncan, Esq., the Proprieter of The Blue Ridge Hotel, one of the oldest citizens of Clayton and a gentleman of influence in Northeast Georgia.

I also met Messrs. J. S. Rainey, J. R. Ritchie, W. S. Long, J. M.

Massengale, J. F. Earl, J. I. Langston, J. A. Reynolds, Dr. W. J. Green, Dr. J. S. Dover of Clayton, James E. Bleckley, R. E. Cannon and H. C. Kirby of Tiger; Hillyer York, H. C. Blalock and Cicero Blalock of Burton; W. T. York, J. B. Dockins, W. C. Scruggs, John Scruggs, Andy Holden, W. R. L. Richie and T. J. Richie of Rabun Gap; John W. Green, A. J. Duncan and M. W. Swofford, and many others belonging to the families of Becks, Bleckleys and Cannons, who have been leading and progressive citizens of Rabun county since its organization.

Messrs. W. S. Paris, R. E. A. Hamby and Jas. A Grant comprise the local bar. Mr. Paris was an ardent supporter of mine.

The newspaper of Rabun and of the country for miles around is the Clayton "North Georgia Tribune," edited by J. A. Reynolds, Esq. The Tribune office is very compact and complete establishment, and the paper is carefully gotten up. Mr. Reynolds was my good friend in the campaign...

Clayton is a nice town, and though it is twenty-five miles by mountain roads from a railroad, I recommend it as one of those places where people from Lower Georgia should go in the summer. It has a bracing, health-giving climate, and the people are courteous and hospitable. Of course, nobody will be treated quite as well as a prospective Governor was, but the traveler can enjoy himself if he is not one of those fellows who will find fault with St. Peter if he ever gets to heaven.

I was told that the mountains are full of game, deer, bear and wild turkeys, and that the streams filled with trout afford splendid sport for the angler.

We arrived at Tallulah Falls at 12 m. [*sic*], and left at 2 p.m., for Turnersville. Mr. P. T. Shore, who is well known throughout the mountain country for the good teams he supplies to travlers, was very courteous to the gubernatorial party.

The hotels of Tallulah Falls are, the Cliff House, of which Messrs. Bain and Montgomery are proprietors; Tallulah Lodge, J. A. Newcomb, Esq., proprietor; the Willard House, Mrs. M. T. Barron, proprietor; the King House, Mr. C. C. King, proprietor; Glen Brook Cottage, Mrs. M. A. Hunnicutt, proprietor. During my visit I stopped at the King House.

The leading merchants are Messrs. H. R. Cannon, W. D. Taylor, R. W. Davison, J. R. Taylor, Hughlett & Co., C. L. Hughlett, T. C. Hampton, Fred Wagoner, and A. B. Long.

§   Dillard.

Mrs. Lura Ritchie leaves to-day for Wago, Texas, where she will join her husband, Mr. Frank Ritchie.

Several people from N. C. passed through here enroute to the barbecue at Clayton Friday.

Misses Arah and Maud Coffee were in the valley the latter part of last week.

Marlor Swofford, Jeff Beck and Julius were in the valley Sunday.

Thomas Kelley has returned from down the country.

Mr. Willie Holden is in the valley canvassing.

Miss Carrie Grist is still improving.

Little Fred Grist is better.

The people report a lively time at the barbecue.

Miss Bertha Scruggs has returned from Gillsville.

Mrs. Amanda Green and son Claude were in the valley last week.

Miss Ida Martin went to the Flats Sunday.

§ Col. Paris is suffering from an acute attack of cold.

§ Arthur McCurry is suffering from an abscess on knee joint.

§ Henry Cannon is quiet [*sic*] sick and has been feeling badly for two days.

§ Strayed from my premises last spring, a muly brindle steer yearling, two years old, crop and split and under bit in the left ear. Any information will be gladly received. W. J. Ramey, Checheroe [*sic*], Ga.

§ Eddie Page returned from the west Tuesday to stap.

§ In regard to a high school at Clayton, Prof. A. J. Ritchie writes us that he is receiving the most encouraging assurance of help for the school outside of the county, and that $1,000 proposed to raise will be forthcoming.

§ Old soldiers' day and the barbecue was a nice affair and in every way a fine success. The ladies did their part nobly. The crowd was large and so was the table. The dinner was spread and piled on a table about 150 feet long. The meats, the cooking of which was superintended by James M. Bell, were delicious. The ladies brung the dinner baskets filled with almost everything imaginable to eat, and smilingly handed it out to the hungry. We saw one lady pick up a cake that looked like a buggy wheel and she, with sweet smiles, sliced it up before she ceased and looked as if she was sorry she did not have a dozen more. We hollowed for a piece ourselves, but we were too late, but Mrs. J. F. Ritchie saw our trouble and we got the cake. Every body looked happy and we believe they were happy. The old soldiers were not an exception. There was a large crowd of them present and the 37 years since the civil war closed has brought most of them close to the grave, though many of them look well and comparatively young.

At the outset of this article we mention day and not night, when men "seek darkness rather than light, their deeds being evil." The stillness of the night was turned into a turmoil, and the sounds that went up from the public square sounded like a lot of raving maniacs. Some of the boys got too much booze and chose the streets and public square for their performance. We believe the whole push regret their conduct and we hope their dramatic act will not be repeated.

§ Wanted. Six energetic capable boys to hold six free scholarships in the Georgia School of Technology; to prepare for paying positions in Southern developments in railroading, mining, electricity, cotton milling, etc. Address, A. J. Ritchie, Waco, Texas.

§ Notice. All persons are hereby notified not to trespass on lot No. 45 in the second land district of Rabun county. James Alman.

§ Burton, Ga., Sept. 27, 1902.
According to appointment services were held at Tallulah Academy at 2 o'clock p.m. After an able sermon by Rev. Frank Loyd, of Mt. Scene, Ga., we proceeded to organize a church by the election of Rev. Frank Loyd Moderator, I. N. Foster Clerk and J. S. Burrell reading clerk. Called for letters and received the following: Eaf Arrendale, M. E. Blalock, Lizzie Blalock, Avery Blalock, Mary Arrendale, Luther Philyaw, G. H. King, V. T. Stonecypher, Wm. Stonecypher, Lucy Stonecypher, I. N. Foster, Edna Foster, J. F. Smith, Sarah Smith, Jas. Smith, J. L. Smith, Thos. Smith, C. A. Smith, S. E. Smith, M. A. Smith, G. E. Smith, R. W. Powell, Lucresia Powell, Bryant Hill, Lillie Hill, Lola Stonecypher.
On motion, resolved ourselves in to a Baptist church by the name of Tallulah Central. Then proceeded to read the articles of faith—on motion adopted the same.
Then read and on motion adopted the covenant.
Adjourned.
Erank [*sic*] Loyd, Mod. I. N. Foster, C. C.
Sunday services begun at 9 o'clock a.m.
The door of the church was opened and the following were received and baptized: John Arrendale, Thos. Powell, 62 years old, Emory Blalock, Augustus Arrendale, Cicero Blalock, Augustus Smith, Elijah King, Homer Denton, Marler Philyaw, Haman King, Hoke Smith, Carrie Blalock, Oda Galbreath, Cora Blalock, Tabitha Parker, Lizzie Tanner, Rozada Blalock.
After the baptismal services were over we went to the house and listened for 45 minutes to a glowing sermon delivered by Rev. Loyd.
The second Sunday in October was appointed for the purpose of ordaining deacons and electing a pastor.
There were supposed to be 700 people at the organization.

§   The election came off yesterday. The day was perfect and the crowd was manly and quiet. Some hard work was done by the friends of the candidates. The State ticket went through with flying colors and there was no opposition to the Democratic ticket, the Republicans voted with us like brothers. We will write up the newly elected officers later. Congratulations to victors and good wishes to the defeated. Below are the returns by distnals [*sic*].

§   Election Returns.

Clayton. Derrick, 150; Bleckley, 85; Baker, 2; Ramey, 218; Ritchie, 68; Dockins, 47; Parker, 65; Carver, 68; Holden, 131; Smith, 115; Marsingale, 146; York, 102; Green, 183; Hollified, 59; McConnell, 51; Welborne, 93; Reynolds, 83; Howard, 6.

Dillard. Derrick, 92; Bleckley, 11; Baker, 2; Ramey, 102; Ritchie, 44; Dockins, 35; Parker, 10; Carver, 12; Smith, 15; Holden, 91; Marsingale, 34; York, 71; Hollifield, 24; Green, 79; McConnell, 23; Welborne, 3; Reynolds, 25.

Stonepile. Derrick, 47; Bleckley, 16; Baker, [blank]; Ramey, 52; Ritchie, 14; Dockins, 22; Parker, 5; Carver, 21; Smith, 60; Holden, 5; Marsingale, 41; York, 23; Hollifield, 17; Green, 45; McConnell, [blank]; Welborne, [blank]; Reynolds, 15.

Tallulah. Derrick, 143; Bleckley, 9; Baker, 10; Ramey, 144; Ritchie, 46; Dockins, 32; Parker, 66; Carver, 15; Holden, 67; Smith, 89; Marsingale, 78; York, 80; Green, 91; Hollifield, 59; Howard, 74.

Tiger. Derrick, 18; Bleckley, 59; Baker, 1; Ramey, 84; Ritchie, 16; Dockins, 20; Parker, 0; Carver, 53; Smith, 79; Holden, 11; Marsingale, 75; York, 14; Hollifield, 9; Green, 81; McConnell, 32; Welborne, [0]; Reynolds, 45.

Chechero. Derrick, 26; Bleckley, 39; Ritchie, 7; Carver, 60; Holden, 20; Smith, 47; Marsingale, 51; York, 15; Green, 62; Hollifield, 4; Welborne, [blank]; McConnell, 27; Reynolds, 32.

Persimmon. Derrick, 80; Bleckley, 5; Baker, [blank]; Ramey, 72; Ritchie, 17; Dockins, 2; Parker, 63; Carver, 2; Smith, 31; Holden, 57; Marsingale, 12; York, 67; Hollifield, 48; Green, 84; McConnell, 41; Welborne, [blank]; Reynolds, 26.

Moccasin. Derrick, 19; Bleckley, 47; Baker, [blank]; Ramey, 52; Ritchie, 5; Dockins, 15; Parker, 27; Carver, 21; Smith, 3; Holden, 65; Marsingale, 51; York, 17; Hollifield, 8; Green, 59; McConnell, 19; Welborne, [blank].

Warwoman. Derrick, 26; Bleckley, 18; Baker, [blank]; Ramey, 43; Ritchie, 4; Dockins, 17; Parker, 3; Carver, 20; Smith, 14; Holden, 33; Marsingale, 30; York, 16; Hollifield, 4; Green, 43; McConnell, 15; Welborne, 1; Reynolds, 14.

§   Stecoah Creek.

School is progressing nicely at Wolf-pen Gap.

Little Ola Taylor, who has been very ill, is well again.

Miss Susie Taylor is staying with her brother V. C. Taylor.

Mr. Jeff McCrackin is making syrup.

Mr. Jable Cannon visited on the creek Sunday.

Mr. G. M. Williams was in this community last Sunday.

We hear Mr. Julius Taylor is very ill with typhoid fever.

We are glad to hear Mr. J. H. Taylor is improving.

§   Chechero.

Miss Maud Coffee went to Clayton last Sunday.

Mr. V. C. Taylor is convalescent.

Miss Zelma Price's school is progressing nicely.

A party visited Stecoah Falls on Stecoah creek last Sunday and report a nice time.

Miss Mattie Price was not at Bethel Sunday.

Mr. Bren Coffee went to Bethel Sunday.

Prof. V. A. Green's school is progressing nicely.

§   Ivory Hill. (Colored School.)

We have decided to write at last.

School is progressing nicely.

Master Newton and Miss Nora Gipson, of Dillard, have entered school here.

Mr. C. H. Fisher, of Franklin, N. C., and son B. C. Fisher, of Tallulah Falls, spent Saturday night with M. W. Bleckley.

Mr. C. E. Bleckley, who has been very ill since he came home from Florida, is some better.

Quite a number of our school and citizens attended meeting in the valley Saturday and Sunday, and report good preaching and a nice time.

Ask Miss Hattie Harper how she likes the rail road boys.

Carrie Bleckley is at Clayton this week.

There is a certain young man came up from the rail road with a horse and buggy to carry a certain girl to the valley Sunday, but by some reason he did not get to take her. He passed on looking very sad and was seen carrying the girl's mother and Aunt Harriet Bleckley.

Ask Miss May Bleckley why she is called "daughter."

October 16, 1902
Volume 5, Number 40

§ Mr. J. F. Earl sold one hundred bushels of apples in one day this week.

§ Chestnuts fell from two dollars [illegible] dollar [per bushel?] Monday [illegible].

§ What is the matter with our correspondents? We have only one letter this week. With such as that to contend with can we make our paper interesting? We offer every inducement we can to correspondents, but nothing seems [to] move them. Oh! but a printer's life is one of milk and honey!

§ Mrs. D. L. Parker, who has been confined to her room for two weeks, is able to be out again.

§ Lost, strayed or stolen. One heifer, one year old, black, white spot near the tail. Mark one smooth crop and one overbit in each ear. Any information as to the whereabouts of heifer will be gladly received by W. E. Swofford, Clayton, Ga.

§ D. L. Parker went to Burton yesterday.

§ Mrs. George Brown, of Tennessee valley, visited Mrs. Parker last Monday.

§ Mrs. J. E. Bleckley is suffering from a severe attack of rheumatism.

§   Hereafter there will be an hour of singing at the Baptist Church Sunday evening at three o'clock.

§   While climbing after chestnuts Sunday John Pelfrey fell out of a tree and hit a bush he had topped, painfully hurting him.

§   Tom Bleckley, who was among a crowd of young people Sunday fell from a tree and could not walk home.

§   Miss Leila Cannon is spending the latter part of the week with her Aunt, Mrs. Emily Wall.

§   Mr. Roy Buchanan, of Elf, N. C., spent Saturday night and Sunday with his Uncle J. F. Earl's family.

§   Miss Emily Wall, we are sorry to report, has a severe attack of rheumatism.

§   We ask readers to excuse the appearance of the Tribune this week. We assure you "it shall not be" again. To our friends we apologize for our blank side. To borrowers and critics we do not. With the support our paper receives you cannot grumble. Remember "to err is human, to forgive divine."

§   Dillard.
   Muddy roads.
   It continues to rain.
   You will have to excuse your correspondent for not writing last week as we were sick.
   Ed Marsingale and John Green were in the valley Sunday (on very important business we supposed).
   Harry Duncan and Chance Vickers passed the Valley Sunday.
   Mr. Porter Green passed through here en route to N. C., Friday.
   Misses Eula and Lizzie Dillard were with home folks Saturday and Sunday.
   Prof. Burrell filled Rev. Brown's place here Sunday.
   Miss Carrie Grist is at home now.
   Miss T. Kelley has returned to her home at Franklin N. C.
   John Holden has moved to the Flatts.
   John Godfrey has made 109 gallons of syrup and still making.
   George Dorsey is off to Gainesville this week.

§   All persons are hereby notified not to enter or trespass in any way on the inclosed [sic] lands where we now reside, it being part of lot No. 1 in the third land district in Rabun county. All persons are further notified not to trespass in any way upon the inclosed of said lot No. 1 by cutting, blazing or marking timber or in any other way whatever. This Oct. 15th, 1902. Mrs. A. A. Swofford, E. D. Swofford.

§ Memorial of Lieutenant F. A. Bleckley.

We, the undersigned committee appointed, submit the following report:

Whereas it has [pleased?] the [great?] Ruler of the universe to call from this earth to the Great Beyond our comrade and brother, Lieutenant F. A. Bleckley, therefore we submit the following resolutions upon the death of our beloved leader and comrade, upon mentioning the following facts:

Lieutenant F. A. Bleckley was born December 6th, 1824, and departed this life August 2nd 1902, aged 77 years. Lieutenant Bleckley was married to Miss Sarah Coffee on the 16th day of March, 1848. The issue of their marriage was six sons and seven daughters.

Lieutenant Bleckley enlisted in Company F, 11th Georgia Cavalry Confederate States of America, and was in Hannon's Brigade, army of the Western Division. Lieutenant Bleckley enlisted in May 25th, 1864, and went out under the command of Capt. W. C. Price. Lieutenant Bleckley was engaged with the enemy in the following battles: At Waynesborough [and?] Jonesborough, Ga., and [illegible] S. C.

Lieutenant Bleckley was a native of Rabun county and spent his entire life here in the service of his comrades and neighbors and for the advancement of his county, and county interests.

Lieut. Bleckley represented this county in the legislature and was Ordinary of Rabun county. Also, he was one of the charter members of Rabun Gap Lodge F. and A. M. No. 265 and was also a Royal Arch Mason. As a legislator, as ordinary, and as a Mason, he was true to his trust, and loyal to his every trust and to his friends, therefore be it

Resolved, first, by this, the United Confederate Veterans of Rabun County, that in the death of Lieutenant F. A. Bleckley, our beloved brother, neighbor and comrade, we have lost a true neighbor, brother and comrade, and that we greatly feel his loss. However, we humbly submit to the will of the great "I am," and humbly bow thereto. And look forward to the time when we shall be again united with our comrade.

2nd. That a copy of these resolutions be spread upon the minutes of the meeting, that a copy be furnished by the secretary to The Clayton Tribune for publication, and to the widow and family of our departed comrade.

This Oct. 7th 1902. M. W. Swofford, Chairman. T. N. McConnell, J. E. Derrick, John W. Green, Jas. R. Grant, Committee.

§   Notice. All of the stockholders of the Masonic Building are requested to meet at the Masonic Hall on Oct. 17th, 1902, at 9 o'clock A. M., to transact some important business. Take due notice and act accordingly. This Oct. 7th 1902. D. T. Duncan, Committeeman.

§   Real Estate.
We are in the real estate business...
1700 acres wild land, good hunting and mountain trout streams. Cliff and cave the line. 100 acres improved, 30 acres of bottom. Residence common, good barn, woodland well timbered. Easy terms to purchasers.
One tract of land. 490 acres, three fine water powers one large creek, good farmhouse, out-buildings, 1 grist mill and saw mill, good white oak and pine timber. 15 acres of bottom land, good orchard of about 100 trees. [One] and one half miles from Chattooga, a good fishing stream. Price $1300. Also 200 acres partly improved on public road. Price $650 acres.

§   Notice. Georgia—Rabun County.
Will be sold in said county on the 28th day of October 1902 between the hours of 10 o'clock a.m. and 4 o'clock p.m. at public outcry at the late residence of Samuel M. Beck, deceased, to the highest bidder, all of the perishable property of said Samuel M. Beck, embracing his stock of mules, cattle, hogs, provisions of every kind, and all his plantation tools etc.
Terms of sale. All amounts under $5 cash. All amounts over $5 note with approved security with 8 per cent interest from date, and due six months after date. This Oct. 13th 1902, M. V. Beck, J. D. Beck, Administrators of the estate of S. M. Beck.

§   Georgia—Rabun County.
To whom it may concern: H. C. Blalock, having made application to me in due form to be appointed administrator upon the estate of N. C. Nichols, late of said county deceased, notice is hereby given that said application will be heard at the regular term of the court of Ordinary for said county, to be held on the first Monday in December, 1902.
Witness my hand and official signature this 9th day of October 1902. W. S. Long, Ordinary.

§   Georgia—Rabun County.
To whom it may concern: M. V. Beck and J. D. Beck, having made application to me in due form to be appointed administrators upon the estate of S. M. Beck late of said county, notice is hereby given that said application will be heard at the regular term of the court of Ordinary for said county, to be held on the first Monday in December, 1902.

Witness my hand and official signature this 9th day of October 1902. W. S. Long, Ordinary.

§   Georgia—Rabun County.

J. E. Derrick has applied for exemption of personalty, and setting apart and valuation of homestead, and I will pass upon the same at 10 o'clock a.m., on the third day of November, 1902, at my office. This Oct. 13th, 1902. W. S. Long, Ordinary.

§   Sheriff's Sales. Georgia—Rabun county.

Will be sold, at the first Tuesday in Nov'r next, at public outcry at the court-house in said county, within the legal hours of sale, to the highest bidder for cash, certain property, of which this is a full and complete description: Part of land lot No. 38 in the fifth land district of Rabun county, containing sixty acres, more or less, and bounded as follows, to-wit: Bounded on the south by lands of Joe Watts, on the west by lands of William Watts, bounded on the north by lands of G. W. Long estate and on the east by lands of J. L. Henson and John Crone, and known as the old Charlie Derrick place. Levied on under and by virtue of and to satisfy a tax fi fa issed from the Superior Court of said county in favor of Sarah L. Sams, for the use of officers of the Superior Court against J. E. Derrick. Said property levied on as the property of the defendant J. E. Derrick and in his possession. Said property pointed out by plaintiff in fi fa. Written notice given the defendant in terms of the law. Levy made and returned to me by E. L. McConnell, Deputy Sheriff.

Also at the same time and place part of lot of land No. 2 in the fifth land district of said county and bounded as follows: Commencing on Big Branch, original line, thence east to a persimmon, thence to top of mountain at L. D. Echol's line, thence Echols line west to the old trail that crosses the mountain; thence down the branch to the beginning corner, containing one hundred (100) acres more or less. Levied on and to be sold as the property of James Gaines by virtue of a fi fa issued by the Superior Court of said county, in favor of Henry Perry and Walter Dickson, for costs. Notice of levy given in terms of the law. Levy made and returned to me by E. L. McConnell, Deputy Sheriff. This Oct. 7th 1902.

Also at the same time and place one Peerless Engine, four to six horse power engine. Also one Kentucky shingle mill. Said mill sold to me by J. S. Carter. Said property levied upon under and by virtue of and to satisfy a mortgage fi fa issued from the Superior Court of said county in favor of J. S. Carter and against the defendants M. B. Ramey and J. D. Woodall. Said property being the property described in said mortgage fi fa and in possession of the said defendants. This 7th day of October 1902.

Also at the same time and place, parts of lots of land No. 18, 19 and 20 situated and being in the fourth land district of Rabun county, Ga., and bounded as follows: On the north by lands of A. M. Jones and Drew Smith, on the east by lands of John Denney, on the south by lands of L. V. Cannon, and west by lands of Mrs. Canada. Also parts of lots of land No. 18, 19 and 20 in the fourth land district of Rabun county and bounded as follows: On the north and east by lands of Jackson Smith, on the south by lands of J. W. Harvey, and west by lands of Allen Turpin, containing 300 acres more or less. Also lot of land No. 4 in the 4th land district of Rabun county and bounded by lands of John Smith, Mrs. Canada and the estate of F. A. Bleckley, containing 50 acres more or less. This land is well timbered. Also part of lot of land No. 22 in the fourth land district of Rabun county, Ga., and bounded on the north and east by lands of Jim Ramey and on the south and west by lands of Wm. Ramey. All these tracts to-gether containing three hundred and sixty five acres more or less. Mineral of all kinds can be found in these lands. Situated on No. 20 is a fine grist mill with good water power, and a good saw mill and shingle mill; also a jig saw and turning lath, all in good running condition. There is also situated on this lot (No. 20) a good two-story house, with a stone chimney and two good fire places and adjoined by a good barn and stables, with outbuildings, and a good orchard. All this land is well timbered, with forty or fifty acres of good improved land.

Said property levied on as the property of Miles Phillips, J. S. Denney and L. V. Cannon, to satisfy a mortgage execution issued from the Superior Court of said county in favor of Nathaniel Phillips and R. B. Collins against Miles Phillips, J. S. Denney and L. V. Cannon. This October 7th 1902.

J. R. Ritchie, Sheriff.

§   Georgia—Rabun County.

By virtue of an order of the court or the court [*sic*] of ordinary of said county, will be sold, at public outcry, on the first Tuesday in November, 1902, at the court house in said county, between the usual hours of sale, the following real estate in said county, to wit:

A certain piece of land, being a part of lot No. 59 in the thirteenth land district of said county, and described as follows: Adjoining lands of Stambaugh on the east, O. G. Porter on the south, T. A. Wilbanks on the west and C. T. Wilbanks on the north, containing 200 acres more or less. Seven popular [*sic*] trees on said land, marked to Stone & Co., not included in this sale. Terms cash.

This Sept. 22, 1902. T. S. Wilbanks, Adminstrator of J. H. Wilbanks, deceased.

§   Notice to the public. The public are warned not to trespass on my premises comprising the parts of lots 53 and 54 in the 4th land district of

Rabun county by hunting, fishing or any other way. Oct. 8th 1902. J. M. Swofford.

§   All persons are warned not to trespass on parts of lots of land Nos. 100 and 101 in the second land district of Rabun county Ga., by hunting, fishing or in any other way. John Keener.

§   See Ritchie's new line of clothing and overcoats.

October 30, 1902
Volume 5, Number 42

§ Miss Effie Duncan says she got a turnip out of her garden one day last week that weighed five pounds.

§ Mr. and Mrs. J. S. Ramey returned from Atlanta Friday.

§ Mrs. H. J. Canup, of Soque, after spending a few days with her children, Mr. and Mrs. D. L. Parker, has returned home.

§ Mr. D. F. Soughard, of Pleasant Hill, Tennessee, was in town Tuesday. He was looking after hardwood timber and is in partnership with W. R. L. Ritchie, who will buy any hardwood timber you may have.

§ W. R. L. Ritchie spent Friday with home people in Tennessee valley.

§ The roads around Clayton are in very good condition now. At any rate, it seems they are being traveled extensively.

§ Mrs. Warren Dunlap has the finest turnip patch we have seen lately.

§ Mrs. W. G. Foster, of Habersham county, will spend a couple of weeks with her sister here, Mrs. Parker.

§ Prof. Virgil Green has been suffering for the last few days with relapse of fever, but is improving.

§   Rev. Landrum has closed his meeting at the Ridge church, with no conversions, we understand.

§   Mrs. Elic Parker and Mrs. M. O. Warlick, who have been at the Parker House (under treatment of our physicians for several days, have returned home.

§   Harry Duncan went to Tallulah Falls Friday.

§   Dr. J. C. Dover and John W. Green left Monday morning to attend a Masonic meeting at Macon Ga.

§   Jesse Langston, of Whetstone, S. C., spent the latter part of last week in town.

§   Miss Lula and Jane Parker, and Rufe and Elic Parker, of Persimmon, visited Mr. and Mrs. Parker a few days ago.

§   Mr. and Mrs. G. W. Allison, of Penrose, N. C., and patrons of The Tribune, have moved to Rabun, near the Falls.

§   Our paper has failed to arrive this week, and we are forced to issue half a sheet or be late.

§   W. K. Rhodes is off on a wagoning trip.

§   Tommy Roane went down to Atlanta last week.

§   Nin Ramey, the popular school teacher, was in the city Saturday.

§   J. C. Green was up from Turnerville Sunday.

§   Mrs. J. R. Ritchie and daughter Mary went to Franklin, N. C., Thursday and returned Friday.

§   D. L. Parker went over to Burton Thursday.

§   Mrs. S. S. Whitmire has been visiting Mrs. D. L. Garland, of Tennessee valley the past few days.

§   On Checheroe [*sic*], near J. M. Swofford's, Oscar Swofford was driving a team across a bridge eight feet from the water a few days ago, when a sleeper suddenly gave way, throwing mules, wagon and all in the creek. The wagon upset in mid-air and the mules hit the water sideways, one on the other. Swofford made a long leap and escaped with no serious injury. The mules, strange to say, also escaped unhurt.

§   Dr. Netherby, of Cornelia, Ga., Drummer Shephard, of Athens, Ga., Mail Route Contractor, Tanker, of London, Tenn., and John Godfrey, of Tennessee Valley, were among the guests of the Parker House last week.

§   J. M. Swofford, of Checheroe [*sic*], was in town Monday.

§   Miss Ada Green was in town Sunday.

§   Women constitute nine percent of the prisoners in the state of Georgia.

§   You will notice the people are requested to meet here on the 8th of November 1902, to take some action about our proposed college. We hope to see a large crowd out. If all will put their shoulder to the wheel there is no reason why Rabun should not have a high school.

§   Mr. H. K. Cannon, who has been sick for several days, is slightly improved.

§   Nelson Tilley went to Atlanta Friday.

§   Bert Paris spent Saturday and Sunday with home folk here.

§   Ned Shirley and S. T. Taylor were guests of The Parker House Friday.

§   Clerk J. S. Ramey has purchased a cow.

§   Rev. Warlick was in town a few ago [*sic*].

§   E. D. Swofford, of Warwoman, was in town Saturday.

§   We had a little cold weather Tuesday.

§   Miles and Henry Parker went to Soque Friday and returned Sunday.

§   Sheriff Ritchie attended the sale at the residence of Mrs. S. M. Beck, of Warwoman Tuesday.

§   Bill York and Jess Dunlap are off "down the country" with a load of apples.

§   D. L. Parker went over to Wolffork Tuesday.

§   Col. Paris returned from Atlanta Friday night.

§   Logan York is off on a wagoning trip.

§   Notice.

We, the committee appointed by the County School Commissioner for the purpose of locating the ground for the high school building for Rabun county, have this day met, in small number. As all districts represented were Clayton, Valley, Warwoman, Checheroe [*sic*] and Persimmon, we now make the following request: That each district meet at an early day and elect one or two men of each district to represent them in all their interest, as to locating and any other business that may be to attend to in this matter. Then all the committees of the entire county meet at Clayton on Saturday the 8th day of November, 1902, by 10 o'clock a.m. Don't fail to come. Let us save the opportunity while we are offered two dollars for one.

School Committee. Clayton, Ga., Oct. 25th 1902.

§   Blue Hights [*sic*].

We guess the readers of The Tribune think the Hights correspondents are all dead, but they are not.

Miss Altha Phillips spent Saturday night in N. C., with her aunt, Mary Ramey.

Mrs. H. B. Dotson is not very well at this writing.

Rev. Landrum has been running a few day's protracted meeting at the Ridge, which closed Thursday night.

Rev. Jay preached a very interesting sermon Thursday night and quite a crowd attended.

Miss Sallie Cathey spent Sunday night with Miss Altha Phillips.

Mr. Elic Roane has made sixty seven gallons of syrup and still making.

Mr. Silas Dotson spent Sunday with his best girl.

Mr. H. B. Dotson killed a fine hog Wednesday.

Ask Mr. Tyra Queen who got disappointed Thursday night.

Mr. Austin Mitchell spent last Sunday with his best girl, on the head of Black's Creek.

Ask Mr. Jesse Rogers who got disappointed the other night.

Guess who sat in the potatoe patch Friday night with their gun?

§   Warwoman.

Fine weather for gathering corn.

Gathering corn, o'possum hunting, and going to market is the order of the day.

Miss Evie Beck is visiting relatives on Warwoman.

Messrs. Hardie and Dave Ledford are off to market with a load of produce.

Ask Arthur Beck where he went Sunday eve.

Mr. Frank Wall is convalescing at this writing.

There was quite a nice crowd at the residence of Mrs. Captain Beck Sunday.

Mr. and Mrs. Jack Duncan were the guests of Mr. Andy Holden Sunday.

Mr. Luther Swofford was at the home of J. C. Turpen Tuesday.

Mr. Jesse C. Turpen and son are gathering corn.

Mr. Ike Pointer killed a nice mutton the other day.

The school at Five Forks is still progressing. Just five weeks of the school remains.

Mr. J. D. Beck is making molasses.

Preaching at Antioch Sunday. We suppose it will be the last service conducted by Rev. Jay.

Success to the Tribune.

§   Grove.

Weather pretty.

Hauling apples and bad reads is about all the news.

Mr. J. M. Arrendale and W. M. Baker went to market with produce this week.

Mr. A. M. Davidson, of Mossey Creek, was in the community Tuesday.

Scarlet fever is very prevalent in this community among children.

Mr. M. L. Arrendale went to Clarkesville Wednesday.

Mrs. Nicholson thinks the alternative road law is not a good one as the wagoners are destroying her fence rails to build bridges.

Mr. Henderson, the popular salesman of John A. Smith, of Gainesville, was at Grove Friday.

We regret the death of Mr. and Mrs. R. N. Dover's little girl who died Wednesday at their home. They have the sympathy of the entire community.

Success to the Tribune.

§   Warwoman.

The weather is fine.

David Ledford has gathered his corn and gone to market.

Dovie Williams and J. D. B. are "in close papers" I think.

Gussie Ledford spent Sunday evening with her cousin Carrie Ledford.

Andy Holden is making up syrup.

Eva Beck is up from Walhalla, S. C.

Miss Della Long, of Whetstone, S. C., is visiting Mrs. S. M. Beck.

Zeb Turpen, one of the best boys in school, got his arm hurt to-day on Sam's cart.

Sam and Estes Holden have gone to market.

Lafayette Dockins is on his journey to Anderson, S. C.

Mrs. D. Y. Ledford visited Mrs. Goebel yesterday.

Mr. Lafayette Wall is up from Atlanta.

I saw Jim Dotson last Sunday and he said he was feeling dull.

Jeff Beck has got his cane fodder pulled and is ready for the mill.

Dovie Williams' toe is improving at this time.

Miss Mary Hamby has returned from Walhalla.

Jesse Speed has got a new pair of boots.

§   Lost—One frostly cow, long horns, very small cow. Mark, two swallow forks and under bit. Any information will be gladly received by L. N. Shirley, Tiger, Ga.

§   All who are due me anything at costs will please come and settle with me and oblige. J. R. Ritchie, Sheriff.

§   Georgia—Rabun County.

Martha Beck, having made application for twelve month's support out of the estate of S. M. Beck, and appraisers duly appointed to set apart the same having filed their return, all persons concerned are hereby requirrd [*sic*] to show cause before the court of Ordinary of said county on the first Monday in December, 1902, why said application should not be granted. This 27th of October, 1902. W. S. Long, Ordinary.

§   Dillard.

Rain and muddy roads.

Messrs. Tom and John Bell were in the valley the latter part of the week.

A singing was enjoyed at Mr. W. E. Powell's Saturday night.

Miss Ethel Powell was with home folks Saturday and Sunday.

Mr. James Fisher is off to Atlanta.

George Dixon, of Tiger, was in the valley Sunday.

Frank Godfrey was with grandparents on Chechero last week.

B. R. Dillard is off to Atlanta.

W. C. Scruggs spent Sunday with John Darnell. Ask him where he spent the Sunday before at.

The school at Fort Hill is to have an entertainment.

Bert Robins pased [*sic*] through the valley Sunday.

§   Georgia—Rabun County.

Will be sold, in said county on the 7th day of November, 1902, between the hours of 10 o'clock p.m. [*sic*], at public outcry, at the late residence of F. A. Bleckley, deceased, to the highest bidder, all of the perishable property of said F. A. Bleckley, embracing one gray mare, one mowing machine, cane mill and a lot of farming tools. Terms of sale, all under $5.00 cash six month's time, with note and approved security with interest from date at 8 of per annum [*sic*]. This Oct. 21st 1902. J. E. Bleckley, Administrator.

November 13, 1902
Volume 5, Number 44

Note: The microfilmed images of this issue were incredibly dark. Many areas were too dark to read.

§   Dillard.

Corn gathering.

Mrs. Malinda Turpen is sick.

Mr. R. T. Green, of Turnerville, was in the valley Friday on business.

Ed Marsingale was in the valley Sunday.

Miss May Donaldson was with us[?] the last part of the week.

Ask [illegible].

[Illegible] Mr. George Martin's Saturday night.

Ed [illegible] [from down the country?].

Ask John[?] [illegible].

[Illegible] George [illegible].

§   [Illegible community name; possibly Grove].

[Illegible section at bottom of page.]

[Continued from illegible section at bottom of page] is the time to settle.

Mr. J. Barrett[?], the popular salesman for John B[?]. Dental Drug Co., was at Grove Friday.

J. M. Arrendale and Mart Baker are off with a load of produce.

Success to the Tribune.

§   Creede.

Dear Editor: I want a few dots in the dear old Tribune, as we never have had any such in the Tribune yet.

We have been having some fine weather but we are having some rain now.

Road working and going to market is the order of the day.

J. C. Benfield is gone to market with his sixth load of apples and produce and every time he comes back with a pocket full of money. J. C. is a hustler.

Mr. R. P[?]. Gragg has got back from Athens, Ga., where he went to attend the United States court.

Mr. F. O. Singleton's school will be out in two weeks and we will [illegible] because he is a fine fellow and a good teacher and his done[?] more for us than we have ourselves in working for our library at Flat Creek. We will miss him when he goes home.

One of Habersham's stock law [illegible] passed through this community hunting [illegible]. That is the way of stock law—you may go hog buying and never get any at all. I hope we will never have it in old Rabun.

§ Death of Mrs. Brown.

Mrs. D. C. Brown, wife of the Methodist Pastor at Blairsville and daughter of Mr. and Mrs. Alex Church, of Clarkesville, died at the home of her uncle, J[?]. E. [illegible], in Town Creek district, Thursday, October 30th, 1902, at 8:35[?] a.m. Mrs. Brown was taken ill about a week before her death on her way to Blairsville from her father's, where she [illegible] short visit of but [illegible] days, and gradually [illegible].

She was married to Rev. D. C. Brown for five years ago last Sept. 14th in the Methodist Church at Clarkesville, at the age of [illegible], and just before the [remainder largely illegible].

§ Lewis N. Shirley had a corn shucking at his land on Tiger Saturday. A very good crowd [illegible].

§ [Illegible] of Walhalla, S. C., was here Monday.

§ [Illegible] from Walhalla, S. C. [illegible]. Lonie[?] [illegible] girl and we think [illegible].

§ [J. S.?] [illegible] and W. J[?]. Neville[?] of Franklin, N. C., [were at the?] Blue Ridge [illegible].

§ W. T. York and R. L. [illegible] of the Valley were in town yesterday.

§ Miss Effie and Eliza [D----] [ex----] to take a trip to Clarkesville, Cornelia and Atlanta in a few days.

§   W. C. [illegible] has been confined[?] to his room for [illegible].

§   [Large section too dark to read.]

§   [Illegible] [Clarke?] of [Spartanburg] S. C. [illegible].

§   Miss[?] May[?] [illegible] of Tennessee Valley was the guest of Mrs. J. S. Ramey yesterday.

§   M. M. Marsingale had a corn shucking at his house on the [Bell farm?] Friday. Sixty-two[?] people helped him eat the new corn and a table loaded with everything it takes to make an old timer dinner.

§   Geo. L. [illegible] of [illegible] Erwin, of Clarkesville, Ga., [illegible] of Atlanta, Capt. W. W. Phillips, of Tallulah Falls, and W. P. [K----], of Clarkesville, Ga., came up Sunday [illegible] to look over the proposed railroad route. They spent Sunday night at the Blue Ridge Hotel and returned Monday.

§   Our town is full of nursery agents this week. Messers Edwards, Brindle[?] and McConnell are registered at the Parker House.

§   My trees have failed to arrive from the nursery in time to deliver them when promised, but will be here for distribution Saturday Nov. 15th and Monday Nov. 17th. Please call and get them. R[?]. C. Clarke.

§   We heard a fellow say the other day that he did not know which was the greatest curse to Rabun county people, the alternative road law or the fruit tree agents with their trees.

§   Mrs. J. I. Langston has been spending the week in Walhalla, S. C.

§   A [illegible] crowd came out to the meeting Saturday. About all done was to [illegible] the college [be built within?] one mile of the court house here, and [illegible] or to-day when it is expected people will be appointed to [illegible] the county for [illegible].

§   Again we are compelled to leave a half sheet and [illegible] we have paper [illegible].

§   W. M. Turpin, the timber man, was at the [illegible] again[?].

§   Lost. One year old [illegible] yellow [illegible] and over bit in the left ear. [Illegible] will be [illegible] by James Pendergrass[?], Wolffork, Ga.

§   [Large section too dark to read.]

§   Dept. Sheriff E. L. McConnell went down to Capt. Hampton's[?] [illegible] who [illegible] in the [illegible] February term of the Superior Court. He [illegible] stealing some dynamite[?] and blowing it up near the camp one night.

§   Lost. One small heifer [illegible] about 8 months old, white[?] [illegible] and ears are [illegible]. When last seen, wore a small bell. Any one delivering it to [illegible] will receive fifty cents. James A. Moore, Wolffork, Ga.

§   Stecoa.
   Mr. W. H. Price went to Clayton last Saturday.
   Russel Woodall is very ill.
   We wonder why Miss Mattie[?] Price was so sad last Saturday [illegible].
   Ask C. E. Woodall if his [illegible] ever cooked.
   Miss Ella Ramey's school will close the 15th of Nov.
   Jable Cannon still [illegible] down on the creek.
   Miss Lassie[?] McCrackin[?] visited her Uncle E. C. Price Sunday.
   V. C. Taylor and family visited L. C. Taylor Sunday.
   If Morgan Moore does not hurray[?] the frost will bite his cane[?].
   Floyd Cannon went to Tiger Monday.
   Ask Ada[?] Ramey and May Price[?] why they are so sorry school will [illegible].
   [---lie] Woodal went to [illegible] Sunday evening.
   Guess who is tired of candy and singings.

§   Old Tiger.
   Dept. Sheriff McConnell [illegible] and carried off Mr[?]. Claude [---y] last Sunday.
   [Little?] Annie Smith and Nory[?] Turpen and Celia Turpin, children of Allen's, have Scarlet fever.
   R. K[?]. McCurry had a corn shucking last week.
   Mr. [illegible] and Henry[?] Taylor [illegible].
   Mr. Will Shirley[?] [illegible].
   [Illegible] Turpen [illegible] Capt. Hampton[?].
   [Henry?] Cleveland [illegible] to Vandiver.
   Capt. Hampton [illegible] completed [illegible] and caught [illegible] another.

Note: The remainder of this issue was largely illegible.

November 20, 1902
Volume 5, Number 45

§   Burton.

Mr. Editor:

Our school is progressing nicely now, numbering about seventy students. Prof Burrell is giving universal satisfaction and in all probability teach for us next year. Also Miss Sallie Smith is very popular as his assistant and if she desires the place will no doubt be in the same place next year.

Tallulah has the best roads she has ever had in her history. People who bucked against the alternative road law are now three-fourths of them for it. Some say it is very hard to go three or four miles and work ten hours per day. But who is to blame for our work all coming on us at once? Nobody but those who held up the law by injunction. Could we have put in three days last spring, four days in August and three days each now our roads would have been better and no one would ever miss the time. Two gentlemen stayed with me a few nights ago from Franklin county Georgia, who tell me that they have had the law there for three years, that it was held up there by injunction and that they paid a lawyer three hundred dollars to kill it but the courts decided against them and that this year they are assessed two dollars each or four days work and that every man who fought it is ashamed of the fact and that nine tenths of their people are for it. I predict the same thing in Rabun. There will no doubt be mistakes and evils that will take some experience to make any system work perfectly. Let all mistakes be corrected next year, let the hands work some in the spring, some when crops are laid by hand some in the fall and the burden will not be so heavily [illegible]. The two great points in favor of the alternative system are first, better roads. We had tried the old system since our county was organized and had never gotten any roads yet. This will give us better roads. Second. Equalization. Under the old system some one had to work ten or fifteen days and furnish tools or be fined from one to three dollars per day. Other hands would do not three days work in the year—would always be sick on road working day. No equalization was about it then. Now every man must do his share. I wish to say that our overseer and superintendent were especially happy in appointing overseers in Tallulah district, as they could never have gotten three better men for the place and they should all be reappointed for next year as they have done so well and gained a lot of experience.

H. C. Blalock

§   Grove.

Weather pretty.

The farmers are very busy gathering corn.

Road working seems to be on a boom in this community.

Mr. W. J. Fuller, of Clarkesville, was at Grove Monday.

V. M. Gipson's baby is very sick at this writing.

Dr. J. K. Barnes, of Clarkesville, was in this community Wednesday.

Mr. E. H. Baker had a corn shucking Thursday and the finest crib of corn was shucked every known on Bridge Creek.

W. J. Evans, of Creede, was at Grove Thursday.

Meeks Arrendale went to Clarkesville with a load of produce Friday.

S. S. Burnett, the popular salesman of Grambling, Spalding and Co., was at Grove Friday.

Success to the Tribune.

§   Mr. J. A. Reynolds, Clayton, Ga.

Kind friend: I write this to inform you that I have found my mule and want you to stop the advertisement and thank you for past favors.

Yours truly, A. A. Darnell, Dillard, Ga.

§   Creede.

Road working and corn gathering is the order of the day.

Mrs. A. Benfield has a turnip that weighs five and three fourths pounds. Now beat that if you can.

Mrs. Loma Gipson, Mrs. Lula Taylor and little folks visited Mrs. A. Befiel [sic] last Sunday.

Miss Zoney Roberts took dinner with Miss Sarah Benfield and they had a nice time.

One more week of school and Prof. F. D. Singleton will go back home. We wish him much success.

We got a red Tribune last week and it a half sheet. We want a whole sheet this week.

Success to the Tribune.

§   Old Tiger.

Miss Ada Green taught school last Saturday.

Manson Turpen caught two o'possums the other night.

Henry Cleveland has moved to Vandiver.

Mrs. T. W. Worley visited [Miss?] Nowell and Miss Sarah Hunnicutt last week.

The trestle at Tiger is almost completed and is an excellent one.

Mr. Miles Phillips has bought a lot of land in Tiger and will begin to improve it soon.

Mr. John Lyle, of Long Creek, S. C., is visiting in Tiger and Stonepile.

We hate to be stuck up for a weather bulletin but it is our fortune. Rheumatism is an unfailing sign of weather—and bad weather, too.

The alternative road system is not a system and half our money and labor will be placed where it will do no good at all. If some people want to put money and labor where it will do no good we dont [*sic*] object to it, but it is not right to compel people to do so to the neglect of the benefit of the county and against their will. But this is the alternative—no system.

We don't like for Stonepile to publish our misfortunes, but he has a head of his own and is a jolly good fellow, and must have his own way.

Mr. James Turpen visited Marcus Turpen Sunday.

Walter Smith killed a fine beef last Saturday.

Mr. E. W. Shirley visited Marcus Turpen Sunday.

Marcus Turpen is building a new house to rent.

§   Poplar Springs.

The rainy weather for the past few days has been very disagreeable for corn gathering.

Mrs. Peter Speed is visiting her sisters Misses Carrie and Lydia Ledford.

Miss Gussie Ledford went to Pine Mountain last Tuesday, on business she said.

Miss Carrie Ledford got a letter the other day that had fifteen pages in it. We would like to know where it came from. There is no more paper there we know.

A large crowd of young folks enjoyed a candy pulling last Sunday night, given by Mr. and Mrs. Pick Norton to Mr. Hardy Ledford on his birthday.

Mr. Arthur Beck visited his best girl last Friday night.

The school closes here to-day.

Mr. Fagant Wall spent a few days with Mr. C. C. Ledford this week.

Success to the Tribune.

§   Dillard.

Still fine weather for corn gathering and wagoning.

Misses T. and Lassie Kelley are here on a visit.

Mrs. Lee Ritchie is very sick with typhoid fever.

Miss Texie York's school closed Friday with an entertainment, which was enjoyed by all who attended.

There is a great deal of sickness in our berg.

[Little] Jackson Dorsey, also Mrs. Octa Greenwood's baby, are very sick with Pneumonia fever.

Bertha Howard is with her sister Mrs. Lula Holden in the Flats.

Leona Hopper was on Mud Creek again Sunday. Lookout Ida.

May Holden had "special" company Sunday.

Misses Frannie and Lizzie Martin are up from Dawson on a visit.

Misses Ethel Powell and Ira Smith were with us Sunday.

§   Tallulah Falls.

Prof. J. S. Singleton opened school on Monday at this place with an attendance of about forty pupils.

Sam Brown, colored, was hit by a stray bullet from a Winchester last Sunday evening. The bullet lodged between the bones on the arm. This happened near the Cainey bottom.

We see the Tribune came out in war colors last week. This is, or should be, looked at as a compliment to the editor and his assistant. It shows how many hardships he has to contend with and how he is persevering to do all in his power to give the people the news and yet some people will grumble and without a cause. If they only had to get out one issue under the same circumstances they would think the subscription price ought to be two dollars per years in stead of one.

Work on extending the railroad is moving along rapidly. Capt. Walker is building the long trestle through the town and will complete it in a very short time.

§   To our dear friends and readers:

We take our pen in hand to drop you a few lines to let you know we are all well and that, after a month issuing on red paper, wrapping paper at that, we have received our paper ordered from Marietta, Ga., in October. We have a bill of lading nearly so long off. Wrapping paper costs about three times as much as news print and we do no aim to be caught any more. Some of our correspondents say we have been putting on war paint and we have not been in much less humor. Finally after ordering twice, once by express, we have paper, and paper, and paper for some time to come.

§ Blue Ridge.

Ask a certain young lady who got up before day Monday morning crying.

There was a certain man of Blacks Creek offered one of our girls a big sweet potatoe if she would marry him. All who want to help eat the potatoe come ahead.

§ We are at home again after over a week's absence. We have been in the employ of Mr. Louis B. Magid, of Tallulah Falls, defining and locating a public road from Tugalo valley to the Lodge on the Tallulah and getting the contour of that part of Tugalo river that bounds the land of Mr. Magid on the east. We also had the pleasure of making a plan of nearly two thousand acres on which about fifty farms are laid off for the purpose of seri-culture.

We are obligated to Mr. and Mrs. W. W. Phillips and Mr. and Mrs. Ivester of the Falls, who cared for us during much of the time we were there.

[*Note: J. A. Reynolds, the Tribune's business manager and editor, was also a surveyor.*]

§ No better sign of progress in Clayton has been seen lately than to-day. There is a committee of our best citizens quietly walking over town selecting a site for a college building. One of the party told us he could have every dollar within ten days to build it. This is surely encouraging and to say the least it seems that we are to have an educational building equal to any country college in the State, if everybody will work.

§ Real Estate. We are in the real estate business and want you to list your property with us...

Two thousand acres of land for sale in Shelby county, Alabama. Six miles from the Southern railway, and the same distance from the Central railway. One thousand acres of bottom land. The remainder of this land is waverly and beautifully so. The land lies on Yellow Leaf river and only a few miles from the famous and beautiful Coosa river. Only 35 miles from the city of Birmingham, Ala., now with a population of one hundred thousand and the coming metropolis of the south. This is an ideal place for a colony of 30 to 50 families. Land is highly productive, and is specially adapted to cotton, wheat, corn and oats. Land is bringing 50 to 75 bushels of corn to the acre. The country is exceedingly healthy. This land is a splendid stock farm. Natural grazing 9 months in the year. This farm is a fortune. For prices and terms apply to J. A. Reynolds Clayton, Ga., or J. C. Jackson, Tallapoosa, Ga. Reason for selling owner retired...

§ J. T. Long is moving to his farm on Scotch Creek to-day.

§   Sine Donaldson has vacated the Wall property on Warwoman St. and occupies a building he has recently built in the same vicinity.

§   C. E. Griggs, of Clarkesville, is here and is interested in a large timber deal in the county.

§   The Thomas Locust Pin Mill will move to town shortly from Persimmon.

§   Mrs. M. C. Warlick, who has been here several days for medical treatment, has returned home much improved.

§   There is an irish potatoe on the mantle at the Blue Ridge Hotel that has seventeen potatoes clustered around a large one, in all weighing nearly two pounds. It grew in the hotel garden.

§   Mrs. L. N. Robins is still drying apples—Nov. 15, 1902.

§   Mr. S. W. Dover continues to spread out in improvements. He is re-covering his residence, extending his crib and painting his well and dairy house, etc. Mr. Dover's words and acts are always forward.

§   Mr. Bill Penland and Miss Rosa Thompson, of Persimmon, were at the Parker House Sunday.

§   J. C. Pickett is making preparations to improve his residence.

§   The friends of Mrs. Lee Ritchie will hear with profound regret that she is very sick with of Typhoid fever. It is reported that her recovery is doubtful.

§   Mrs. A. C. Godfrey was adjudged insane by a jury last Tuesday. For more than fifteen years Mrs. Godfrey has been in a more or less demented condition.

§   Miss Mamie Grant, of Clarkesville, is the guest of Mrs. J. R. Grant.

§   Sheriff Ritchie has shown that he is not only a good sheriff but an excellent salesman. For some time he has been selling goods for his brothers Lee and Tom.

§   The railroad news continues encouraging. Another contract has been let to Capt. Hampton, the distance we have not learned.

§ Our readers will see in another column the beginning of an address by Louis B. Magid, of Tallulah Falls. The address was delivered before The Farmer's National Congress. Mr. Magid is president of the Seri-Culture and Manufacturing Co., of Tallulah Falls, and is doing much to build up our section. Mr. Magid will soon publish a twenty four page magazine devoted mainly to silk culture. The address will be continued in the Tribune and is a highly interesting account of the manufacture of silk. [*Note: Those articles were not abstracted. Please see the full issue.*]

§ Dr. Green, Judge Long, Jesse McCurry, D. L. Parker and L. C. Hollifield attended as jurymen at the lunacy trial on Chechero last Tuesday.

§ Webb Johnson left for his home in Hartwell Tuesday. He will add two thousand apple trees to his Blue Hights farm the coming winter. A good sign of prosperity.

§ About a year ago Eddie Ritchie took out to the Nantahala Mountains seven pigs three weeks old. On last Tuesday evening he came in town with them and they are large sleek fellows and at present price of pork would bring about a round hundred dollars. They have not been fed but twice since they left here about a year ago.

§ I will buy poplar, whire [*sic*] oak and spotted oak in this section, and chestnut and all timber in boundaries of other timber. Half cash and half within six months. T. J. Ritchie, Clayton, Ga.

§ The friends of Capt. W. W. Phillips will be pleased to know that he has full charge of the engineering of the Tallulah Falls Railway extension. Capt. Phillips' friends are numbered by his entire acquaintance in Rabun county.

§ The stockholders of the Masonic building are requested to meet in Clayton on Tuesday the 25th inst., for the purpose of transacting important business. D. T. Duncan.

§ Lost—One year old past calf, yellow brindle, swallow fork and over bit in the left ear. Any information will be gladly received by James Pendergrass, Wolffork, Ga.

§ I will be at the following named places for the purpose of collecting the state and county taxes for the year 1902: Clayton, November 13th; Valley law ground, Nov. 14th; Persimmon law ground, Nov. 15th; Tallulah law ground, Nov. 17th; Stonepile law ground, Nov. 18th; Tiger law ground,

Nov. 19th; Checheroe law ground, Nov. 20th; Warwoman law ground, Nov. 21st; Moccasin law ground, Nov. 22nd.

Second round. Clayton, December 1st; Valley, the second; Persimmon, the third; Cross Roads, Dec. 4th, from 9 to 11 o'clock a.m.; Dick's Creek, the fourth, from 2 to 4 p.m.; Burton, the 5th; Stonepile, the 6th; Tallulah Falls, the 8th; Tiger law ground, the 9th; Chechero, the 10th; Warwoman, the 11th; Moccasin, the 12th; Hale Ridge, Dec. 13th, from 9 to 11 a.m.; Bettie's Creek, Dec. 15th, from 9 to 12 a.m.; Tiger P. O., the 16th, from 9 to 11 a.m.; Germany church, the 16th, at 2 p.m.; Close out at Clayton, Dec. 17th to 20th. Joseph L. Dickerson, T. C.

§ John Massingill has moved his residence from J. B. Murray's to the Wall block on the Warwoman road. He has rented land from J. F. Earl for next year.

§ Capt. S. S. Hall has returned from Saulbery, N. C.

§ I have harness, shoe and leather oil and will sell it at a reduced price for the next ninety days. S. S. Whitmire.

§ Strayed from my premises. Three stock hogs, fifteen month old. One red and black stotted, two black with white feet. Mark, a crop and overbit in the right and a split in the left. Any information gladly received by James H. Ramey, Dillard, Ga.

§ Miss Carrie Cannon's school at the Pines closed Saturday with an entertainment.

§ William Gilds and Sam Welborn have been granted a new trial. Welborn and Gilds, it will be remembered, were charged with rape and convicted of assault with the intent to rape, and were sentenced to twenty years in the penetentiary [sic]. Judge Estes has fixed a bond of five hundred dollars, which it is thought they will soon make and be given their liberty after nearly a year's confinement in our county jail.

§ All persons due James H. Ramey please come and settle at once or they will find their accounts in the officer's hands.

§ All persons who are due me anything in this county are urgently requested to make immediate settlement with me, as I need the money and the notes were due the 15th inst. D. L. Parker, Tallulah Falls, Ga., Nov. 18th 1902.

§ Editor Clayton Tribune

Dear Sir: Will you kindly inform the readers of your paper that our picture gallery at Tallulah Falls will remain open all winter and that we make almost any kind of photographic pictures that they may want and at reasonable prices, and latest styles and sizes.

Old pictures copied. If the picture you wish to have copied is a good one the copy will be a good one. We can make the copp [*sic*] the exact size, smaller, or we can enlarge them. So if you should send them write plainly instructions, or if you come yourself you can tell me. Respectfully, Walter Hunnicutt.

§ Lost—One small heifer calf, about 8 months old, white specked and ears are pale red unmarked. When last seen, wore a small bell. Any one delivering it to me will receive fifty cents. James A. Moore, Wolffork, Ga.

§ Mrs. Nettie Hess and children, of Walhalla, S. C., are the guests of Mr. and Mrs. J. I. Langston.

§ Georgia—Rabun County.

To whom it may concern: J. C. Pickett, having made application to me in due form to be appointed permanent administrator upon the estate of S. A. Beck, late of said county, notice is hereby given that said application will be heard at the regular term of the court of ordinary for said county, to be held on the first Monday in December, 1902.

Witness my hand and official signature, this 3rd day of November, 1902. W. S. Long, Ordinary.

§ Notice to debtors and creditors.

Notice is hereby given to all creditors of the estate of F. A. Bleckley, late of said county, deceased, to render in an account of their demands to us within the time prescribed by law, properly made out. And all persons indebted to said deceased are hereby requested to make immediate payment to the undersigned. This the 5th day of November 1902. J. E. Bleckley, J. N. Bleckley, Adminstrators of F. A. Bleckley, deceased.

§ Notice is hereby given to all credictors of the estate of Cal Conley, late of said county, deceased to render in an account of their demands to us within the time prescribed by law, properly made out. And all persons indebted to said deceased are hereby requested to make immediate payment to the undersigned. This the 18th day of Nov. 1902. Logan Turpen, Administrator of Cal Conley, deceased.

§ Georgia—Rabun County.

Adaline Long, having made application for twelve month's support ento[?] the estate of G. W. Long, and appraisers duly appinted [sic] to set apart the same having filed their return, all persons concerned are hereby required to show cause before the Court of Ordinary of said county on the first Monday in December, 1902 why said application should not be granted. This 6th day of November, 1902. J. S. Ramey, C. S. C. and Ex-Officio Ordinary.

§   Sheriff's Sales.

Georgia—Rabun County. Will be sold, on the first Tuesday in December next...

Also at the same time and place: one half (½) undivided interest in part of lot of land No. 107 in the second land district of said county and bounded as follows: Commencing on the southeast corner of lot No. 107 thence north the original line to the top of the mountain a southwest course to the east and west original line of said lot to a conditional corner, thence east said line to the beginning corner, containing one hundred acres more or less. Levied on as the property of D. D. Turpen by virtue of a fi fa issued from the justice's court of the 556th district G. M. of said county in favor of Virgil Green against D. D. Turpen and W. T. York. This Nov. 6th 1902.

Also at the same time and place about 7 bushels of corn, more or less, levied on and to be sold as the property of M. A. Hopkins by virtue of a fi fa issued from the Superior Court of Hart County, Ga., in favor of A. D. Candler, Governor the State of Georgia against the said M. A. Hopkins, principal, and J. I. Langston, security on forfeiture recognance [sic]. This Nov. 6th 1902. J. R. Ritchie, Sheriff.

§   Notice to Teachers.

I am to-day sending out report blanks. You will please follow these directions in making out your reports:

1st. Make them out with pen and ink.

2nd. The time for which you have not made a report, make that on the monthly blanks.

3rd. Then make a report for the school year on the annual report blanks.

4th. Make these reports in full, placing the number of pupils that studied each of the branches of study, etc.

5th. Then have these reports properly signed and turned into my office at your earliest convenience after the close of your schools.

This Nov. 18th 1902. A. A. O'Kelley, C. S. Com'r.

November 27, 1902
Volume 5, Number 46

§   William Gilds and Sam Welborn were given their liberty last Friday and we bear no regrets.

§   Thanks to D. T. Duncan for the largest turnip yet reported. It weighs five and three fourths pounds.

§   Spart Ramey was at Franklin, N. C., several days last week.

§   Chance Vickers and Harry Duncan attended the closing exercises of Miss Lena Bleckley's school Saturday.

§   Miss Ada Green closed her school at Tiger with an entertainment last Thursday.

§   Miss Fannie Donaldson has returned from a visit of two weeks in the valley.

§   Miss Zelma Price's school closed with exercises Saturday.

§   James Green and F. D. Singleton closed their schools Saturday.

§   James E. Bleckley has been busily engaged gathering corn on Tiger Creek.

§   Miss Reed Bleckley is home after teaching a successful term at Pine Mountain.

§ There was an educational rally at Burton Saturday night.

§ J. R. Grant attended Turnerville Court Friday of last week.

§ W. C. Scruggs sold to Col. R. E. A. Hamby a set of fine mill stones some time ago and they were delivered to Col. Hamby's mill last Saturday. The rocks were cut by Mr. Scruggs and W. E. V. Cathey. They are said to be beauties.

§ Miss Martha Wall, of Warwoman, was the guest of Mrs. Ramey Saturday.

§ N. J. Thomas, of Franklin, N. C., and Mr. Partial, of New York, N. Y., were at The Wall House last week.

§ Mr. Millard M. Marsingale has had two corn shuckings this fall and his corn is not near shucked yet.

§ Mr. and Mrs. J. F. Earl went down on Chechero Friday.

§ Prof. Foster has been suffering with inflammatory rheumatism in his [illegible] for several days.

§ The negro school at Ivy Hill, one mile from town, closed Tuesday the 18th inst., with an entertainment on that day and night. Several recitations and dialogues and some fine music kept the attention of a large crowd.

§ O. W. McDade is in town.

§ W. C. Smith, of Knoxville, Tennessee, is registered at The Parker House. Mr. Smith is here for the railroad[?] purchasing land. He has bought forty thousand acres [illegible] McDade and Turpen, and will buy [illegible] more as he can get it.

§ Mr. J. F. Godfrey of Checheroe made our office a business call Saturday. Mr. Godfrey has been one of our best friends and supporters since we have been in this county.

§ Prof. Foster spent Saturday and Sunday with home folk on Burton.

§ Miss Mamie Grant has returned to her home in Clarkesville, Ga.

§   It is reported that Mr. A. C. Godfrey, former postmaster at Tallulah Falls, is in failing health. Mr. H. R. Cannon has been appointed postmaster at the Falls and Mr. Godfrey has moved to his farm on Chechero.

§   We are obligated to Mr. J. M. Carver, of Chechero, for a sweet potatoe that measured twenty five inches in length. It is all potatoe and not vine and string.

§   Post office Inspector R. E. Barry was examining into Uncle Sam's business here last week. Clayton and Rabun Gap post offices had been reported, but Capt. Barry reports they have been correctly kept.

§   John B. Dockins passed through town Friday last with a drove of hogs.

§   J. E. Derrick has a turnip that measures twenty-three inches in circumference.

§   John Burton is on the road, wagoning for Nelson Tilley, all the time these days.

§   Miss Stella Langston will be the guest of friends in Walhalla for a month.

§   Nelson Tilley sold fifteen head of cattle to Tom Ritchie last week.

§   Mrs. John Wilson has been quite sick for several days.

§   Sheriff Ritchie is having a sale in clothing.

§   We have heard quite a number of farmers over the county talk of the yield of corn this year and about all say the crop is the best in years. The hay and fodder crop has been gathered in excellent condition, owing to the dry weather. The apple crop has been a superior and large one, which has been mainly marketed. Irish and sweet potatoes are an average crop. The cabbage is in the finest condition in many years. The continual dry weather kept the growth back until the late rains and consequently they will keep better for this and for many months yet the people will continue to market them. The chestnut crop proved to be short but many hundred dollars' worth were sold. We think we are safe to say that thousands of beef cattle have been and will be sold at good price. Droves of sheep have been driven to the markets and hundreds of hogs are being driven and at present prices will bring in a large sum of money. There are many other products of the county, such as dried fruit, wool, beeswax, etc. There is a large yield of turnips and in fact there is a good crop of everything that grows in this section. Besides the large yield and good prices there are good schools almost in every nook[?] of the county, and with an increased salary. In addition to all of this for the past year a large amount of money has been paid for timber, and still there are men buying almost daily, and to add to all this there will be paid out an enormous amount the coming year on the extension of The Tallulah Falls Railroad. The southern part of the county is now experiencing an era of prosperity in this line. So when we stop to think of all these blessings and the prosperity of our citizens our heart leaps with joy and we congratulate the citizens upon their condition financially. So we, for the next year, at least as citizens, will enjoy an era of prosperity as never before.

§   Post Master Duncan will kell up about forty bushels of turnip.

§   Misses Vinnie and Florence Marsengale raised thirty-five wagon loads of corn with a small help from Jesse Smith.

§   Gibson—Thompson.
The marriage of Miss Annie Jeanette Gipson [*sic*], of Beta, N. C., and Mr. Henry Edward Thompson, of Asheville, which occurred at the Second Baptist Church in Atlanta, Sunday evening, Nov. 16th, was a surprise to their many friends.
Mrs. Thompson has been a frequent visitor in Atlanta, where she has received many charming attentions.
Mr. Thompson is a young man of sterling worth and [illegible] is successfully engaged in business in Asheville.
The bride was becomingly gowned in a gray cloth suit with white silk trimmings, with a picture hat to match, and carried a bouquet of bridal roses. Her traveling suit was of blue and white.
After a delightful luncheon at the Aragon, Mr. and Mrs. Thompson left on the midnight train for Asheville, where they will be at home to their many friends after December first at 320 Bailey street.

§   Tallulah.
Mrs. Fannie Harkins and Miss Daisy Gipson were at Eden Sunday and spent Sunday night with Mrs. F. A. Taylor.
Mr. Hilton Roberts' baby is very ill.
Mr. A. Benfiel fell off his mule a few days ago and seriously hurt himself.
Mr. F. D. Singleton's school will close Saturday. We wish him a nice time.
Mr. Houston Gosnell's baby is very ill.

Mrs. Fannie Harkins is gone to Roswell to work in the [illegible] department.

§   Poplar Springs.

We are having some fine weather. We believe it is the warmest we ever saw for the time of year.

Mr. John Speed is off down the country again.

Mr. and Mrs. Sam Thomas and Miss Ada Kell, from the Flats, have been visiting friends and relatives here for a few days.

Mr. Jeff and Judson Speed went hunting the other night and they caught two o'possums and a coon.

The boys are working the road this week.

Mr. Arthur and Julius Beck visited Mr. Jeff Speed Wednesday night.

Mrs. Mary Ledford and Misses Carrie, Lydia and Guffie Ledford visited our singing Sunday. Come again.

Mr. Arthur Beck visited his best girl the other evening again.

We heard two girls say they went to singing last Sunday in the wheel barrow on purpose to hear Mr. Thad Kell sing. He said he would be there if he was living. Some body find out if he is dead, for he wasn't there.

§   Grove.

News scarce.

People are mostly done gathering corn.

Right Burton was at Grove Monday.

Meeks and Lester Arrendale are off with a load of produce this week.

R[?]. J. Denney went to Clayton Tuesday.

Richard McClain was at Grove Wednesday.

Lester and Fred Arrendale and Henry Smith went o'possum hunting and caught a rabbit.

W. M. Baker went to Clayton Friday.

The Revenue officers were raiding on Bridge Creek Friday.

Mrs. C. C. York was at Grove Friday.

John and Mart Baker went to Clarkesville Friday with a load of produce.

Mr. T. H. Smith went to Buiton [*sic*] Friday.

§   Stonepile.

The firm of Taylor and Fincher, hunters, returned Saturday with ninety-nine squirrels, six coons, ten o'possums, three rabbits and seven partridges. The squirrells held meeting while the boys were out in the woods. The old squirrels thought all of them would be killed, so the old captain ordered a meeting. While in session, one squirrell said he heard one of the firm wish they were out in the Nantahala mountains and all of the squirrells said they wished so too. One of the members said there was only one man that had any mercy in the crowd and that was when they hit a hard tree. He would beg them to let it go. The squirrels tried to haunt them with the hooting owl and there was a regiment of dogs come out of the camp and the owl got killed next day.

Mrs. Wall and daughter were around getting signers to a petition. They found bad roads in this part.

The boys are working the roads now. Mr. J. I. Langston passed last week. We know he is in sympathy with the boys and road hands.

The people are about all done gathering corn and it turns off very well.

Mr. F. D. Singleton's school will close the 22nd of this month with an entertainment.

Mr. Thomas Worley was seen some time ago coming out of the woods with a dead pork on his back. So look out for something else soon.

We were very sorry to learn Mr. Pitts was quarantined on account of the distemper tick.

§   Old Tiger.

Mr. Steven Gambol, who has been sick for a long while, died last Monday evening about four o'clock.

Mrs. N. C. Smith has scarlet fever very badly.

The rest of the scarlet fever cases are better.

Miss Ella Ramey and her mother attended Prof. Singleton's school entertainment at Flat Creek last week.

Mr. V. C. Taylor and wife and Miss Susie went to Cornelia last week on a pleasure trip.

Nevitt and Henry Taylor are getting better of fever.

R. F. McCurry and Jeff Taylor returned from Athens last Saturday.

Mr. C. L. Taylor sold a fat hog to Hughlett and Co.'s commissary this week.

Capt. Hampton has done the finest railroad work on the line.

Tiger looks lonely since Miss Ada Green closed school.

The bible says, be subject to the laws of the country. The legislature ought to make a law for us to steal, so we can steal legally as well as the alternative road system can rob legally.

Last week some one shot a Winchester rifle at a distance of about five hundred yards on Ginn's works and tore a negro's arm and elbow all to pieces. The man who did the shooting was a white man and shot the negro for stealing whiskey, as to the best information we can get.

§   North Chechero.

Weather pretty.

Miss Zelma Price's school closed Friday with an entertainment enjoyed by all who attended.

Prof. V. A. Green taught school Saturday.

Miss Ella Ramey was in this community Tuesday.

Mr. James York and son Lester are off to Anderson with a load of apples.

Mr. Charley and Bren[?] Coffee attended preaching at Bethel Sunday.

Mr. George Dixon, of Tiger, is a Sunday visitor at Mr. A. J. Duncan's now.

Mrs. F. A. Bleckley is visiting relatives on Tiger this week.

The school is progressing nicely here.

Miss Mary Green and her brother Roy visited home folks on Warwoman Sunday.

Charley York, of Clayton, is on Chechero this week.

Ask Miss Lizzie York how she enjoyed last Sunday.

Ask Mr. Charley Coffee what time he got home Sunday night.

Mr. J. M. Bleckley was among friends here Saturday.

Success to the good old Tribune.

§   Dillard.

News scarce this week.

Mr. James Hopper had a corn shucking Thursday.

Mrs. Lela Ritchie is some better.

Fannie Donaldson was at Clayton Sunday.

Mrs. Fannie Fisher is here from Turnerville.

Will Penland was over from Persimmon Saturday and Sunday.

Prof. O'Kelley was in the valley Friday.

W. E. Powell had a corn shucking Tuesday.

§   Wylie.

Mr. J. H. Ramey is off to market.

We all miss Miss Ada Green since her school is out.

The corps of engineers are at work here with Capt. Phillips as Chief Engineer. Capt. Barry, Superintedent of Construction, is with the corps. They are all pleasantly quartered with Mr. J. H. Ramey. They are re-locating the line and, we understand, making a big improvement on it.

Miss May Ramey returned from Clayton Tuesday.

Capt. Hampton is grading the road about as fast as the way can be blazed out.

Mrs. Anna Clore is the guest of Mrs. Ramey.

Jas. E. Bleckley has been gathering corn.

Jesse Green has purchased another mule and gone to railroading. So has Joshua Worley.

§   Gainesville, Ga., Nov. 19th, 1902.

Editor Tribune: At their last meeting the Daughters of the Confederacy of Longstreet Chapter decided to erect a monument in loving memory of the Confederate dead of the 9th Congressional District. Than the heroic sons of this section no braver soldier ever faced a foe. Constituting a part of the grandest army known to history it is but fitting that a shaft be erected in commemmoration [*sic*] of such soldiery.

Subscription lists are being furnished the County Clerks in the district and the movement is well under headway. Those in charge of the lists are to forward all collections to Col. C. C. Sanders, President State Banking Company, Gainesville, Georgia, to be deposited to the credit of the Daughters of Confederacy and to be used exclusively for the erection of above named monument.

Kindly aid us in this noble cause by bringing the matter before the people through your most estimable paper and we shall ever feel grateful and appreciate the same.

Very truly, Mrs. Jasper N. Dozier, Mrs. A. W. Van Hoose, Miss Kate Dozier.

§   For sale. 300 acres of land lying on Tallulah River, 30 acres of bottom, reasonably good timbered, common farm buildings. One mile from Tallulah Falls. The place [is] well watered. Price $1,000 cash. Apply for terms.

§   Mr. M. L. Shirley was in town Tuesday.

§   H. K. Cannon is off on a wagoning trip, down the country.

§   Newton Thomas, of Franklin, N. C., spent Saturday night at the Wall House.

§   Bring on your eggs to W. R. L. and T. J. Ritchie.

§   A. J. Duncan and J. H. Coffee of Chechero attended the meeting here yesterday.

§   John W. Green and daughter, Miss Ada, were in the city yesterday.

§   A singing was enjoyed by a number of young people at J. M. Marsingale's Saturday night.

§   Julius Parker, of Persimmon, was attending the school meeting here Wednesday.

§   The hands are working the Warwoman road beyond the saddle gap this week, under the alternative system.

§   Thanks to Sydney Bradley, of Rabun Gap, for favors.

§   Only one prisoner in jail now.

§   Ed Marsingale spent Sunday on Burton.

§   Only three weeks more of our school.

§   Moses Shirley sold to Nelson Tilley yesterday one hog weighing 278 pounds, and bringing at the present price of pork $22.24.

§   W. F. Holden, of Pine Mt., was here yesterday.

§   J. F. Ezelle, of Memphis Tenn. and a nursery agent, is in town.

§   Capt. Wm. Berry, of Clarkesville, was in town Monday.

§   C. D. Hughes, Dept. U. S. Marshal, left Tuesday morning for Gainesville with two prisoners, McClain and English.

§   Lester Blalock, of Persimmon, was at the Parker House Monday.

§   F. A. Bell spent Saturday night and Sunday with home folk east of town.

§   Tom Mitchell attended court in Macon county, N. C., last week.

§   Rabun County is destined to get a big boom.

§   The Carolina Locust Pin and Mica Company's plant, located at Spruce, was destroyed by fire last Saturday morning about three o'clock. The fire was not discovered until the building was about half burned and consequently no machinery was saved. The engine, however, escaped injury. About 40,000 pins were burned. The loss is heavy. The exact amount is not known, but will run into thousands of dollars.

§   Today is thanksgiving day.

§   The editor is now engaged with the surveying corps of the Tallulah Falls Railway Extension, as levelman for Chief Engineer W. W. Phillips.

§   A. B. Forrester, of Persimmon, as at the Parker House Saturday night.

§   Mr. and Mrs. J. R. Ritchie spent Sunday at the bedside of of Mrs. W. R. L. Ritchie, in Tennessee Valley.

§   The engine for the Thomas Locust Pin Mill has been moved here and the mill will be at the old tannery stand shortly.

§   Any person knowing anything about a halter Dr. Ellenburgher left somewhere belonging to me, will do me a favor by saying something about it. J. R. Ritchie.

§   Bill Penland was over from Persimmon Monday.

§   Apple tree agents by the car load.

§   The committee selected some time since to locate site for the erection of the Clayton high school buildings will resume labor here Wednesday. The committee decided to build the college in East End, near J. F. Earl's.

§   Several days ago, while climbing a tree I accidentally fell, breaking my leg. I would advise all boys to be careful about climbing, as there is no fun in breaking a leg. Luther Turpen, Tallulah Falls.

§   Eugene Mozely, of West End, was on the streets Wednesday.

§   John Carter, of Toccoa, came up Monday to visit his sister Mrs. Lee Ritchie, in the valley, who has been confined for some weeks with Typhoid fever.

§   Thanksgiving turkey dinners are very popular here to-day.

§   It is rumored that John Burton, of Rabun, will succeed Hon. Farish Carter Tate in the House of Congress.

§   Mrs. R. A. Parker, of Persimmon, who has been quite sick for some time, is reported to be much improved.

§   Mrs. Lee Ritchie, who has been very ill with Typhoid fever, is reported as we go to press to be resting much more comfortable with fair chances of an early convalescence.

§   Thanks to Horace McCurry for some wood.

§   Notice to Teachers. The Rabun County Teachers Association will meet in the court house December 6th 1902. We will try to have something in which every teacher should be interested. Let every one come without fail. If you have not brought in your reports, bring them in on that day. This Nov. 27, 1902. A. A. O'Kelley, C. S. Com'r and President of Rabun Co. Teachers' Association.

§   Georgia, Rabun County.

J. F. Godfrey, administrator upon the estate of Ancel Godfrey, late of said county, deceased, having filled his petition for discharge, this is to cite all persons concerned to show cause against the granting of the discharge, at the regular term of the court of Ordinary for said county to be held on the first Monday in Jan. 1903, this 22nd day of November, 1902. W. S. Long, Ordinary.

§   Stecoa.

Mr. Russell Woodall, who has been sick for some time, is convalescent.

Mr. and Mrs. V. C. Taylor are spending a few days in Cornelia having some dental work done.

Mrs. Gussie Cannon, of Tallulah Falls, is visiting relatives on the creek this week.

Misses Zelma Price and Laura Wall and Messrs. Tom Singleton and Marcus Taylor spent last Saturday night with Mattie and May Price.

Miss Ella Ramey's school closed the 15th with an entertainment. Everything was all O. K.

Ask Adolphus Ramey if he ever received any answer to his letter.

Ask Ada Ramey if it is alright, just so it is in the family.

The young folks enjoyed a candy drawing at Mr. Thomas Ramey's Saturday night.

Miss Lillie Whitmire spent last Wednesday night with May Price.

§   J. M. Bell. The Blacksmith. Two miles east of Clayton. All kinds of blacksmithing done at reasonable prices.

December 4, 1902
Volume 5, Number 47

§   We hear it talked that our friend W. H. Duncan will build a large hotel in Clayton. "Bud" is hustler enough to build it and can command the wherewith.

§   Mrs. Mary B. Watts, of Tiger, is in very poor health. She has been under the treatment of Dr. J. C. Dover for some time.

§   W. C. Donaldson still continues in feeble health.

§   The social event of the past week was the assembling of quite a number of young people of the town at the residence of Mr. J. F. Earl Saturday afternoon.
    There were present Miss Leila and Zoie Cannon, Misses Vinnie and Florence Marsingale, Miss Lillie Norton, Misses May and Lizzie Donaldson, and Miss Hannah Whitmire.

§   There will be a lot of changes to some people in the coming year.

§   It is amusing to hear some say we are going to have a railroad.

§   Misses Eliza and Effie Duncan are the guests of their sister Mrs. Swofford at Demorest. They probably will visit in Atlanta before they return.

§   J. E. Derrick is in very poor health. He has been confined to his home for several days the past week.

§   The School Building.

After viewing the different grounds offered by the citizens in town the committee appointed for the purpose of locating a building site for the college accepted the proposition made by J. F. Earl, which is eight acres of land with the right of a spring that can be easily thrown into the building. In addition to this he gives to the college a handsome cash donation. The site selected is what as known as the Norton hill, which lays about seven eights of a mile east of the court house. The site selected is a commanding one and so far as we know satisfactory to all concerned. Mr. Earl's donation is a liberal one and now it is to be hoped that in the near future that a handsome building will adorn the beautiful elevated plot of ground selected by the committee and so generously given by Mr. Earl. We have made no inquiry as to the size of the building but we hope that every citizen in the county can point to with pride. Just now is a good time to call the attention of the philanthropist. There are millionaires who are trying to get rid of their fortunes by donating to charitable institutions and no doubt if the proper efforts are made we can get aid from them. But we are going to have a college. With a railroad nearly here and a college assured we do not see why Clayton should not begin to get on a hustle.

§   J. R. Ritchie killed a fine porker Monday. It weighed about two hundred and seventy five pounds.

§   [Illegible] [Singleton?] is clerking for [remainder cut off].

§   North Chechero.

Muddy roads.

Rainy weather.

Miss Ada Ramey and her three brothers have entered school here.

Ask Lucy Duncan why she is so anxious for school to close.

Mr. W. J. Smith went to Clayton Tuesday.

Mr. J. W. Ramey and daughter Ada went to town last Saturday.

Miss Helen Dotson is visiting relatives on Chechero this week.

Mr. Jesse Smith went to S. C., last Saturday.

Ask Misses Callie York and Effie Smith why they are so sorry school will close soon.

Minnie Smith spent Monday night with Miss Lucie Duncan.

Prof. F. D. Singleton went to Clayton Monday.

B. E. Ramey and his better half have returned home from Blue Hights.

Ask Willie Carver where he went last Sunday evening.

E. L. McConnell went to Warwoman Monday.

§   Warwoman.

Corn shuckings, candy pullings, and road working is the order of the day.

We are having some rainy weather now.

Mr. A. M. Holden is off down the country with a load of apples.

Mr. Sam Beck killed a fine pork last week.

Mr. John Carver was on Warwoman a few days ago.

Mrs. J. A. Wilson is in feeble health.

Miss Gussie Ledford was all smiles last Sunday.

Mr. Julius Beck is at Fort Hill, S. C., guarding convicts.

Ask Sam Holden who passed the road while he was working the roads.

A nice sociable was enjoyed at the home of Jeff D. Beck last Saturday night.

Luther Swofford caught a wild cat last week that measured four feet in length.

Miss Fannie Turpen knocked the bark off her finger with a hammer while cracking walnuts the other night.

Everything seems lonely since Miss Dovie Williams closed her school.

Mr. Jeff Beck has made four hundred gallons of syrup and is still making. Hurrah for Jeff!

Mr. Sam Bowers will soon have his new house completed.

Miss Lena Bleckley is at home after teaching a successful term of school in Germany.

Success to our county paper.

§   Bert Paris was at home from the railroad survey Sunday and Mon[day] [remainder cut off].

§   J. E. Derrick killed a fine porker [remainder cut off].

§   Tallulah Falls.

The railroad is completed except the bridges and Captain Walker is pushing the work right along with them.

The piers in the Tallulah river are nearing completion. The spans will be 125 feet long.

One of the jolliest and most rushing men at the Falls is Mr. Magid, president of The Seri-Culture Company.

The merchants are all enjoying a good trade.

General William Phillips, of Marietta, is the guest of his son, Captain W. W. Phillips, several days last week. The General is in robust health and is one of Georgia's honored citizens. He is a highly honored Christian gentleman.

C. L. Hughlett is among the busiest men about the Falls.

Miss Sarah E. White expects to leave for an extended visit north after the holidays.

§   Mr. Almond and daughter, of Franklin, N. C., were the guests of Mr. and Mrs. S. S. Whitmire Sunday night. Miss Almond was on her way to Alabama.

§   All persons due M. B. Ellard anything are requested to make immediate settlement with me. [Remainder cut off.]

§   J. C. Pickett was appointed permanent administrator of the estate of Capt. S. M. Beck, deceased, last Monday.

§   Miss Tinnie Ledbetter killed a strange and large what is supposed to be a seafowl Tuesday at her home on the Blue Ridge. It made a noise like the bleating of a goat. It was web footed, and weighed 20 pounds.

§   A prominent delegation of citizens from the Valley are in town to-day purchasing goods. They say there never was as much money in Rabun county in its history.

§   A. L. Beck, of Cullasaga, N. C., called to see us Wednesday and gave us encouragement as usual.

§   We are obligated to Charlie Derrick, of Stonewall, for favors extended us.

§   Moses Shirley killed, Wednesday, a wild turkey, five partridges, one squirrell and a rabbit.

§   We spent Monday and Tuesday of the week grading a public road in Pine Mountain section. We find the people over the county largely in favor of the new road law, and especially the grading part. They say they can work with hope that they will have a good road when worked. The cry with the people is now graded roads.

§   We have long necks, short necks, big necks and little necks, but the longest neck we have seen lately is a gourd that Mrs. Nelson Moore of Wolffork brought to our office to-day that has a neck or handle that is 38 inches long and as [straight] as an arrow.

§   Old Tiger.
Capt. Hampton and some friends celebrated Thanksgiving with a fine dinner. It is reported that they had turkey, rabbit, squirrell and 'possum.

Hon. J. H. Derrick passed up last Saturday to spend the night with his father, and returned to Atlanta Sunday. He said the House of Representatives had passed a resolution not to let any member off for anything. He also said a great many bills were up in the house.

Judge W. S. Long passed down toward Tallulah Falls last Saturday.

We understand that John A. Reynolds, Editor and Surveyor, is engaged with the rail road engineers.

Mr. W. D. Taylor, of Tallulah Falls, did not sell out for nothing but has bought a fine stock of new goods.

Esq. Wyly Pitts has got the south quarantine line discontinued indefinitely.

We understand that Hughlett and Co. have the contract of building the railroad in Clayton and hope it is true if they want it.

A gentleman of Cornelia has promised a young lady of Rabun a Cornelia lawyer. Wouldn't that be nice! But would it be lawful for non-residents to intermeddle and cross the quarantine line?

§ A Big Deal in Real Estate.

C. W. McDade and W. M. Turpin made one of the largest if not the largest sale of land ever consumated [*sic*] in Rabun county last week to W. C. Smith of Knoxville Tenn. The tract consists of forty thousand acres and all in Rabun county. Up going to press, titles have been passed upon, by their attorney Jas. R. Grant, of about twenty thousand acres, of the forty thousand acres and deeds deposited in the Cornelia Bank and the money will be paid within ten days. McDade and Turpen have been engaged in making the deal since Sepr. 1902, and have worked unceasingly. Success has crowned their efforts. We do not know what the consideration is but it foots up an enormous sum.

§ Strayed from my premises, one heifer yearling, one year old past, white specked and red. Marked, crop and split in the left ear, white face and horned. Any information will be gladly received by John W. Green, Clayton, Ga.

§ Lost. One two year old past steer, a brindle. When he left he had on a small bell. Mark, a crop and a split in the left, and a swallow fork and overbit in the right. Also one year old past steer, red with white tail. Mark, a crop and and split in the left, and a swallow fork and overbit in the right. Any information will be gladly received by C. C. Ledford, Pine Mountain, Ga.

§ Georgia, Rabun County.

To all whom it may concern: J. N. Crunkleton, administrator of C. J. Crunkleton, deceased, has in due form applied to the [undersigned] for leave to sell the lands belonging to the estate of said deceased, and said application will be heard on the first Monday in January next. This 2nd day of Dec., 1902. W. S. Long, Ordinary.

§   Tallulah Falls.

As we have seen no communication from our little berg recently we decided we would give you a few items. Our railroad is progressing nicely and we hope to be able to ride the iron horse to Franklin, N. C., before twelve months elapse.

Mr. Thomas Ramey and daughter Miss Ella, from Stecoa Falls, were in our town Monday, shopping.

Ordinary W. S. Long was at the Falls one day last week.

Col. R. E. A. Hamby and Prof. A. A. O'Kelley gave us a call on Tuesday.

Messrs. Augustus Ginn and Willard Taylor have opened a new commissary under the name of Ginn and Taylor with a large and varied stock of goods.

Mr. D. T. Duncan visited kins people at Tallulah a few days ago. Mr. Duncan is one of our best citizens and we were glad to see him.

Mr. Cecil R. Cannon returned from the Gate City Tuesday where he had been purchasing merchandise for the firm of Cannon and Hughlett.

Messrs. H. B. Stonecypher, of Tiger, and John Burton, of Clayton, were among us recently.

Chance Vickers came to the Falls Tuesday, "the rough rainy day."

Capt. W. W. Phillips returned from a trip below on Tuesday.

Col. John A. Reynolds gave us a call a few days ago.

Mr. James Bleckley passed through a few days ago enroute to the lower county carrying apples to market.

Mr. James A. Turpen returned from market Saturday.

'Squire Marcus Vandiver was in town a few days ago.

Miss Allie Stone has a few boarders for the winter season.

Mrs. James King has moved from the Robinson Hotel to the Robinson dwelling house. Hereafter travelers will find her in the place above stated, with plenty to eat and that that's [sic] good.

Mr. and Mrs. W. D. Young departed Sunday eve for Atlanta where they will perhaps stay for a-while. They have gone for medical assistance for Mr. Young's health, as it is known he has been in feeble health for some time.

Mr. J. Claude Green, a nice young man and merchant of Turnerville, was with us a few days ago.

Mr. L. B. Magid, the silk man, has several men at work under the directions of Mr. J. F. Robinson on his silk farm. Mr. Magid is a thorough going man in the silk business and an all around gentleman. We need more such men among us!

Success to your valuable paper!

December 11, 1902
Volume 5, Number 48

§   W. P. McCrackin, a former citizen of Rabun county, now of Demorest, was here Friday of last week. He kindly remembered the editor.

§   Allen S. Williams has moved to town and will occupy J. E. Bleckley's cottage until he can build on the property he purchased of J. B. Murray some time ago. Others have Clayton in view and we welcome all good citizens.

§   Our friend Ranson C. Smith, of Burton, sent us by Oliver Vickers two fine large strawberries just from the vine. Mr. Smith sent us word that he has a lot of them growing and ripening now, Dec. 6th. They must be a new variety or else a very late second crop.

§   We are obligated to our townsman J. C. Pickett for his sixth year's subscription. Mr. Pickett leads in paid up subscribers among our five hundred names on our book.

§   J. A. Wall, our clever constable, has moved to the cottage belonging to L. N. Robins in east Clayton.

§   The Carolina Locust Pin Company has moved to the Canup block in North Clayton.

§   Dr. W. J. Green is in Atlanta viewing old scenes at the capital city, and attending to business matters.

§   Judge Long is in the Gate City for the holidays on business.

§   J. S. Ramey is in Atlanta for a few days.

§   Miss Lizzie Duncan is gone to the Gate City.

§   Col. J. H. Estill, of Savannah, Ga., a candidate for governor, has been appointed a member of the trustees of the soldier's home by Governor J. M. Terrell.

§   Mr. Langston, road superintendent, returned from Pine Mountain Monday evening and reports that seventy-five men are at work on a change of the public road. The change is seven thousand feet long and a grade of four feet in one hundred. The change is at the Pigpen Gap. So much interested are the people in the change that men of sixty years and over are at work and of course voluntarily.

§   Miss Blanche Wall has returned from Atlanta.

§   Misses Ella and Effie Duncan have returned from visiting in Demorest and Cornelia.

§   Henry Burrell and family, of Burton were visiting in the first of the week.

§   Mrs. Lee Ritchie is very much improved.

§   Mrs. Watts, an aged and [illegible] lady, who lives but two miles west of Tiger, is very feeble. Her recovery is [illegible].

§   The [illegible] resulted in the election of Bill Holcomb and C. O. Gilds. Holcomb got sixty votes of the sixty seven that was polled. He said he used printer's ink and that he has learned something about the printing business.

§   There was a regular stampede here Saturday evening after the close of the Bailiff's election. There were loud threats and for a while it looked like there would be murder but fell short and only a little accidental blood was spilt. Of course some of the boys got too much booze which was the cause of all the trouble.

§   We are told that it is the intention of the leading citizens of our town to hold an election for Mayor and Councilmen the first of next year. If the report is true that we are to have protection it will be news gladly received by every law abiding citizen in this community. Such scenes and conduct as is at times carried on is simply disgusting, not only to the man who loves order but to the participants in the conduct. As little as you may think of municipal government it is not only a protection to the civil element but it is a safeguard thrown around those who are disposed to criminate themselves in an intoxicated condition. Hundreds of the best men in this country have weaknesses and the law should step in as their guardian when they are not properly at themselves. A man when intoxicated is temporarily insane and they should not be allowed to have their way and roam in this condition. In the name of decency and good order and for the protection of our children do not let up in the matter of a municipal government. It is a good and wholesome move and as the intelligence of the town are the movers and as intelligence governs the world we are hopeful of the long needed law of protection. In all ages [past] and all ages to come, people, when congregated, will, more or less, violate the law, and the only thing that can be done is to marshal them. The Tribune stands ready to publish, free of charge, any notice necessary to effectually carry out the intentions of the good citizens of this town.

§   Germany.

Mr. Isaac Justus and James Collenback are gone to Athens with a load of apples.

Mr. A. E. Dickerson, Leila and Letha, went to Clayton Wednesday.

Mr. Jess Page and Austin Carnes were pleasant callers among friends of this community Wednesday night.

Mr. Samuel Taylor had a corn-shucking Thursday.

Mr. Damascus Alman went to Clayton Saturday. We wonder if he won the bet.

Mr. Lex Justus and sister Della from Persimmon, went to Clayton Saturday.

Miss Mary Pitts visited home folks Sunday, after a stay of a week or two in the valley.

Mr. Rockaway Keener and Jesse Taylor, from Wolffork, were at preaching Sunday.

Mr. G. N. and J. N. Justus started bright and early Sunday morning for Persimmon. We wish the boys much success in their early start.

Mr. and Mrs. C. F. York were in this community Sunday.

(Germany news, intended for last week.)

Rain is plentiful in Germany nowadays.

Most all of the roads have been worked recently.

J. O. [illegible] and Ed Almon have just returned from a market trip.

A. E. Dickerson had a corn shucking Saturday.

Mr. George Bleckley made a flying trip through this section Saturday night.

Mary Pitts and Florence Justus have just returned from Habersham on a business trip.

James Colenback purchased a new wagon a few days ago.

John McCurry was up with us attending to business Saturday.

We wish Mr. Jesse Justus much success in his western home.

C. F. York passed through the community last Thursday.

Prof. J. Marcus Bleckley made a flying trip through Germany Monday morning. We hope he will go slower by the time he gets to the foot of the mountain.

Mr. Damascus Almon spent Sunday with James Colenback and family.

§   Stonepile.

It is raining. This is my fifty fourth birthday and I have been confined to my room two weeks. I can not do anything but write or talk and set in the house and study. Those who have rheumatism know how to sympathize with me.

This is the first day of December, 1902. What my dinner will be is unknown to me. Fifty four years ago I guess it was milk.

There have been many lonely days passed my life. Many times have I wished that I had been carried from my mother to the grave. One time I would have changed places with the cur that lay in the yard. At other points I would not have swapped places with the President of the United States. I have worked very hard to make a living and now I am not able to enjoy it but some one else may. I have thought at times would write all my ups and downs, griefs and sorrows and the many changes that have passed with me and send it to some editor, but I thought it would be too lengthy for them. I often think of Arp's old trees falling and where they are all gone and how soon we will all be gone and what have we left behind, as it seems most people want to leave a fortune for their children, though it might be best to leave good schools and churches and a good government for the people to live under. What it takes to make up all these things others say can.

We missed all the entertainment and the potatoe wedding. We guess the girl that woke up crying dreamed of the big potatoe.

§   Quartz.

Intended for last week.

We have rain plenty.

Road working is over with some of the boys and they say they are not sorry of it.

John Teems likes to work so well he says he would not care if road working would last all year long.

John Dillingham and his daughter Mary are just back from Cornelia. Mary brought back with her a fine sewing machine.

J. C. Howard reports more corn than usual and he has it all gathered up and shucked it.

We are glad to learn that Miss Matildy Parker is improving after having a long spell of sickness.

M. H. James says he did not get to see all of his children in a week during road working as he had to leave home before they got up in the morning or they would be gone to bed when he got home at night.

Gather up your corn.

Christmas will soon be here.

§   All persons due M. B. Ellard anything are requested to make immediate settlement with me. F. A. Taylor.

§   A copy of The Mountaineer, Vol. 1, No. 1, published at Cleveland, Ga., is before us. The Mountaineer is a semi-monthly, and a bright little sheet. We bespeak for it a long life.

§   It will be remembered by our citizens that Clayton had less drinking, rioting, etc., last Christmas than for many years previous. The cause of this decrease in drinking is unknown to us, but we remember printing an article in The Tribune as to whether it is the proper way to celebrate Christmas or not. Almost every one of our exchanges also discussed the matter. And everywhere it seems there was, comparatively speaking, nice conduct. We believe that our people here will stay sobor—at least we hope so. Is getting drunk the way to celebrate the birth of Christ, who died to save you? We say, "No." And yet we know people who will not take a drink through the year, and we find them in a manner crazy, due to intoxication. Gentlemen, if you will stop and think this over, we believe you will feel better after the holidays are over.

§   On Thanksgiving day [of] the year 1901, one of our foremost citizens happened to be in Cornelia, so the story goes. He was mingling with the people in the town and ran across Mr. Candler, a resident of Cornelia and a brother of Governor Candler. Candler was invited to a thanksgiving dinner given by Rev. C. C. Spence, of Demorest, Ga., and thought he would take along our Rabun man with him. They went together and when all were seated at the table Rev. Spence announced that instead of a blessing each one would repeat a verse from the Bible. The member at the head of the table repeated a vere [sic], each on following. The person next to our Rabun man was almost as ignorant of the Bible as he. So when it came around to him he repeated a verse: "Jesus wept." Our citizen could not think of any verse to repeat, so he looked around for several moments until the eyes of the guests were on him, when he slowly remarked: "He sure did."

§ Atlanta was visited by a very destructive fire Tuesday morning, the damage is estimated at $350,000.

§ All persons interested in the progress of the high school in Rabun county are invited to attend our next meeting on the third Saturday in this month, the 20th. We will be glad to have you with us. J. F. Earl.

§ We are rather late in telling it, but the North Georgia Conference which convened in Atlanta some time ago, called new preachers to this territory, names, Pendergrass and Gaines. We failed to see what disposition was made of Revs. Jay and Landrum.

§ Stecoah.
  Mr. Gus Brewer passed through this community Friday.
  Mrs. Lulu Perry visited Mrs. J. W. McCrackin Saturday.
  Mrs. Mattie Ramey, an aged widow, died at her home Sunday morning. The community will mourn her loss.
  Mr. G. M. Williams spent Saturday evening at Mr. W. H. Price's.
  Ask Ada Ramey if she was in a hurry Sunday.
  Mr. Marlor Whitmire and C. Woodall spent Sunday with Miss Mattie and May Price.
  Mrs. J. W. McCrackin and Mrs. E. C. Price visited Mrs. Ramey Saturday evening.
  Ask Miss Ada and Ella Ramey and Lizzie McCrackin if they like peanut candy.
  Miss Ella Ramey went to Tiger Saturday.
  Mr. E. C. Price has returned from the market.
  William Ramey spent Sunday night with Thomas Ramey.
  Little Jerry Ramey visited Wesley Stubblefield Monday night.
  Ask Henry Smith who he saw pass the road Tuesday.

§ Green apples hanging on the trees yet, Dec. 8th.

§ John Hooper, of Burton, was at The Parker Hotel Monday.

§ The sky was crimson at sunset Monday.

§ [Illegible] J. E. Derrick is [illegible] seriously inflicted.

§ [Illegible] in Atlanta for several days.

§ Fred Smythe, of New York, was at The Parker House Friday night.

§ Ed Ritchie went to Westminster Tuesday.

§ Ranson Smith was over from Burton Monday.

§ J. W[?]. Jones, of Tallulah Falls, was in town Saturday.

§ Miller Ritchie spent Saturday night with Sheriff and Mrs. J. R. Ritchie.

§ D. L. Parker went to Burton Saturday.

§ Samuel Chastain, Bill Chastain and Hut Chastain, of Burton, were in town Monday.

§ Misses Lucy Duncan and Lizzie York, of Checheroe, were in the city Saturday, attending Teachers' meeting.

§ Prof. Foster spent Sunday with home folks on Burton.

§ J. H. Coffee, of Checheroe, is in town to-day.

§ Mrs. J. M. Long, of Tiger, was shopping in town Saturday.

§ Asbury Henson, of Habersham county, was here yesterday.

§ Elihue Parker, of Persimmon, was in the city Tuesday.

§ Miss Lulu Parker and brother Rufe, of Persimmon, spent Saturday in town.

§ From the appearance of our stores, one would suppose Christmas was here.

§ Sheriff-elect Tom Carver, of Checheroe, is in town to-day.

§ Jesse Dunlap left last Friday for Little Rock, Arkansas. He will be gone some time.

§ John W. Green was in town Saturday.

§ Geo. P. Erwin, Gov. Terrell's secretary, died Sunday night in Atlanta. Consumption was the cause of his death. His remains were interred in the cemetery at Clarkesville Monday. Mr. Erwin was an exceedingly smart lawyer, and had many friends in this county who will regret to hear of his death. We extend sympathy to the bereaved family.

§   Miss Mary Scruggs has been spending the most of the week in town, the guest of Mrs. J. S. Ramey.

§   Miss May Donaldson left Tuesday for Westminster, S. C., where she will spend some time.

§   Nelson Tilley has from five to ten wagons going all the time now, hauling goods from the railroad.

§   J. F. Earl went to Chechero Tuesday.

§   Webb Johnson is up from Hartwell. He is still setting out apple trees.

§   Mr. Ed Poole, of Buffalo, N. Y., a timber inspoctor [*sic*], is here examining land for a large company. He was at The Parker House Friday and Saturday.

§   J. B. Jones, of Burton, was in town Tuesday.

§   Guy Wykle, son of Bud Wykle, was accidentally killed last Saturday, near their home in the Tennessee Valley. He and Young Neville were out with some hogs and it is supposed laid his gun down with the muzzle on a log while he headed off the hogs and when he went to take up his gun the hammer struck the boy, firing and practically blowing off the top of his head. Young Neville was some distance ahead and heard the report of the gun, and after waiting for a while went to where Wykle lay dead. The accident is a sad one and we extend sympathy to the bereaved.

§   Misses Ada and Nora Justus, and Horley and Miss Rosa Thompson, of Persimmon, were at The Parker House Saturday night.

§   Dillard.
     You will have to excuse your correspondent for not writing last week on account of the bad weather.
     Christmas is here, we think, by the way we see so many people passing the road with plenty of tangle foot.
     Misses Eula and Lizzie Dillard, Misses Mary Neville and Ethel Powell, accompanied by Mr. Frank Dillard, attended the Teachers' meeting at Clayton Saturday.
     Thomas Kelley is very sick with Typhoid fever.
     Mr. John Ritchie, of Wolffork, is moving to his farm on Kelley's creek.
     D. D. and J. A. Turpen were in the Valley the first of the week on business.
     Mr. Sexton White, of Warwoman was in the valley the latter part of the

week.

Misses Fannie and Lizzie Martin are with Miss Ada Green on Warwoman.

On last Saturday Mr. Wykle, while hunting got his head blowed off by the gun going off in his face. The bereaved family has our sympathy.

§   Mud Creek.

Here we are knocking at your door again.

We are having some rainy times.

Mr. Lon Dillingham has moved to Tennessee.

Mr. Tom Kelley has Typhoid fever.

Mrs. John Darnell is sick with Typhoid fever.

Mr. John Howard passed through this section Friday.

Guess what young girl walked a half of a mile to get to ride with a certain boy Sunday.

Will Dorsey is up from Gainesville.

Mr. Charlie Grist was on Mud Creek Saturday after a [load] of fodder. Hurrah for Charlie!

Misses Pearl and Laura Martin who has been spending a few days in the Flatts have returned home.

§   North Checheroe.

Mr. J. F. Earl was on Checheroe Monday and Tuesday.

Miss Lizzie McCrackin entered school here.

Miss Zelma and Geneva Price and Lucy Duncan went to Clayton Saturday.

Arlis Marsongale was with his best girl Sunday.

Charley Coffee spent Saturday night on Warwoman.

Messrs. Thomas Singleton and C[?]. C. Dickerson visited our school last Tuesday.

Zelma Price spent Sunday with May and Arah Smith.

Miss Callie York spent Wednesday night with Miss Effie Smith.

Miss Lucie Duncan spent Sunday with Mrs. W. S. Price.

J. L. York and daughter, Miss Lizzie, went to South Carolina last Tuesday.

§   Georgia—Rabun County.

To all whom it may concern: W. B. Watts having made application to me in due form to be appointed administrator upon the estate of G. W. Long, late of said county, notice is hereby given that said application will be heard at the regular term of the court of Ordinary for said county, to be held on the first Monday in January, 1903.

Witness my hand and official signature. This 9th day of December, 1902. W. S. Long, Ordinary.

§ Rabun Sheriff Sales. Georgia—Rabun County.

Will be sold, before the court house door in said county, on the first Tuesday in January, 1903, between the legal hours of sale, the following real estate situated in said county to wit: (1) one half undivided interest in part of land lot No. (26) in the first district and first section of said county and bounded as follows: On the north by lands which was sued for in ejectment by A. J. Trusty against Owen Coleman, on the east by Manuel Nichols, on the south by lands of Coleman Justice, on the west by lands of Wm. Metcalf, and containing 75 acres more or less. Levied on and to be sold as the property of A. J. Trusty, by virtue of a fi fa issued from the Superior court of said county in favor of Owen Coleman against A. J. Trusty. Levy made and returned to me by E. L. McConnell, Dept. Sheriff notice given in terms of the law. This Dec. 10th 1902. J. R. Ritchie, Sheriff.

Index

Items are indexed only once per page on which they appear. Wild and domesticated animals were indexed together.

agriculture (cont.)
dew berries, 111
eggs, 171, 195, 237
farmers, 27, 33, 37, 49, 52, 61, 73,
74, 81, 90, 95, 96, 103, 121,
131
farming, 70, 71, 73, 74, 75, 76
fields, 88
fruit, 40, 74, 80, 111, 114, 121,
133, 150, 179, 192, 233
fruit trees, 53, 74, 93, 100, 113,
154, 193, 218
garden, 51, 57, 68, 110
gooseberry, 131
gourds, 186, 244
grape vines, 110
hares, Belgian, 67
hay, 62, 232
heifer, 104, 202, 219, 245
hog (ham, pig, pork, porker), 9, 16,
34, 38, 43, 57, 58, 99, 101, 103,
114, 151, 182, 183, 194, 205,
212, 217, 226, 227, 232, 235,
238, 242, 243, 254
horse, 22, 30, 51, 61, 114, 127,
132, 185
huckleberries, 103, 111
lambs, 118
milk, 195, 250
molasses, 213
mules, 18, 34, 35, 50, 69, 108,
115, 149, 205, 211, 215, 221,
233, 236
oats, 195, 224
onions, 110, 122
orchards, 88, 205, 207
oxen, 14, 18
peaches, 80, 101
peas, 8, 187
cow, 194
ground, 194
persimmons, 9, 16, 182
potatoes, 195, 212, 250
Irish, 140, 147, 171, 225, 232
new, 123
sweet, 123, 194, 224, 232
produce, 35, 71, 103, 122, 142,
146, 147, 173, 188, 191, 192,

agriculture, produce (cont.)
213, 216, 217, 221, 234
rhubarb, 115
rice, 194, 195
rye, 1, 49, 126, 132, 187, 195
seri-culture, 224, 226, 243
sheep (mutton), 33, 88, 147, 149,
151, 185, 186, 187, 213, 232
silk, 161, 226, 246
steer, 61, 245
stock, 69
strawberries, 247
sugar, 132, 194, 195
syrup, 187, 190, 191, 201, 203,
212, 213, 243
tobacco, 122, 189, 194
turkey, 17, 34, 79, 197, 239, 244
turnips, 122, 209, 221, 230, 232,
233
watermelon, 167, 174
wheat, 195, 224
yearling, 185, 198, 245
Alabama, 244
Anniston, 122
Birmingham, 131, 224
Shelby County, 224
Albert, Prince, 88
Albridge
Rev., 42
Allen
A. K., 130
A. S., 58
Thomas, 54
Allison
G. W., 140, 210
G. W., Mrs., 140, 210
Allman, Alman, Almon, Almond
D. B., 41
Damascus, 41, 249, 250
Ed, 1, 147, 190, 249
Essie, 37
J. A., 18, 37, 39, 49, 59, 115, 162
J. W., 18, 41, 67
James, 37, 199
John W., 32, 162
Miss, 244
Mr., 41, 244
Pearl, 37

Allman, Alman, Almon, Almond (cont.)
  Rev., 134
Anderson
  Elinor, 122
Angel
  Ed, 96
Apple, 128
  Mess., 127
Aragon, the, 233
Arkansas, 51, 62, 101
  Elem Springs, 24
  Ledwedge[?], 160
  Little Rock, 253
  Taylor, 48, 88
Arnold
  Raney, 150
Arp
  Bill, 35
Arrehdale
  M. L., 8
Arrendale
  Augustus, 199
  Basha, Mrs., 71
  Eaf, 199
  Eliza, 6, 26, 112
  Fred, 234
  Gus(s), 71, 118
  J., 150
  J. F., 16, 76
  J. F., Mrs., 16, 135
  J. M., 6, 11, 32, 71, 141, 188,
    213, 216
  J. V., 118
  Joal M., 157
  Joel M., 93
  John, 7, 55
  John V., 7, 12, 112
  Lester, 8, 234
  Liza, 13
  Lizzie, 26
  Lula, 16
  M. L., 13, 35, 158, 188, 213
  Mary, 13, 26, 79, 94, 96, 112,
    199
  Meaks, 81, 135
  Meeks, 141, 221, 234
  Ramey, 142
  Roney, 65

Arrendale (cont.)
  Rufus, 34
  S. M., 11
  T. A., 118
  Thos., 199
  Vig, 5
  Vig, Mrs., 91
  Viola, 118
  W. L., Mrs., 76
  Will, 10
ash, prickly, 172
asylum, deaf and dumb, 108
Atkins
  B. H., 77
  Sutton, 127
Atkinson
  J. M., 190
Australia, 178
B.
  J. D., 213
B[?]
  John, 216
Bagle
  Tom, 82
Bain, 197
Baird
  N. B., 62
Baker, 200
  Candidate, 167
  E. H., 23, 24, 81, 188, 193, 221
  Eli H., 32
  F. R., 162
  Hoyl, 119
  J., 188
  John, 234
  Mart, 216, 234
  W. M., 112, 213, 234
  W. S., 3
Ballew
  Belle, 28
  Mr., 108, 115
  Prof., 99
Bancroft
  George, 153
Barclay
  H. W., 33
Barnard, Bernard
  Annie, 116

Bradshaw
  Horace, 45
  J. E., Sr., 162
Bramblett
  J. B., 77
  R. W., Mrs., 74
Bransom
  E. C., 174
Brewer
  Gus, 252
Brindle
  Mr., 218
Bron
  Charlie, 32
Brooksher
  Rev., 10
broom sage, 139
Brown
  Berry, 134
  Chas. H[?]., 67
  D. C., 88, 217
  D. C., Mrs., 217
  Fay, 134
  Geo., 184
  George, 164
  George, Mrs., 202
  Mrs., 112, 162, 217
  Oscar, 65
  Rev., 22, 57, 62, 82, 89, 93, 110,
    124, 126, 134, 152, 160, 167,
    203
  Sam, 223
Brownlee
  W. V., 153
Buchanan
  Roy, 203
Bugle
  Sam, 75
Burch
  R. D., 102
  Susie, 102
  W. D., 115
Burnett
  S. S., 131, 221
  Shered, 159
Burrel, Burrell
  A. E., 174
  A. J. M., 162

Burrel, Burrell (cont.)
  Bright, 157
  George, 51
  H. M., 158
  Henry, 135, 248
  Henry, Mrs., 135
  Henry N., 32
  J. A., 134
  J. S., 111, 114, 117, 165, 168,
    199
  John A., 157
  Mr., 37
  Mrs., 37
  Prof., 28, 118, 135, 203, 220
  T. M., 150
  Thomas, 26
  W. J., 105, 165, 189
  W. P., 105
Burton
  [---nn], 190
  J. M., 37
  Jerry, 14, 162
  John, 34, 47, 185, 232, 239, 246
  Right, 234
  Vicey, 188
  William, 87
  Willie, 96
business and industry, 74
  [Illegible] Bros. Nursery and
    Orchard, 24
  A. L. Dillard store, 62
  Alladain Mining and Milling Co.,
    55, 78
  A. T. Morris Wholesale Company,
    15
  attorney at law, 66, 88, 109, 127
  B. B. and Stone, 90
  Barclay gold mines, 15
  blacksmith, 57, 88, 126, 146, 240
  Brobston Fendig and Co., 161
  cane making, 187
  Cannon and Hughlett, 246
  Cannon and Thompson, 24, 185
  Carolina Locust Pin and Mica Co.,
    238, 247
  coal field, 180
  Cornelia Bank, 80, 86, 245
  cotton mills, 33

Cumberland Mountains, 180
    Coal Creek mine, 180
    Walden Ridge mine, 180
[D---]
    Effie, 217
    Eliza, 217
Daniels, Daniel
    Graver, 16
    Graves, 55, 71
    Jennie, 55
Darnell, 82
    A. A., 18, 130, 147, 174, 221
    Asbury, 118
    Bry, 147, 174
    Bud, 147
    Della, 174
    G. H., 125
    G. W., 38, 150
    G. W., Mrs., 38
    Icy, 174
    John, 172, 214
    John, Mrs., 255
    Lex, 118, 174
    Lizzie, 125
    Sallie, 68
    W. H., 87, 96
Daughters of the Confederacy
    Longstreet Chapter, 236 – 237
David
    John H., 88
Davidson
    A. M., 213
    Andy, 11
    Mr., 115
Davis
    John H., 87, 145
    Mr., 32
Davison
    R. W., 197
Dean
    H. H., 21, 88, 145, 168
debate, 151 161
    F. C. Tate Debating and
        Declaining[?] Society, 74
    society, 134
deer, 197
DeEsteshaxy, 111

Democrat Party (Democrats), 12 – 13,
    19, 22, 23, 44, 47, 53, 57, 60, 77,
    84, 85, 108, 145, 146, 151,
    180 – 182, 186 – 187, 200
Denney
    Carrie, 46
    J. S., 164, 165, 207
    John, 46, 164
    May, 46
    R[?]. J., 234
Denton
    Homer, 199
Derrick, 200
    C. W., 81
    Charlie, 206, 244
    J. E., 24, 76, 122, 132, 185, 204,
        206, 232, 241, 243, 252
    J. E., Mrs., 132
    J. H., 12 – 13, 45, 82, 245
    J. H.
    J. W., 132
    J. W., Mrs., 132
    John H., 115, 167
    John H. Jr., 14
    Joseph W., 24
    Mrs., 110
    Squire, 110, 131
devil shoestring, 174
Dewey's army, 90
Dickerson, Dicerson, Dickesson
    A. E., 1, 41, 69, 89, 165, 249
    Bryant, 20
    C. C., 255
    E. A., 37
    Hindy, 33
    J. L., 97
    Joseph L., 3, 5, 46, 54, 85, 151,
        226 – 227
    Jos. L., 60
    Leila, 249
    Letha, 41, 249
    Luther, 20
    M. L., 4
    W. T., 4
Dickson
    Alfred E., 32
    Clara, 124
    Emory, 24

Dickson (cont.)
George, 17
George W., 87
Harold, 124
J. C., 86
J. L., 65
J. S., 71, 90, 118, 141
Lafayette, 93, 96, 130, 172
Rev., 42
Robert, 141
W. A., 42
W. S., 96
Waller, 57
Walter, 87, 130, 166, 206
Dillard
[Illegible], 172
A. L., 62, 75
B. R., 12, 76, 84, 98, 134, 214
B. R., Mrs., 75, 134
Bob, 12
Eula, 62, 89, 112, 123, 175, 203, 254
Frank, 26, 254
George, 50
Hiram, 9, 33
Ida, 175
J. H., 62
James H., 45 – 46
Jas. H., 32
Lizzie, 26, 68, 79, 117, 168, 203, 254
Mattie, 62, 175
May, 175
R. B., 82
R. E. L., 37
Reed, 11
Reed, Mrs., 11
Z. B., 45, 51, 92, 99
Zack, 12
Dillingham
Emory, 50
Hade, 119
John, 250
Lizzie, 1
Lon, 255
Mary, 50, 175, 250
Nancy, 61 – 62
Sarah, 50, 175

Dills
M. A., 188
disease and illness
abscess, 198
accident, 116, 140, 166, 167, 172, 243, 254
affection of the eye, 177
boil, blood, 192
broken ankle, 64
broken leg, 45
bronchial trouble, 166
burns, 22, 25, 186
cold, 109, 198
critical, 132
cut, 26, 160
declining, 177
Erysipelas, 10
feeble, 1, 5, 37, 65, 81, 127, 132, 142, 147, 172, 176, 189
feeling badly, 192, 198
fell, 203
fever, 82, 126, 149, 152, 166, 176, 192, 209, 223, 235
grip, the, 73
health, 32, 56, 70, 74, 80, 90, 111, 118, 127, 147, 151, 161, 188, 232, 241, 243, 246
heart failure, 31
hurt, 149, 214, 233
ill, 38, 42, 48, 66, 78, 80, 101, 135, 142, 175, 187, 201, 217, 219, 233
illness, 38, 177
inflicted, 252
injury, 160
lame foot, 138
measles, 37, 61
medical treatment, 185, 186
not well, 5, 21, 30, 212
pneumonia fever, 223
poor health, 147, 179
quarantine, 235
rheumatism, 56, 110, 166 – 167, 202, 203, 222, 231, 250
scarlet fever, 15, 82, 147, 166, 176, 180, 213, 219, 235
sick, 10, 11, 12, 17, 20, 22, 23, 25, 26, 27, 31, 33, 34, 42, 61, 68,

disease and illness, sick (cont.)
71, 75, 76, 82, 88, 89, 94, 99,
103, 108, 109, 112, 118, 131,
134, 138, 142, 145, 147, 164,
165, 166, 171, 176, 178, 183,
184, 203, 211, 216, 221, 223,
232, 235, 240, 251, 255
  smallpox, 30
  sty, 10
  surgery, 7, 73
  toothache, 10, 187
  Typhoid fever, 16, 24, 134, 135,
  149, 166, 167, 175, 177, 178,
  179, 187, 188, 201, 223, 225,
  239, 254, 255
  very bad, 18, 37
  wound, 193
Ditzel[?]
  H. P., 85
divorce, 13, 95, 109, 113, 119
Dixon
  Beulah, 24
  George, 214, 236
  Lafayette, 32
  V. G., 16
Dockin(s), Dockens, 25, 200
  Ballenge, 126
  Benjiman, 5
  Dud, 26
  Emma, 69
  H. D., 126
  Henry, 55, 69, 90
  Henry, Mrs., 69
  Hepsey, 55
  Irene, 25
  J. B., 25, 157, 197
  J. B., Mrs., 25
  James, 38, 51
  Jim, 57, 190
  John, 67, 101, 103
  John B., 5, 23, 25, 232
  Lafayette, 124, 158, 214
  Laura, 22
  Mathey, 126
  Maube, 138
  Maud, 69
Dodgins
  D. L., 1

Dodgins (cont.)
  Jim, 11
dogs, 118, 235
Donaldson, Donalson
  Fannie, 6, 57, 75, 79, 82, 230, 236
  John, 57
  John H., Mrs., 31
  Lizzie, 241
  May, 9, 143, 216, 241, 254
  Sine, 74, 75, 140, 189, 225
  W. C., 56, 57, 74, 241
  W. C., Mrs., 6, 57, 79
  W. G., 177
Dorsey
  G. L., 167
  G. L., Mrs., 167
  Geo. L., 182
  George, 51, 203
  Ida, 175
  Jackson, 223
  Will, 255
Dotson
  Ada, 57
  H. B., 81, 89, 212
  H. B., Mrs., 212
  Helen, 242
  J. H., 34
  Jim, 214
  John, 57, 132, 186
  John H., 32, 56, 93
  Julius P., 32
  Silas, 212
  Thomas, 18
Douglas, Duglass
  Sarah, 91, 156
Dover
  Bulah, 6
  D. G., 20, 101, 130, 185
  Dan, 23, 41
  Dr., 34, 80, 103, 135, 139, 146,
    165, 176
  Ema, 6
  J. C., 5, 75, 92, 103, 112, 117,
    124, 161, 163, 210, 241
  J. S., 197
  Jesse, 49
  Mr., 8, 41
  Prof., 16

The Clayton Tribune, 1902

Dover (cont.)
R. N., 37, 126, 213
R. N., Mrs., 213
S. W., 76, 102, 109, 191, 225
S. W., Mrs., 76, 102, 109, 132
Dozier
Jasper N., Mrs., 237
Kate, 237
Drymon
Mary, 50
Duglass
See Douglas
Dummon
J. A., 102
Duncan
A. J., 84, 116, 123, 142, 197, 236, 237
D. J., 5
D. L., 196
D. T., 68, 191, 205, 226, 230, 246
Dave, 49
Effie, 82, 209, 241, 248
Eliza, 241
Ella, 248
Harry, 134, 190, 203, 210, 230
Jack, 42, 191, 213
Jack, Mrs., 42, 213
Jeff, 5, 179
Jesse, 190
L., 172
Lizzie, 248
Lucie, 242, 255
Lucy, 27, 39, 56, 242, 253, 255
Post Master, 233
W. B., 26
W. H., 86, 93, 144, 175, 177, 241
Dunlap
Jess, 211
Jesse, 253
S. C., 2
Warren, 101, 209
Dyer
Mr., 190
dynamite, 219
Earl, 49
[--rett], 160
Amanda, 23, 74
Everett, 74, 172, 183

Earl (cont.)
Heman, 13
J. F., 56, 60, 74, 93, 109, 113, 132, 159, 162, 190, 197, 202, 203, 227, 231, 239, 241, 242, 252, 254, 255
J. F., Mrs., 171, 184, 190, 231
Leila, 130, 131, 142, 190
M. E., 172
Maud, 131
Mr., 94, 150
Nora, 132, 190
Eason
Thomas, 98, 100, 155
Echols
L. D., 206
Edge, 92
education and schools
See also: Rabun County, education and schools
Athens, GA, 96
Atlanta medical college, 9
Banks Co., GA, 159
Baylor University, 133, 149
Blue Ridge, GA, 17
Brenau Female College, 24
Carnot, GA, 159
Cornelia, GA, 17, 67
Dahlonega, GA, 12, 22
deaf school, 192
Demorest, GA, 9, 12
Epps, GA, 67
Franklin, NC, Institute, 114
Georgia School of Technology, 199
Harvard, 133
Hiawassee, GA, high school, 133
Normal School, 67, 174
North Georgia Agricultural College, 7
Public School, 100 – 101
State University of Texas, 133
Sylva, NC, college, 99
University of Georgia, 133
Edwards
J. C., 88
J. E., 145
Mr., 218

Ford (cont.)
J. Z., 13, 162
Rev., 26
Forester, Forrester
A. B., 77, 98, 111, 238
M. B., 84
forgery, 101
Foster
Edna, 199
I. N., 159, 168, 199
J. H., 253
Prof., 171, 190, 231, 253
Sam, 64
W. G., Mrs., 209
Fowler
Luke, 1
Mary, 156
fox (animal), 188, 193
Fox
Prof., 182
Frady
John, 61, 73
Sarah, 156
Frank
William B., 153
Franklin
Judge, 72
Franks
Willie, 33, 89, 182
Free
L. L., 65
Mart, 71
Freeman
J. O., 160
Fuller
Addie, 11
J. H., 76
J. H., Mrs., 76
Mr., 66, 71
W. J., 221
Gable, Gables, 37
Paloma, 24
Tom, 35, 76, 112, 118
Gains, Gaines, 252
James, 206
Lydie, 156
P. T., 80
Tom, 149

Galbreath
Oda, 199
gambling, 136
Gambol, Gambols
Mr., 9
Steve, 64, 235
Gard
Gus, Mrs., 51
Gardner
H. H., 122, 127
Garland, 92
C. F., 174
D. L., Mrs., 67, 210
Dr., 83, 103, 112, 167
Geo. N., 32
H. P., 144, 164
J. B., 114
Judge, 65
Mrs., 182
Noah, 86, 96
Pulaski H., 32
Riley, 174
Garlet
Maggie, 27
Garrett
Claud, 174
geology
coal, 180
gems, 127, 142 – 143, 180
minerals, 142 – 143, 180
Georgia, 132, 133
Acworth, 102, 106, 109, 117, 131
Alpharetta, 192
Anandale, 2, 168
Athens, 96. 109, 116, 171, 175,
185, 211, 217, 235, 249
Atlanta, 5, 9, 12, 13, 23, 25, 31,
34, 46, 55, 58, 61, 62, 71, 76,
78, 80, 85, 86, 93, 94, 96, 97,
101, 102, 109, 116, 118, 121,
122, 124, 136, 139, 140, 152,
160, 171, 172, 173, 177, 180,
188, 189, 190, 192, 209, 210,
211, 212, 214, 217, 218, 233,
241, 246, 247, 248, 252, 253
Banks County, 159
Bethlehem Church, 176
Blairsville, 9, 36, 53, 145, 153,

Green, Ada (cont.)
222, 230, 235, 236, 237, 255
Amanda, 198
Beulah, 6, 14, 26, 68, 79, 80, 82,
96, 125
Claude, 159, 198
D. M., 6, 40, 51, 89, 96
Dr., 23, 51, 56, 73, 80, 135, 139,
146, 147, 166, 172, 185, 226
J. C., 86 – 87, 98, 157, 210
J. Claude, 246
J. W., Mrs., 75
James, 6, 12, 74, 117, 138, 168,
230
Jesse, 26, 76, 236
Jesse F., 139
Jesse W., Mrs., 172
John, 203
John W., 5, 7, 23, 32, 36, 39, 47,
48, 49, 79, 144, 149, 163, 164,
166, 197, 204, 210, 237, 245,
253
Mary, 26, 70, 111, 236
Porter, 203
Poter, 96
Prof., 125
R. T., 96, 172, 216
Roy, 236
V. A., 15, 187, 201, 235
Virgil, 117, 139, 209, 229
W. J., 5, 91, 92, 99, 161, 164, 171,
197, 247
W. J., Mrs., 171
Greenwood
B. H., 152, 182
G. W., 144, 164
Harrison, 58
J. J., 175
Mrs., 182
Ocia, 112
Octa, 134, 144, 223
W. H., 12, 37, 74, 112, 152
Will, Mrs., 175
Griggs
C. E., 225
Grist
A. J., 6, 12, 39, 65, 158
A. J., Mrs., 12

Grist (cont.)
Andrew J., 32
B. F., 65
Beulah, 9, 125
Carrie, 26, 40, 58, 68, 89, 125,
126, 152, 162, 167, 174, 175,
182, 198, 203
Charley, 126
Charlie, 9, 65, 255
Fred, 167, 175, 198
G. H., 152
G. H., Mrs., 152
G. W., 50
George, 11, 65
George, Mrs., 65
Homer, 65, 152, 175
Julia, 11
Laura, 11, 65
May, 51
Miller, 65
Rush, 134, 175
Rush, Mrs., 175
Sallie, 9, 125
Tom, 50
W. J., 39
Willie, 125
groundhogs, 186
guns, 41, 60, 90, 116, 212, 254, 255
Winchester, 223, 235
Guerry
Dupont, 98
Guy
James[?], 26
Hall
S. S., 15, 227
Hamby
Bob, 112, 118
Col., 57, 78, 80, 103, 177
Ella, 28
J. L., 2 – 3, 77
Jeff, 95
Jesse, 15
John, 95
Mary, 214
R. E. [missing], 5
R. E. A., 5, 7, 8, 39, 49, 63, 99,
111, 161, 163, 168, 197, 231,
246

Hamby (cont.)
  R. E. A., Mrs., 66, 74
  Rob, 49
  Samuel, 32
  T. J., 164
  Tom, 28
Hamlim
  Charlie, 96
Hamlin
  Wade, 12
Hammond
  W. R., 173
Hampton, 48, 219
  Capt., 146, 219, 225, 235, 236, 244
  T. C., 197
Haney
  J. W., 84
  Liz, 112
Haralson
  Bro., 36
Hard
  J. C., 125
Hardeman
  Judge, 147, 174
Harkins
  Fannie, 233, 234
  John, 51, 112, 174, 185
  Oliver, 71
Harper
  Hattie, 201
Harris, 171
Hart
  J. C., 98
  John C., 155
Harty, 128
  Mess., 127
Harvey
  Erastus, 37
  J. W., 164, 207
Hawkins
  Rev., 160
Heaton
  Mr., 136
Henderson
  Albert, 27
  E. V., 146
  Mr., 213

Henderson (cont.)
  Mrs., 146
Hendrix, Hendricks
  Mr., 118, 138
  Murray, 138
  Murry, 141
Hensely
  Guss, 33
Henson
  Asbury, 253
  Dr., 79
  Dutch, 76, 184
  J. L., 66, 206
  Mrs. Dr., 93
  Son, 146
Hess
  Nettie, 228
Hicks
  James B., 32, 93
Hidden
  Elmina, 156
Hill
  Bryant, 76, 199
  Bryant, Mrs., 76
  Byrant, 45, 71
  Byrant, Mrs., 71
  Jeff, 76
  Lillie, 199
  ex-Ordinary, 51
  W. B., 166
  W. D., 170
Hillier
  Mr., 62
Hogshed, Hogsed
  Clarey, 51
  D. E., 66, 75, 96, 151
  D. F., 65
  Dan, 86
  Lula, 82, 89, 175
Holcomb
  Bill, 248
  Carrie, 37
  Cintha, 95
  James, 69
  Jeffie, 1, 26
  John, 1, 26
  Julia, 37
  W. H., 190

King
C. C., 197
Della, 8
Dora, 8
Elijah, 199
G. H., 55, 199
G. H., Mrs., 55
Haman, 199
Hanon, 110
James, Mrs., 246
Jim, 8
Jimmy, 28
Joe, 102
Lee, 39
Lige, 110
T. E., 77, 98, 158
Thos. E., 17, 32, 92
Tom, 8
Kirby
See Kerby
knitting, 14
Knowell
Adaline, 46, 105
Kragg, *see* Cragg
Lacount, Lacounte
D. P., 54, 96
Lamb[?]
John, Mrs., 22
Mary, 24
R[?]., Mrs., 22
Landrum, 122
B. H., 102, 117, 168
L. L., 5, 34, 47
Prof., 125
Rev., 33, 81, 82, 94, 101, 125,
142, 210, 212, 252
Langston
J. [Illegible]., 190
J. C., Mrs., 68, 74
J. I., 7, 34, 49, 86, 94, 99, 127,
131, 133, 166, 170, 172, 179,
184, 197, 228, 229, 235
J. I., Mrs., 6, 34, 131, 139, 166,
218, 228
Jesse, 210
Mr., 248
Mrs., 116
Stella, 23, 79, 139, 232

Laprade
J. H., 162
John, 55
Mrs., 132
Lasure
J. W., 153
laws, 40 – 41, 43, 178
Acts of 1892, 152
alternative road, 14, 25, 35, 36, 64,
66, 73, 94, 115, 131, 141, 179,
213, 218, 220, 222, 235, 237,
244
compulsory school, 99
internal revenue, 149
Proclamation, 45
stock, 69, 217
Ledbetter
Tinnie, 244
Ledford
C. C., 222, 245
Carrie, 213, 222, 234
Columbus C., 32
D. Y., Mrs., 214
David, 213
G. W., 174
Gussie, 193, 213, 222, 234, 243
Hardie, 213
Hardy, 222
Hary, 95
John, 146
Lydia, 222, 234
M. L., 145, 181, 183, 186 – 187
Mary, 234
Sam, 166
Lee
Dovie, 42
Sarah, 42
W. M., 84
Wesley M., 59, 166
Leon
Prof., 123
Leonard
Mr., 72
Syd, 102
Lewis
J. T., 173
Lindsay
W. E., 103

Liner
  John, 38
Littleton
  Ara, 156
  Charlie, 61
  Ruth, 91
  Sam, 151
Lloyd, Loyd
  Frank, 118, 125, 199
  J. C., 48
locusts, 14
log rolling, 20, 73, 82
Long
  A. B., 197
  Adaline, 228 – 229
  Ben, 11
  Beth, 183
  Bob, 11
  Charley, 44
  Della, 44, 213
  Dr., 176
  G. W., 206, 228 – 229, 255
  Henry, 13, 86
  J. M., 57
  J. M., Mrs., 56, 68, 78, 253
  J. Marion, 109
  J. T., 110, 161, 184, 224
  John, 42, 49
  John T., 101, 173
  Judge, 49, 51, 68, 149, 184, 226,
    248
  Lafayette, 147
  Marion, 30, 68, 138, 178, 184
  Ordinary, 6, 38
  Susie, 184
  W. E., 192
  W. S., 4, 5, 7, 20, 39, 49, 57, 63,
    77, 79, 84, 104, 114, 119, 130,
    148, 158, 159, 183, 196, 205,
    206, 214, 228, 240, 246, 255
  W. S., Mrs., 165, 190
Louin
  Ambrose, 1
Love
  Joe, 65
Lovell
  Albert, 126
  Bud, Mrs., 138

Lovell (cont.)
  Dalton, 138
  G. H., 16, 88
  Geo. W., 5
  Gussie, 10
  Isaac N., 32, 93
  Leonard, 8
  Marion, Mrs., 71
  Rebecca, 10
  Robert, 71
  Virgil, 172
  Virgil N., 157
Loyd
  See Lloyd
Lumpkin
  Samuel, 98, 155
lunacy, 91
Lunchford
  Rollie, 151
Lunsford
  H. R., 42
  Robert[?], 27
Lyle
  John, 222
  Leo, 22
Lyon
  Mr., 16
Magid
  L., 160
  Louis B., 224, 226, 246
  Mr., 161, 243
Mahaffey
  J. A., 31
  W. S., 92
Majors
  Mr., 72
Manley, Manly
  E. M., 13, 46, 68, 105
  W. D., 13
Marcus
  John, 37
Marlatt
  C. L., 14
Marsingale, Marsongale, 49, 200
  See also Massengale
  Arlis, 255
  E. O., 8
  Ed, 65, 81, 203, 216, 238

McCurry, McCurray (cont.)
  W. J., 49
  W. J., Mrs., 78
McDade, 102
  C. W., 58, 110
  Col., 41, 245
  D. M., 31
  G. W., 101
  O. W., 190, 231
McHaffey
  J. A., 48
McKinley
  President, 96
McKinney
  Sol, 185
  Solomon, 74
McMillan
  Robt., 145
McWhorter
  W. J., 157
  Will, 42, 120
Meece
  A. J., 74
  J. A., Mrs., 37
  Josey, 11
Merck
  A. W., 85
Merritt
  W. B., 98, 100, 155
Metcalf
  William, 96
  Wm., 256
Methodists
  Epworth League, 44
  Methodist Episcopal, 44
  missionaries, 44
  Workers' Conference, 44
Miller
  Gen., 194
  H. V. M., 196
Mills
  F. C., 102
Mississippi River, 44, 194
Mitchel, Mitchell
  Austin, 212
  L. T., 102, 110, 135, 186
  T. L., 168
  Thos., 47

Mitchel, Mitchell (cont.)
  Thos., Mrs., 47
  Tom, 87, 114, 168, 238
mole (animal), 71
money order, 191
Montgomery, 197
moonshine, 60
  See also: beverages, illicit, making
  mountain dew, 22
moonshiners, 168, 178
Moore
  Alvin, 39, 86, 121
  Della, 18, 20
  Draper, 85
  E. A., Mrs., 20, 33
  Ella, 20
  H. V., 164
  J. B., 20, 41
  James, Mrs., 89
  James A., 219, 228
  John, 28, 81, 112
  Lillie, 70
  Marsh, 50
  Marshall, 134
  Morgan, 219
  Mrs., 26
  Nelson, Mrs., 244
  V. L., 73, 134
  Willie, 175
Morris
  A. T., 15
  Newt, 145
Morton
  Mr., 6, 15
Mosely
  See Mozely
Moss
  R. L., 99 – 100, 109
Mozely, Mosely
  Dora, 89, 117
  Eugene, 62, 192, 239
  James, Mrs., 164
  Nancy, 70
  Terrel, 112
  Terrel, Mrs., 112
Murray
  H. V., 104
  J. B., 124, 227, 247

music, 58, 111, 125, 163, 184, 231
  See also: singing
  banjo, 134, 184
  organ, 76, 175
  piano, 58
Nesbitt
  R. T., 94, 98
Nesby, 162
Netherby
  Dr., 211
Neville
  J. E., 158
  Mary, 47, 89, 117, 123, 254
  W. J[?]., 217
New Year's, 16, 17
New York, 35, 160, 252
  Buffalo, 254
  New York (city), 231
Newcomb
  J. A., 197
newspapers, 53
  Atlanta Constitution, 124
  Baptist Banner, 43
  Blairsville Herald, 36, 53
  Clarkesville Advertiser, 29, 108, 176
  Cleveland Courier, 192 – 193
  Franklin Press, 80
  Gainesville Eagle, 66
  Home and Farm, 58
  Morning News, 194
  Mountaineer, The, 251
  Mt. Airy Protectionist, 179 – 180
  Rome Tribune, 88
  Semi-Weekly Journal, 58
  Toccoa Anagraph, 72
  Wrightsville Headlight, 44
Nichols
  Charley, 95
  Emanuel, 103
  H. M., 118
  Lester, 8
  Manuel, 256
  N. C., 205
  S. M., 103
  Thomas, 27, 158
Nicholson
  Bailess, 32

Nicholson (cont.)
  Balis C., 93
  Mrs., 213
Nimmons
  Hamp, 192
Nix
  J. A., 105, 165
Norris
  Mary, 110, 134
  Mollie, 68
North Carolina, 20, 37, 38, 51, 52, 62, 65, 83, 89, 96, 99, 112, 134, 142, 147, 161, 175, 179, 185, 194, 197, 203, 212
  Asheville, 58, 110, 122, 190, 233
    Bailey Street, 233
  Beta, 233
  Bryson City, 132
  Bushnell, 180
  Cherokee, 174
  Cullasajah, 34, 165, 166, 244
  Dillsboro, 174
  Elf, 203
  Franklin, 37, 51, 52, 62, 72, 81, 92, 102, 110, 111, 112, 114, 122, 124, 127, 133, 143, 144, 175, 179, 194, 201, 203, 210, 217, 230, 231, 237, 244, 246
  Highlands, 50, 140
  Horse Cove, 140
  Macon County, 28, 238
  Nantahala, 174
  Nantahala Mountains, 122, 226, 234
  Otto, 23
  Penrose, 210
  Saulbery, 227
  Scaly, 30, 40, 50
  state line, 3
  Sylva (Sylvia), 99, 102, 111
  Waynesville, 132
  Webster, 167
North Georgia Conference, 252
Norton
  Bill, 1
  E. B., 76
  E. B., Mrs., 76
  Ed, 1, 126

Powel, Powell (cont.)
Ethel(l), 26, 68, 79, 117, 125, 126,
135, 162, 182, 214, 223, 254
F. A., 55
Fannie, 75, 82
Georgia, 20
J. B., 70, 85
James, 18
James B., 32
Lucresia, 199
Marvin, 1, 20, 25 – 26, 41, 50
Mr., 152, 175
Mrs., 152, 175
Oscar, 9, 12
Oscer, 152
R. W., 199
Sallie, 22
Sarah C., 45
W. E., 77, 145, 157, 214, 236
Powers
Mr., 20
Mrs., 20
Prentiss
Geo. L., 81, 160, 170
Mr., 40, 166
Price
E. C., 219, 252
E. C., Mrs., 252
Eddie, 46
Geneva, 46, 255
Irvin J., 131 – 132
Mattie, 26, 79, 80, 187, 201, 219,
240, 252
May, 138, 219, 240, 252
W. C., 204
W. H., 219, 252
W. S., 84, 98, 146, 158
W. S., Mrs., 255
Zelma, 26, 32, 46, 80, 187, 201,
230, 235, 240, 255
prisoners, female, 211
Profitt
W. A., 186
prohibition, 161
quarantine line, 74, 87, 145, 187, 245
Queen
John W., 157
Patton, 186

Queen (cont.)
Patton, Mrs., 186
Tyra, 212
Quillian
J. W., 34
quilting, 69
rabbits, 1, 9, 32, 34, 42, 191, 193,
234, 244
Rabun
Governor, 194 – 197
Rabun County, cemeteries
Baptist, 96
Baptist, Dillard, 136
Clayton, 164, 184
Gipson, 24
M. E., 52
Wolf Creek, 136
Rabun County, churches
Antioch, 67, 166, 213
Baptist, 195
Baptist, Chechero, 163
Baptist, Clayton, 23, 57, 87, 93,
110, 124, 160, 184, 203
Baptist, Dillard, 22, 62, 88 – 89
cemetery, 89
Baptist, Persimmon, 95, 118
Baptist, Quartz, 71, 90
Baptist, Tallulah Central, 199
Bethel, 115, 135, 138, 201, 236
Blue Ridge, 5
Clayton, 5
Clayton Methodist, 34
Cross Roads, 188
Eden, 17, 99, 127, 233
Flat Creek, 17
Germany, 62, 227
Ivy Hill, 76
Liberty, 65
M. E., Dillard, 89
M. E., South, 125
meeting, protracted, 122, 125, 141,
142, 150, 160, 162, 167, 212
Methodist, 47, 101, 195
Mount Pleasant, 38
Mountain Grove, 26, 69
New Hope, 5
Pine Mountain, 5
Ridge, 58, 79, 210, 212

Rabun Co., communities, Valley
(cont.)
    230, 236, 239, 244, 249, 254
  Vandiver, 18, 219, 222
  Warwoman, 20, 27, 31, 33, 34, 42,
    44 – 45, 51, 55, 70, 76, 77, 79,
    80, 82, 84, 96, 99, 102, 111,
    130, 147, 164, 172, 178, 193,
    195, 211, 212 – 213, 213 – 214,
    227, 231, 236, 237, 242, 243,
    254, 255
  West End, 239
  Wiley (Wylie), 236
  Wolf Creek, 17, 90, 136, 140
  Wolffork (Wolf Fork), 18, 20, 26,
    33, 34, 37, 58, 59, 70, 71, 82,
    87, 90, 97, 140, 151, 152, 191,
    212, 218, 219, 226, 228, 244,
    247, 254
Rabun County, courts, 30, 39, 78, 80,
    90, 94, 96, 138, 147, 149, 178,
    183, 188
  Clayton, 168
  court week, 29, 79, 95, 146
  courthouse, 30, 56, 60, 64, 77, 78,
    88, 111, 119, 122, 144, 145,
    149, 155 – 156, 161, 164, 182,
    196, 206, 218
  jurors, 32, 33, 162, 183, 188, 226
  jury, 94
  Grand Jury, 27, 32, 33, 88,
    91 – 93, 94, 102, 107, 110, 145,
    155 – 157, 159, 160, 161
  Justice's, 68, 142
    509th district, 65
    556th district, 45, 119, 229
    597th district, 46, 105
    1014th district, 92
    1275th district, 3
    Chechero(e), 191
  Ordinary, 114
  special jury, 94
  Stonepile, 16, 34, 75
  Superior, 73, 87, 88, 91, 93, 109,
    113, 145, 155, 173
  Supreme, 92
  Tiger, 9, 176
  Traverse, 32, 162

Rabun County, districts
  1st land, 46, 65, 85, 89, 111, 193,
    256
  1275th, 3, 28, 55 – 56
  13th land, 2, 3, 85, 207
  2nd land, 45, 46, 85, 89, 114, 119,
    121, 127, 144, 164, 165, 192,
    199, 208, 229
  3rd land, 3, 54, 85, 165, 204
  4th land, 4, 10, 31, 54, 85, 100,
    143, 164, 165, 207
  5th land, 31, 46, 54, 55, 78, 105,
    143, 206
  556th, 46, 229
  597th, 46
  Chechero, 90, 200, 212
  Clayton, 92, 199, 212
  Dillard, 200
  militia, 116
  Moccasin, 200
  Persimmon, 200, 212
  Stonepile, 18, 108, 200
  Tallulah, 200, 221
  Tiger, 66, 200
  Valley, 92, 212
  Warwoman, 166, 200, 212
Rabun County, education and
    schools, 10, 13, 14, 23, 24,
    25 – 26, 30, 39, 40, 51, 57,
    58, 67, 71, 94, 96, 102,
    107 – 108, 125, 139, 140, 142,
    147, 149, 159, 171, 193, 195,
    230, 233, 237, 238
  Academy, 71, 76
  Betty's Creek, 147
  Blalock, 167
  Board of Education, 6, 59, 92, 108,
    116
  Boiling Spring(s), 8, 115, 134
  Burton, 16, 71, 118, 125, 135, 220
    Academy, 117
  Chechero, 17, 201
  Chechero, Lower, 187
  Chechero, North, 235, 242, 255
  Clayton, 12, 14, 28, 38, 43, 75,
    76, 79, 99, 129, 137, 160
    college, 160, 211, 212, 218,
    224, 242

Rabun Co., geography and landforms (cont.)
Scotch Creek, 224
Scott's Creek, 1, 92, 147, 172, 184, 190, 192
Screamer Mountain, 81, 93, 100, 196
Simpson valley, 194
Stekoa (Stecoa) Creek, 219
Stekoa (Stecoa) Falls, 138, 201, 246
Tallulah Gorge, 123
Tallulah River, 73, 195, 237, 243
Tennessee River, 88, 133, 180
Tennessee valley, 194
Tiger Creek, 81, 92, 136, 146, 195, 230
Tiger Tail valley, 194
Timpson Creek, 1
Tugalo(o) River, 195, 224
Tugalo Valley, 224
Warwoman Creek, 34, 38, 67, 80, 147, 193
Warwoman valley, 194
Wolf Creek, 1
Wolf-pen Gap, 201
Rabun County, lodging
Blue Ridge Hotel, 15, 40, 74, 86, 102 – 103, 110, 140 – 141, 160, 166, 190, 196, 217, 218, 225
Cliff House, 99 – 100, 109, 197
Glen Brook Cottage, 197
hotel, Clayton, 241
King House, 197
Langston House, 151
mountain resort, 111
Parker Hotel, 102, 110 – 111, 117, 149, 190, 210, 211, 218, 225, 231, 238, 252, 254
Robinson Hotel Place, 2, 246
Tallulah Lodge, 2, 168, 197, 224
Wall House, 49, 73, 103, 111, 122, 131, 196, 231, 237
Willard House, 197
Rabun County, Masons, 5, 13
Masonic Festival, 101, 106
Masonic Hall, 6, 205, 226
Rabun Gap Lodge, 7, 39, 49, 106,

Rabun Co., Masons (cont.)
204
Tallulah Chapter, 38 – 39, 49, 63
Rabun County, roads and bridges, 59, 92, 94, 157, 203, 209, 213, 217, 221, 234, 235, 242, 243, 249, 250, 251
Betty's Creek bridge, 92
big road, 165
Blalock road, 17
bridge, Chechero, 210
Chechero road, 7
Clayton to Tallulah Falls road, 92
Dicks Creek road, 70
Germany road, 69
James Kell road, 92
Main Street, 184
mountain roads, 197
Pine Mountain road, 244, 247
private road, 92
public road, 4, 7, 22, 33, 62, 69, 92, 102, 127, 154, 172, 179, 184, 224, 244 248
Quartz road, 50
Rabun Gap and Franklin road, 92
River Street, 2
Russell Bridge, 38
Scott's Creek bridge, 92
Spring Street, 2
Tallulah, 220
Tallulah Falls, 48
Tallulah Falls iron bridge, 195
Tallulah Falls trestle, 223
Tallulah River road, 73
Tiger road, Old, 69
Tiger trestle, 222
Tiger Creek bridge, 92
Tiger Creek road, 195
Valley road, 58
Warwoman Road, 100, 109, 154, 227
Warwoman Street, 26, 140, 225
Rabun County Singing Convention, 163
Rabun County Union Meeting, 6
raccoons (coons), 193, 234
railroads, 15, 33, 34, 39, 41, 58, 61, 62, 68, 69, 71, 72, 73, 75, 77,

railroads (cont.)
81, 87, 88, 93, 96, 99, 103, 110,
131, 134, 136, 140, 142, 146,
159, 160, 161, 166, 171, 176,
178, 179, 179 – 180, 182, 194,
197, 201, 218, 223, 225, 235,
236, 241, 242, 243, 245, 246,
254
[Illegible] Ridge, 180
Blue Ridge and Atlantic, 81
Carolina and Tennessee Southern
Railway, 179 – 180
Central of Georgia, 195
Centrail Railway, 224
iron horse, 246
Missouri, Texas & Kansas Railway
Company, 131
R. and D., 64
Rabun Gap Railroad, 194
Southern Railway Company, 109,
179, 180, 224
Southern and Tallulah Railway,
189
Tallulah Falls Railway Company,
2, 40, 48, 67, 86, 100, 124, 127,
133, 139, 147, 154, 160, 166,
168, 180, 189, 190, 194, 226,
233, 238
Tennessee, South Carolina and
Georgia Railroad Company,
152, 180, 194 – 195
railroad commissary, 136
Rainey
J. S., 196
Ramey, 200
Ada, 219, 240, 242, 252
Adolphus, 27, 240
Americus, 15
Andrew, 26
Ara, 34
B. E., 242
Berry, 42
Carry, 34
Charlie, 48
Dol, 32
Ella, 26, 32, 138, 187, 219, 235,
236, 240, 246, 252
Elsie, 39, 79

Ramey (cont.)
Gramma, 42
H. C., 9, 55
H. J., 84
Horace J., 157
I. A., 157
Isaac, 1
J. H., 236
J. M., 184
J. M., Mrs., 184
J. S., 2, 3, 4, 5, 13, 20, 21, 22 –
23, 26, 79, 105, 109, 113, 119,
121, 133, 158, 159, 209, 211,
229, 248
J. S., Mrs., 30, 159, 184, 209, 218,
254
J. W., 242
James, 89
James H., 170 – 171, 227
James M., 157
Jas. M., 127
Jeff, 142
Jerry, 252
Jim, 164, 207
Leander, Mrs., 42
Lex, 46
Lillie, 27
Lula, 156
M. B., 66, 206
Mary, 212
Mattie, 252
May, 13, 93, 147, 236
Mrs., 231, 236, 252
Nin, 74, 79, 90, 159, 210
Polly, 26
Spart, 79, 230
Spart, Mrs., 93
Sug, 38
Sylvester, 46
Thomas, 240, 246, 252
Thomas A., 138
Tillman M., 32
W. J., 158, 198
William, 164, 252
Wm., 207
rape, 95, 227
Redmond
Mr., 68, 72 – 73, 136, 146

Reed
    George P., 164
    Napoleon, 51
Rembert
    Walter, 1
Republicans, 19, 95 – 96, 130, 150,
    159, 169, 178, 196, 200
Retail Merchants Association, 11
revenuers, 33, 50, 61, 96, 102, 112,
    147, 176, 178, 185, 193, 234
Reynolds, 200
    J. A., 5, 49, 72, 100, 154, 197,
       221, 224
    John A., 72, 245, 246
Rhodes
    W. K., 210
    W. K. "Kirk," 189
Rholetter
    J. B., 162, 166
Rice
    J. M., 46
Richards
    J. C., 24 – 25
Richardson
    H. L., 102
Rickman
    D. W., 77, 84, 98
    Jas. E., 32
Ritchie, Richie, 121, 123, 124, 132,
       133, 159, 161, 171, 200, 208
    A. J., 67, 129, 133 – 134, 137,
       140, 143, 149, 166, 198, 199
    A. J., Mrs., 167
    Andy, Mrs., 191
    Bob, 175
    Charley, 95
    Charlie, 57
    Ed, 122, 252
    Eddie, 226
    Frank, 143, 146, 149, 197
    Frank, Mrs., 191
    J. F., 84, 87
    J. F., Mrs., 198
    J. R., 3, 5, 46, 55, 56, 59, 61, 65,
       66, 73, 78, 85, 95, 105, 116,
       119, 122, 144, 147, 158, 165,
       188, 196, 207, 214, 229, 239,
       242, 253, 256

Ritchie, Richie (cont.)
    J. R., Mrs., 48, 210, 239, 253
    John, 254
    John F., 145, 157
    Lee, 56, 144, 171, 185, 186, 225
    Lee, Mrs., 114, 134, 223, 225, 239,
       248
    Lela, 236
    Lura, 197
    Mary, 210
    Miller, 253
    Mr., 19, 187
    R. B., 65
    R. J., 76
    R. J., Mrs., 76
    R. L., 12, 191
    Rile, 152, 167
    Rile, Mrs., 152
    Sheriff, 20, 49, 56, 66, 70, 152,
       211, 225, 232
    T. J., 116, 173, 197, 226, 237
    Tom, 86, 151, 162, 167, 186, 225,
       232
    W. R., 131, 149, 166
    W. R. L., 114, 173, 197, 209, 237
    W. R. L., Mrs., 239
    William, 41
    Wm., 8
Roane
    Alex, Mrs., 81
    Elic, 212
    Marvin, 101
    Mrs., 138
    Tommy, 116, 210
    W. F., 122, 138, 189
    W. F., Mrs., 139
Roberts
    Hilton, 233
    Tom, 34
    Zoney, 221
Robin, Robins, 25, 49
    Bert, 23, 214
    Daisy, 131
    James, 138
    Jesse, 23
    Katie, 131, 192
    L. M., 192
    L. N., 23, 24, 49, 148, 247

Swetman
Mrs., 81
swimming pool, 109
Swofford, Swafford
A. A., Mrs., 203 – 204
Ben, 46
Charley, 95
Charlie, 158
E. D., 10, 32, 34, 42, 68, 70, 164, 203 – 204, 211
Ethel D., 93
J. M., 70, 84, 165, 207 – 208, 210, 211
Jeff, 42, 93, 99
Jeff, Mrs., 45
Jeff D., 145, 157
Josia, 27
Josie, 20, 44
Lottie, 27. 32
Luther, 26, 213, 243
M. W., 10, 60, 77, 84, 197, 204
Marlor, 46, 198
Mary, 27
Mrs., 241
Oscar, 210
Turner[?], 26
W. E., 202
Talley
Antony, 156
Aunt, 91
Cloey, 156
Mr., 28
tanglefoot, 254
Tanker, 211
Tanner
Lizzie, 199
Mary, 96
Tate
F. C., 98, 149, 155
Farish Carter, 239
Taylor, 108, 234
[---ford], 190
Amanda, 138
Balor[?], 55
C. L., 168, 235
Clinton, 122, 179
D. D., 9, 141
Dial D., 150

Taylor (cont.)
Dock, 99
F. A., 9, 13, 18, 51, 73, 84, 88, 90, 98, 104, 113, 132, 141, 150, 162, 233, 251
Farret, 69
H. J., 18
Henry, 135, 219, 235
Hillyer, 41
Ira, 147
J. H., 77, 162, 176, 187, 201
J. R., 1 – 2, 197
Jeff, 235
Jennie C., 20
Jesse, 249
Jeptha, 178
Julius, 92, 126, 201
L. C., 219
L. N., 103
Lucie[?], 55
Lula, 221
Marcus, 138, 240
Matilda, 138
Nevitt, 235
Ola, 138, 142, 201
Palestine, 4
S. T., 77, 99, 211
Samuel, 249
Sanford, 25, 57
Susie, 18, 69, 168, 173, 176, 201, 235
V. C., 3, 26, 127, 138, 176, 179, 192, 201, 219, 235, 240
V. C., Mrs., 240
Virgil, 25, 38, 57
W. D., 197, 245
Willard, 64, 246
Wm. G., 4
Teems, Teem
John, 73, 82, 90, 250
L. T., 50, 95
Lee, 61 – 62
Teens
Leander T., 32
telegraphs, 179
telephones, 179
temperance, 103

Tennessee, 53, 76, 255
    Charleston, 153, 180, 195
    Chattanooga, 69, 102 – 103
    Ducktown, 58, 153
    East, 179
    Knoxville, 67, 73, 180, 231, 245
        5th Avenue, 67
    London, 211
    Maryville, 180
    Memphis, 238
    Montvale Spring, 180
    Pleasant Hill, 209
    Winstead, 24
Tennessee River, 194
Terrell
    Gov., 253
    J. M., 98, 100, 248
    Joseph M., 155
Texas, 16, 62, 133
    Dallas, 62
    Mineola, 10
    Sabo, 47
    Waco, 67, 133, 166, 191, 197, 199
Thanksgiving, 238, 239, 244, 251
Thomas, 83, 225
    Ben, 51, 52, 125
    E. W., 46
    John, 112
    Little, 38
    Mr., 111, 118
    N. J., 231
    N. S., 62, 111
    Newton, 237
    Sam, 234
    Sam, Mrs., 234
Thompson, 24, 167, 185
    G. E., 151
    G. H., 27, 95, 118
    G. W., 39
    Harley, 8
    Henry Edward, 233
    Horley, 17, 118, 254
    James W., 45
    Lizzie, 27
    Luther, 27
    Milas, 8
    Miles, 188

Thompson (cont.)
    P. E., 167
    Peter E., 32, 93
    Plena[?], 27
    Rosa, 8, 167, 225, 254
    S. E., 42
    Walter, 102
Thomson
    G. H., 8
Thos
    J. M., 31
tick
    cattle, 74, 166
    distemper, 235
Tilley, 65, 131
    Nelson, 23, 28, 31, 39, 47, 49, 66, 70, 78, 94, 109, 115, 171, 211, 232, 238, 254
    Nelson, Mrs., 94
timber, 41, 42, 60, 62, 67, 69, 86, 90, 100, 101, 121, 127, 154, 161, 166, 179, 190, 204, 205, 207, 218, 225, 226, 233, 237, 254
    hardwood, 100, 209
    oak, spotted, 226
    oak, white, 205, 226
    pine, 205
    poplar, 73, 226
Tow
    Margaret, 91, 156
trailing arbutus, 111
trout, 116, 197, 205
Trusty
    A. J., 256
Turner
    J. A., 162
Turpen, Turpin, 102, 219
    A. P., 68
    A. P., Mrs., 68
    Allen, 12, 32, 141, 164, 168, 173, 176, 207, 219
    Allen, Mrs., 12, 135
    Celia, 219
    Charles, 156
    Col., 41
    D. D., 37, 167, 229, 254
    Drew, 139
    Effie, 33

Turpen, Turpin (cont.)
Fannie, 243
J. A., 77, 254
J. C., 51, 213
James, 222
James A., 246
Jesse C., 213
John, 82, 193
Logan, 12, 33, 228
Luther, 239
Malinda, 216
Manson, 222
Marcus, 222
Mrs., 175
Nopolean, 167
Nory, 219
W. M., 31, 218, 245
Wm., 156
Zeb, 214
United States, 73, 145, 161
See also: revenuers
Congress, 239
Court, 101, 168
Department of Agriculture, 14, 74
Marshall, 238
Post office, 24, 59, 60, 146
inspector, 232
mail carrier, 33, 37
mail contract, 140
postmaster, 95, 232
President, 250
Revenue Department, 6
Supreme Court, 53, 94
Utah, 34
Van Hoose
A. W., Mrs., 237
Vance
E. M., 176
Vandiver
Marcus, 246
Vaugn
Athens, 113
Frank, 113
venison, 116
Vernadoe
L. C., 122
Mrs., 116

Vest
Frederick W., 20
Vicker, Vickers, Vickors
Chance, 34, 140, 203, 230, 246
Jerry, 16, 57, 65
Oliver, 247
Virginia, 45, 102
Wise County, 132
Wagoner, Wagener
Fred, 72, 197
Mr., 41, 110
Walker
Capt., 223, 243
J. A., 189
Wall, 73, 140, 225, 227
A. M., 147
Blanch(e), 49, 74, 131, 172, 184, 248
Bud, 95
C. C., 57
C. C., Mrs., 67, 68, 109
Chub, 31
Drew, 30, 58
E., Mrs., 58
Ella, 46, 144, 164
Emily, 31, 159, 185, 203
Fagant, 222
Fajan, 91
Fojan, 156
Frank, 33, 70, 102, 213
Gus, 44, 79, 147
J. A., 56, 247
J. M., 106
Jess, 118
L. M., 46, 144, 164
L. P., 118
L. P., Mrs., 160
L. T., 164
Lafayette, 23, 34, 101, 121, 214
Laura, 135, 240
Lillie, 110
Lily, 95
Lula, 44, 68
Mart, 88, 185
Martha, 34, 38, 231
Miss, 26
Mrs., 196, 235

Wall (cont.)
  T. F., 162
  William, 86
walnut tree, 172
  walnuts, 243
war
  1812, 121
  Civil, 170, 198
  Revolutionary, 121
Warlee
  M. C., 27
Warlick
  Harold, 166
  M. C., 166
  M. C., Mrs., 166, 225
  M. O., Mrs., 210
  Rev., 32, 33, 71, 76, 112, 211
Washington, 50, 179
Washington, D.C., 179
Watkins
  Eva, 3
Watson
  M. C., 73
Watts
  Andrew, 150
  Fannie, 37, 150
  Fanny, 38
  Henry F., 86
  J. S., 130
  Jno. L., 162
  Joe, 206
  M. O., 54, 65
  Mary, 65
  Mary B., 241
  Mrs., 248
  W. B., 56, 65, 80, 255
  William, 81, 206
  Willie, 135
  Wm. B., 32, 93
  Wm. J., 32
weather (inclusive), 6, 8, 9, 11, 12, 15,
  16, 17, 27, 31, 32, 33, 34, 37, 38,
  42, 43, 50, 55, 61, 65, 66, 70, 71,
  73, 75, 76, 80, 86, 89, 96, 99, 103,
  108, 111, 112, 115, 117, 118, 120,
  125, 126, 132, 135, 136, 138, 139,
  140, 141, 142, 148, 149, 150, 151,
  161, 167, 171, 173, 174, 178, 182,

weather (cont.)
  183, 184, 187, 188, 193, 203, 211,
  212, 213, 214, 217, 219, 221, 222,
  223, 232, 234, 235, 242, 243, 246,
  249, 250, 254, 255
Webb
  Mrs., 146
Welborn(e), 200
  A. F., 69
  Bill, 1
  Frank, 69 – 70
  M. F., 61, 71
  Sam, 115, 191, 227, 230
West, the, 8, 14, 17, 23, 48, 86, 198,
  250
White
  Mr., 33
  Pat, 65
  Sarah E., 244
  Sexton, 254
Whitmire, 26, 124
  A., 84
  Alf[?], 38
  Hannah, 241
  Hannie, 135, 187
  L. C., 119, 130
  Lillie, 240
  Marlor, 252
  Mary C., 119, 130
  R. L., 5, 17, 62, 106, 122, 157, 177
  Rufa[?], 95
  S. S., 96, 124, 130, 227, 244
  S. S., Mrs., 210, 244
  W. S., 2 – 3
Wilbanks
  C. T., 3, 207
  J. H., 207
  S. B., 84, 98, 162
  Samuel, 95
  Susie, 88
  T. A., 207
  T. S., 115, 207
Wilborne
  Jack, 49
  Sam, 95, 150
wildflowers, 80
Willhite
  Emma, 91

Wilkerson
J. M., 131
J. M., Mrs., 131
Williams, 122
A. J., 46, 105
Abel, 120
Albert, 9
Allen, 64, 176
Allen S., 247
Dennis, 96, 120
Dovie, 17, 26, 46, 193, 213, 214,
243
E. H., 158
Edward, 121
Ellick, 120 – 121
G. M., 201, 252
J. H., 174
John, 120, 162
Lenton, 185
M. A. F., 165
Rev., 125
T. R., 162
W. E., 9?
Wiley, 98
Wilson
J. A., Mrs., 243
John, 147
John, Mrs., 232
Rosa, 16
Wimpey
Col., 28
Wimpsey
Col., 34
wine, 9
Winters
Henry, 49
Wood
Callie, 55
Coloma, 16
Frank, 34, 76
Frank, Mrs., 135
Marion, 45
Pink, 96
Pink, Mrs., 96
Prof., 125
T. M., 76
Texie, 16
Tom, 34

Wood (cont.)
W. R., Mrs., 55
Woodall, 219
C., 252
C. E., 219
Georgia, 8
J. D., 66, 206
Morgan, 72
Russel(l), 219, 240
Wooten
John, 156
Worley
G. W., 156
Isaac, 9
Joshua, 236
Lawrence, 103
Mary, 18
Sabrina, 90
T. W., Mrs., 222
Thomas, 235
Wright
W. A., 98, 155
Wm. A., 97
Wykle
Bud, 254
Guy, 254
Mr., 255
Neville, 254
Yellow Leaf River, 224
YMCA, 40
York, 200
A. J., 177
B., 175
Belle, 17, 111, 117, 125, 152, 168
Bentley, 125, 162
Bill, 211
C. C., 78
C. C., Mrs., 234
C. F., 1, 18, 26, 41, 81, 249, 250
C. F., Mrs., 249
Callie, 142, 242, 255
Carlton, 192
Carrie, 26, 37
Charley, 236
Cicero C., 32, 93
Clara, 156
Dessie, 10
Fannie, 37

York (cont.)
  G. F., 10, 61, 103
  Helena, 17
  Henry, 17
  Hillyer, 197
  Ira, 180
  J. C., 40, 47, 61, 66, 71, 89, 112,
    126, 151, 167, 180
  J. C., Mrs., 82
  J. C. "Cal," 48 – 49
  J. C. "Cal," Mrs., 48
  J. D., 8
  J. F., 17, 151
  J. L., 142, 255
  J. Lee, 61
  J. M., 1, 70, 132
  J. M., Mrs., 190
  James, 42, 108, 236
  James L., 15
  John C., 59
  John M., 33, 67, 70
  John M., Jr., 162
  John M., Mrs., 132
  Jno. M., Sr., 60 – 61
  Julius F., 32
  Lester, 73, 236
  Lizzie, 236, 253, 255
  Logan, 172, 212
  Lula, 66

York (cont.)
  M. B., 10, 14, 18, 73, 165, 168,
    175
  M. C., 61, 66, 70, 71, 188
  M. L., 175
  M. N., 42
  M. V., 10, 82, 90, 126, 164
  Major, 25, 75, 116
  Mollie, 37
  Montine, 10
  Mr., 71
  Mrs., 60 – 61, 182
  Nancy, 26
  Otto, 167, 188
  Prof., 175, 182
  Richard, 17
  Roy, 26
  Rutha, 37
  Sarah, 59
  Texie, 10, 17, 103, 134, 152, 168,
    223
  W. H., 102, 110
  W. Hillyer, 61
  W. T., 5, 124, 138, 186, 197, 217,
    229
  W. T., Mrs., 124, 134
  Wm. H., 32, 93
Young
  W. D., 246
  W. D., Mrs., 246

Made in the USA
Middletown, DE
15 February 2023